Film, Hot War Traces and Cold War Spaces

Film, Hot War Traces and Cold War Spaces

Maurizio Cinquegrani

EDINBURGH
University Press

Edinburgh University Press is one of the leading university presses in the UK. We publish academic books and journals in our selected subject areas across the humanities and social sciences, combining cutting-edge scholarship with high editorial and production values to produce academic works of lasting importance. For more information visit our website: edinburghuniversitypress.com

© Maurizio Cinquegrani, 2022, 2024

Edinburgh University Press Ltd
The Tun – Holyrood Road
12 (2f) Jackson's Entry
Edinburgh EH8 8PJ

First published in hardback by Edinburgh University Press 2022

Typeset in Garamond MT Pro by
Cheshire Typesetting Ltd, Cuddington, Cheshire, and
printed and bound by CPI Group (UK) Ltd,
Croydon, CR0 4YY

A CIP record for this book is available from the British Library

ISBN 978 1 4744 7519 8 (hardback)
ISBN 978 1 4744 7520 4 (paperback)
ISBN 978 1 4744 7521 1 (webready PDF)
ISBN 978 1 4744 7523 5 (epub)

The right of Maurizio Cinquegrani to be identified as author of this work has been asserted in accordance with the Copyright, Designs and Patents Act 1988 and the Copyright and Related Rights Regulations 2003 (SI No. 2498).

Contents

List of Figures — vii
Acknowledgements — ix

Prologue: Tranquillity Base, Mare Tranquillitatis, Moon, 20 July 1969, 8:17 p.m. (UTC) — 1

Part 1: Hot War Traces
Chapter 1: Latin Bridge, Sarajevo, Austria-Hungary, 28 June 1914, 11:00 a.m. — 15
Chapter 2: Huesca, Aragón, Spain, 20 May 1937, 5:00 a.m. — 35
Chapter 3: Sobibór, Generalgouvernement, Occupied Poland, 14 October 1943, 4:00 p.m. — 55
Chapter 4: Hiroshima, Chūgoku Region, Japan, 6 August 1945, 8:15 a.m. — 75

Part 2: Cold War Spaces
Chapter 5: San Fernando, Buenos Aires, Argentina, 11 May 1960, 8:05 p.m. — 97
Chapter 6: Olympiapark, Munich, Germany, 5 September 1972, 4:30 a.m. — 117
Chapter 7: Via Mario Fani, Rome, Lazio, Italy, 16 March 1978, 9:02 a.m. — 137
Chapter 8: Bornholmer Straße, East Berlin, GDR, 9 November 1989, 11:30 p.m. — 159

Epilogue: Venice, Los Angeles, California, USA, 10 January 1914, 1:30 p.m. — 181

Bibliography — 185
Films by Location — 193

Index — 200

Figures

1.1	The wintry landscape of *Tra le Nevi e i Ghiacci del Tonale* (*Amid Snow and Ice on Mount Tonale*, 1918)	21
1.2	The *Farina* cuirasses in *Uomini Contro* (*Many Wars Ago*, Francesco Rosi, 1970)	24
1.3	Gianni and Du in *I Recuperanti* (*The Scavengers*, Ermanno Olmi, 1970)	28
2.1	The ruins of the old town of Belchite in *The Adventures of Baron Munchausen* (Terry Gilliam, 1988)	36
2.2	Florence 'Fifi' Roberts returns to Guernica in *Battleground for Idealists* (John Blake, 1983)	40
2.3	Exhumation at the municipal cemetery in Guadalajara in *El silencio de otros* (*The Silence of Others*, Robert Bahar and Almudena Carracedo, 2018)	46
3.1	Lublin Castle in *The Tragic City Of Lublin* (British Pathé, 1944)	58
3.2	The site of the Majdanek camp in *Lublin. Uroczystości na Majdanku* (*Lublin: Commemoration at Majdanek*, Ludwik Perski and Jerzy Bossak, 1948)	63
3.3	The site of the Majdanek camp in *The Reader* (Stephen Daldry, 2008)	64
4.1	Illustration by Melton Prior titled 'Back from the Wars: A Street Scene in Hiroshima' (*The Illustrated London News*, 13 August 1904)	76
4.2	Ruins of the Hiroshima Prefectural Industrial Promotion Hall at dusk in *Genbaku no Ko* (*Children of Hiroshima*, Kaneto Shindo, 1952)	82
4.3	Ruins of the Hiroshima Prefectural Industrial Promotion Hall in *Kono Sekai no Katasumi ni* (*In This Corner of the World*, Sunao Katabuchi, 2016)	90
5.1	Footage filmed by American lawyer David Glick for the Jewish Joint Distribution Committee (1939)	101
5.2	Alicia and T. R. Devlin in Praça Floriano Peixoto in *Notorious* (Alfred Hitchcock, 1946)	104

5.3	Desert route in *Wakolda* (*The German Doctor*, Lucia Puenzo, 2013)	108
6.1	ABC television coverage of the Munich Massacre (1972)	123
6.2	Advertisement for the Munich Tourism Bureau in *One Day in September* (Kevin Macdonald, 1999)	126
6.3	The Connollystraße apartment in *Munich* (Steven Spielberg, 2005)	130
7.1	The aftermath of the ambush in Via Mario Fani (ANSA)	143
7.2	The Via Montalcini apartment in *Buongiorno, notte* (*Good Morning, Night*, Marco Bellocchio, 2003)	146
7.3	The dead body of Aldo Moro in Via Caetani (Rolando Fava, 9 May 1978)	150
7.4	TG1 coverage of the discovery of Aldo Moro in Via Caetani (9 May 1978)	151
8.1	Bricked-up windows of Bernauer Straße in *Funeral in Berlin* (Guy Hamilton, 1966)	164
8.2	Cassiel and Homer in Potsdamer Platz in *Der Himmel über Berlin* (*Wings of Desire*, Wim Wenders, 1987)	169
8.3	Robin Day in a *Panorama* report (BBC TV, 30 October 1961)	171
8.4	The replica of Checkpoint Charlie in *The Spy Who Came in from the Cold* (Martin Ritt, 1965)	174

Acknowledgements

The research for *Film, Hot War Traces and Cold War Spaces* was undertaken in my capacity as Senior Lecturer in Film at the University of Kent; I am thankful to my Division for a Research Leave which enabled me to complete the book. I wish to thank all my colleagues at the School of Arts for shaping a creative, inspiring and rigorous research environment even during the challenging times of the COVID-19 pandemic. I also wish to thank staff at the Templeman Library, the BFI Reuben Library, Senate House Library, and the Imperial War Museum Archive and Research Room. Finally, I would like to express my gratitude to everyone at Edinburgh University Press for their support in the process of completing this book.

PROLOGUE

Tranquillity Base, Mare Tranquillitatis, Moon, 20 July 1969, 8:17 p.m. (UTC)

> *A thirty-eight-year-old man from Wapakoneta, Ohio, descends a ladder and plants the first human foot on the Moon. His name is Neil Armstrong and this happens on the evening of 20 July 1969.*

A parody of science, an anti-imperialist satire and a legacy of *féerie*, the early fantasy film *Le Voyage dans la Lune* (Georges Méliès, *A Trip to the Moon*) was first screened on 1 September 1902 at the Théâtre Robert-Houdin in Paris. Sixty-seven years later, when the Apollo Lunar Module *Eagle* landed on the Moon, that impossible journey became reality. On the fiftieth anniversary of that event, the documentary *Apollo 11* (Todd Douglas Miller, 2019) and fiction film *First Man* (Damien Chazelle, 2018) returned to the unfolding of the historical landing; *Apollo 11* consists solely of archival material focusing on the lift-off at the Kennedy Space Centre (Merritt Island, Florida), the landing of the *Eagle* on the Moon, its reconnection with the Columbia spacecraft, and its re-entry into Earth's atmosphere. The landing of the *Eagle* is also staged in the long sequence of *First Man* where the action is intertwined with scenes showing the family of astronaut Neil Armstrong (Ryan Gosling) and which is followed by archival footage of the crowd watching the event on a large screen in Trafalgar Square, London. The combination of archival footage and fictional re-enactment emerging from these cinematic narratives of the Moon landing captures a historical moment rooted in space and articulates a visual memory of Armstrong's first step on the Moon or, as Roger D. Launius has put it, 'the climax of humanity's greatest adventure to date.'[1]

The Moon landing was a major triumph for the United States in the space race against the Soviet Union and a pinnacle of that process which, since the turn of the century, had seen technological advancements exponentially invade everyday life; its imagery offered a glimpse of that future which was predicted by those who lived immediately before the First World War and which was expected to be defined by a proliferation of technological progress. And yet, had the future offered a glimpse of itself to those who lived at that time, the Moon landing and other achievements would have been dwarfed by a much darker picture of things to come. The escalation of scientific progress witnessed at the turn of the century would shift towards warfare and result in previously unseen carnage and in the most horrific conflicts in human history. The early-twentieth-century vision of a bright future defined by innovation in the sciences leading to a leisured and scientifically advanced society was thus to meet the destruction of hopes, ideals and illusions at the hands of those catastrophic human decisions which plagued the century and which were enhanced by technological upheaval. In the novel *Nineteen Eighty-Four* (1949), George Orwell uses a fictitious book titled *The Theory and Practice of Oligarchical Collectivism* in order to illustrate this broken promise: 'The world of today is a bare, hungry, dilapidated place compared with the world that existed before 1914, and still more so if compared with the imaginary future to which the people of that period looked forward.'[2] Orwell's prose functions both as a reflection on the dystopian world envisaged in the novel and as a commentary on the ways in which war and totalitarianism betrayed the real world's expectations for a luminous future.

Eric Hobsbawm's history of what he calls the Short Twentieth Century (1914–91) echoes the words written by Orwell and argues that the twentieth century was the most murderous:

> … of which we have record, both by the scale, frequency and length of the warfare which filled it, barely ceasing for a moment in the 1920s, but also by the unparalleled scale of the human catastrophes it produced, from the greatest famines in history to systematic genocide.[3]

Hobsbawm identifies, in the years between the outbreak of the First World War and the aftermath of the Second World War, an Age of Catastrophe during which humanity 'stumbled from one calamity to another' and when 'even intelligent conservatives would not take bets on its survival;'[4] humanity did survive and yet, as Hobsbawm evocatively explains:

> [The Short Twentieth Century] was marked by war. It lived and thought in terms of world war, even when the guns were silent and the bombs were not exploding. Its history and, more specifically, the history of its initial age of breakdown and catastrophe, must begin with that of the thirty-one years' world war. For those who had grown up before 1914 the contrast was so dramatic that many of them – including the generation of this historian's parents, or, at any rate, its central European members, refused to see any continuity with the past.[5]

As Hobsbawm concludes, for several generations '"peace" meant "before 1914": after that came something that no longer deserved the name.'[6] Like Orwell, Hobsbawm thus sees the outbreak of the First World War as a watershed leading to an Age of Catastrophe which was followed by the Cold War or by what Hobsbawm calls a 'contest of nightmares' built on fears which were part of the age of revolution born in Russia in October 1917 and whose epitaph would only be written forty years after the end of the Second World War with the fall of Communism in the Eastern Bloc.[7]

With a focus on that something which could no longer earn the right to be called peace, in *Film, Hot War Traces and Cold War Spaces* I want to travel back in time to the Short Twentieth Century and reflect upon the ways in which film has built a visual aftermath for a diverse range of incidents which exemplify the century of violence dissected by Hobsbawm in *Age of Extremes*. The events of the Age of Catastrophe and of the Cold War were captured on newsreels and, later, on television news reports. Like the Moon landing, other key historical incidents of the Short Twentieth Century were addressed in later documentaries which used and repurposed footage taken at the time of their happening and often combined that material with the testimonial performances of those who lived through war. The same episodes would have been re-enacted, often on the basis of the visual record provided by newsreels and television reports, in live-action and animated fiction films of hot and cold war. By means of a spatial reading of these narrative flows, I want to investigate the aftermath of incidents whose visual memorialisation has been shaped by the intertwining of factual and fictional footage.

The use of film as a source for historical pursuit has been discussed in multiple contexts by film scholars and cultural historians. As Marcia Landy suggests, the 'social and cultural transformations rooted in economic catastrophes, wars, revolution, counterrevolution, colonization, and decolonization have marked this century and are part of the history of cinema and cinematic uses of the past.'[8] Film, Landy continues, does not reflect 'history through verisimilitude' but rather it mirrors 'our received notions of the past'.[9] Landy's words intervene in the extensive debate on the merits of film as historical source, a discussion which has seen multiple and often contrasting views. In 1978 Ian C. Jarvie expressed his suspicion of film as a tool for historical research:

> Film is a more cognitively dense medium than music or painting, to be sure, but in its imagery and descriptive bias it resembles poetry rather than prose. For another thing, and perhaps most decisively of all, its discursive weakness means that it cannot participate in the debate about historical problems, which is what history is really all about.[10]

Five years later, Richard C. Raack expressed a diametrically-opposed view and explained the potential of film as a 'way of sensing past reality':

> Present historical study should be able to report this. It should give an empathetic reconstruction to convey how historical people witnessed, understood and lived their lives. It should seek to recover all the past's liveliness – partly

that of dream and memory, of time decomposed and recomposed, all corrected and interpreted, of course, and then rejoined to the external 'reality' by the multiple perspectives the mass of historical source materials so often affords. These are the aspects of the past least perceptively reflected in traditional history. And they are what film reports best.[11]

Robert A. Rosenstone would later join this debate and conclude that film has the ability to effectively represent history despite the fact that contemporary scholarship had shown little interest in this framework of analysis: 'Current theories of cinema [...] all seem too self-contained and hermetic, too uninterested in the flesh-and-blood content of the past, the lives and struggles of individuals and groups, to be directly useful to the historian.'[12]

I am taking the dispute about the value of film as a historical record as a starting point for an investigation rooted in a spatial reading of films dealing with historical events of the Age of Catastrophe and of the Cold War and entrenched in the places whose histories shaped the twentieth century. My study embraces the idea of using film as a historical source and as a suitable tool to recover what Raack called 'all the past's liveliness' and to address what Rosenstone named the 'flesh-and-blood content of the past'.[13] In doing so, I aim at building an argument for film as a historical source on the basis of a methodology based on two main premises. First, the memories inscribed in space are made to emerge from a predefined genre or type of film; the visual polyphony stemming from amateur and archival footage, documentary and fiction films alike has the potential to delve deeper into the history of a specific location and into the aftermath of events which took place there.[14] The image of specific filmic spaces unfolds in sources as different as short amateur films or mainstream dramas in interconnected ways, and the diverse perspectives on place inherent in this plurality of sources can provide a multilayered reading of events inscribed onto their location. Exemplified by the interwoven lunar space of *First Man* and *Apollo*, the richness of an approach to filmic spaces which goes beyond a compartmental distinction between fiction and non-fiction is the basis of the journey through time and place unfolding in the eight chapters of this book.

The second premise of *Film, Hot War Traces and Cold War Spaces* is the use of space as an interpretative category which should be given a role akin to that of time in the attempt to unlock memories and exhume history through film. I thus plan to apply to a diverse range of spaces the notion which James Hay has used in regard to the cinematic city and which claims that 'films serve as maps within (and thus territorialize) the places where they are engaged' and states that 'the "cinematic" is defined by a relation among sites and flows'.[15] François Penz and Andong Lu have built upon this framework of analysis in their own theorisation of 'urban cinematics', an idea which they define as the moving image's ability 'to reveal a new spatial and narrative structure, to challenge the traditional organization of the city as new geographies and new thematic connections may emerge.'[16] According to Penz and Lu, these geographies can be unwrapped by means of what they call 'cinematic urban archaeology', a retrospective longitudinal way of making visible filmic spaces of the past and the present by means of digging through chronological layers of cinematic representations of a particular place.[17] Penz and Lu have also discussed the relationship between the real site and its cinematic image in terms of creative geography and topographical coherence, two distinct ways of reorganising multiple spaces into narrative geographies with a different impact on the spatial perception of the viewer.[18] The former term implies a departure from the real locations in films where specific cities, squares and streets are creatively connected and often called on to play the role of other places. The latter reflects the process of using locations in a way which is closely connected to the real places and which, through cinematic intervention, provides a coherent experience of how a given space is organised.

In *Film, Hot War Traces and Cold War Spaces*, I adopt the terminology suggested by Penz and Lu while departing from its exclusive focus on the urban in order to apply the notion of cinematic archaeology to a broader range of the filmic spaces, including smaller towns, abandoned places, natural landscapes and battlefields. My investigation of these spaces merges the dissection of archival footage, documentary and fictional re-enactments in the attempt to map a series of events unfolding on the sites of memory of the Short Twentieth Century. According to Pierre Nora, sites of memory, or *lieux de mémoire*, are places where memory is seized by history and by the consequent requirement for every group to redefine its identity through the re-elaboration of its own past.[19] In the first volume of the collaborative project *Les Lieux de Mémoire*, Nora explains how a site of memory is defined by the interplay between history and memory and by their material and symbolic nature determined through constant reworking of memory and by means of the need to remember the events inscribed in place; here the past is absorbed by the present in order to create a meaningful history.[20] As it engages with sites of memory dug through chronological layers of filmic space, *Film, Hot War Traces and Cold War Spaces* also responds to and is shaped by Edward W. Soja's attempt to promote a meaningful way to think about the 'significance of space and those related concepts that compose and comprise the inherent spatiality of human life.'[21] Soja coined the notion of Thirdspace as a 'tentative and flexible term that attempts to capture what is actually a constantly shifting and changing milieu of ideas, events, appearances, and meanings.'[22] In this book I try to answer the invitation to think about the spatiality, historicality and sociality of human life as part of what Soja calls a 'three-sided sensibility' aimed at 'bringing about a profound change in the ways we think about space' and leading to 'major revisions in how we study history and society'.[23]

The spatiality of history is at the core of my investigation of eight historical events of the Short Twentieth Century divided into two parts focusing, respectively, on hot wars (1914–45) and the Cold War (1945–91). The first part looks at events of the Age of Catastrophe and includes four chapters investigating the filmic spaces and the physical traces of war inscribed on the Italian front of the First World War and those emerging from the films focusing on the Spanish Civil War, the Holocaust in occupied Poland, the bombing of Hiroshima and their aftermath. The second part of the book explores four incidents which unfolded against the background of the Cold War, including the escape of Nazi war criminals to Latin America, the Munich Massacre at the Olympic Games, the kidnapping and murder of former Italian Prime Minister Aldo Moro in Rome, and the construction and fall of the Berlin Wall. Transversal spatial themes are intertwined across the eight chapters and range from studies with a narrow spatial focus on individual buildings to the investigation of larger spaces and territories. Throughout the book, I establish thematic connections between the filmic spaces of the events examined in each chapter, in the attempt to probe the close-knit historical and topographical ties binding the century from the beginning of the Age of Catastrophe to the end of the Cold War.

I introduce each chapter with an episode exemplifying the significance of the historical event investigated. These episodes are used to set in motion the analysis of the incidents addressed in the investigation which follows. Chapter 1 opens with the assassination of Archduke Franz Ferdinand of Austria and his wife Sophie at the hands of Slavic nationalist Gavrilo Princip on 28 June 1914 in Sarajevo. The event which started the Age of Catastrophe is used to introduce one of the battlefields of the First World War, the front at the border between Austria-Hungary and Italy. This chapter investigates the ways in which the northeast of Italy during the war has been captured in a diverse range of films serving different purposes in the different historical contexts of their making. In particular, it focuses on how the same locations were used for patriotic and nationalist narratives during the war and the years of the fascist regime and how the implied values of the films made at that time later gave way to dramas with pacifist and antimilitarist messages. The chapter reflects on the ways in which the sites of battles between Austria-Hungary and Italy saw history repeating itself and considers how filmic space can reveal scars and traces of war.

Chapter 2 is introduced by the incident which saw George Orwell being shot and severely injured by a sniper on 20 May 1937 during an offensive on the Aragón front of the Spanish Civil War. This episode introduces the political and historical complexities of the war and opens an investigation charting the topography of the conflict across a range of locations, including Guernica, Lérida, Badajoz, Madrid, Guadalajara and Toledo. This chapter also looks at how the portrayal of the Spanish Civil War has changed from the Nationalist perspective which characterised films made during Francisco Franco's dictatorship and the later emergence, upon the return to democracy in the late 1970s, of what had previously been repressed. This chapter also articulates a discourse on how films made by international filmmakers during and after the conflict provide alternative political perspectives and often embrace the Republican cause.

Chapter 3 begins with the killing of a *Schutzstaffel* officer by Jewish prisoner Yehuda Lerner at the Sobibór death camp on 14 October 1943. The uprising which took place in the camp on that day is the defining event of a chapter which looks at three sites of memory of the Holocaust and includes a space which was exploited by the Nazis during the Holocaust and two locations which were created for the purpose of forced labour and extermination, namely the Old City of Lublin and the camps in Majdanek and Sobibór. Lublin and Majdanek are explored in regard to the opposition between creative geographies and topographical coherence; Sobibór, a site obliterated by the Nazis in the attempt to hide the mass murder, is discussed with a focus on the ways in which fiction films and testimonial performances included in documentaries are intertwined in the process of memorialising a place where no tangible trace bears witness to the events which unfolded on its grounds.

Chapter 4 opens with the moment when Paul Tibbets dropped the atomic bomb codenamed Little Boy on city of Hiroshima on the morning of 6 August 1945 and focuses on the site of a domed building which was located below the hypocentre of the detonation of the bomb. The Hiroshima Prefectural Industrial Promotion Hall was largely destroyed by the atomic blast, its ruins eventually preserved and used to memorialise the bombing under the name of Atomic Bomb Dome. The role of this building in the urban fabric of Hiroshima is explored through film in relation to its significance and its altered role from a symbol of Hiroshima's civic pride and Japan's imperialism to a monumentalised site of memory of the atomic bombing and an emblem of pacifism. This chapter investigates the image of the building in amateur films made in the 1930s, in newsreels made after the bombing, and in live-action and animated dramas set in Hiroshima in the aftermath of the attack.

Chapter 5 is introduced by the actions of three Mossad agents who ambushed and kidnapped *SS-Obersturmbannführer* Adolf Eichmann on 11 May 1960 in Buenos Aires. The capture of Eichmann, one of the architects of the Final Solution, is used as a starting point for a discussion focusing on the aftermath of the Holocaust in Latin America; the chapter looks at the ways in which amateur films, newsreels, documentaries and fiction films have addressed the relocation of Nazis and Holocaust survivors alike in Brazil, Argentina and other countries. In particular, this investigation considers the connections between fiction films articulating fantasies of Nazi resurgence in Latin America and factual films addressing the complexities of the topographical interrelations between the war in Europe and remote Latin American landscapes. This investigation also dissects the connection between the Nazi escapees and the emergence of totalitarianism in post-war Latin America as it surfaces in film.

Chapter 6 begins when wrestling referee Yossef Gutfreund was awakened by the noise made by the terrorists who, on 5 September 1972, were breaking into the apartment hosting the Israeli team at the Munich Olympic Village. This chapter focuses on Apartment 1 at 31 Connollystraße, in the Olympic Village, and the Fürstenfeldbruck airfield, the two places where the assassination of eleven Israeli athletes, coaches and referees unfolded. Along with the dissection of the ways in which these locations have been used in documentaries and fiction films, this chapter looks at the relationship between later films and the live coverage of the event broadcast on the ABC. This investigation anchors the memory of the event to the aftermath of the Second World War and establishes topographical connections between the locations of the massacre and the past; it also uses documentary to chart the historical significance of the return of the Olympic Games to Germany thirty-six years after the Berlin Olympics hosted by the Nazi regime.

The attack perpetrated by *Brigate Rosse* (Red Brigades) on 16 March 1978 in Rome, the kidnapping of Aldo Moro and the assassination of his five bodyguards, opens Chapter 7. This investigation looks at the intertwining of factual accounts and fictional representations of Via Fani, the place where Moro was taken, Via Montalcini, the location of the apartment where he was kept prisoner for fifty-four days, and Via Caetani, the street where his body would be found in the boot of a car. This chapter focuses on documentary and fiction films of the incident and uses the live coverage of the events which was broadcast on Italy's public television from the day of the kidnapping to that of the assassination. Akin to the case of the Munich massacre, the television reports on the Moro case were used in documentaries and in re-enactments of the events, and have also been shown on television as part of the *mise-en-scène* of a fiction film.

Chapter 8 starts with the raising of the barrier at the Berlin Wall border crossing in Bornholmer Straße on the evening of 9 November 1989. This study looks at the juxtaposition of television news reports on the building of the Wall, and later documentaries and fiction films set in its shadow. In particular, this chapter focuses on the function of the Wall as a location in a number of international spy films. Historical and topographical connections are made to emerge from a study of the urban fabric of the divided city, and the chapter travels back to the building of the Wall and to its impact on three locations profoundly altered by its construction (Bernauer Straße, Potsdamer Platz and Friedrichstraße). Topographical accuracy and creative geographies emerge from these three locations and the chapter aims at capturing an image of the Cold War as it surfaces from films of its most emblematic location.

This journey in time and space from the outbreak of the First World War to the fall of the Berlin Wall is rendered through a multitude of images, a polyphony of depictions mirroring a selection of episodes which gave shape to the Short Twentieth Century. In doing so, *Film, Hot War Traces and Cold War Spaces* uses film to capture the unfolding and the significance of historical events and builds on Soja's claim that 'historicality and historiography are not enough' to understand the world we live in and that this pursuit requires 'a deeper appreciation for the spatiality of human life.'[24] With this book I also aim to expand the scope of my own work on the use of a spatial framework for the study of film; in my previous monograph, *Journey to Poland: Documentary Landscapes of the Holocaust*, I mapped the unfolding of the Holocaust in Poland through a wide range of documentaries and with a focus on the places which were destroyed in the process of the genocide (the *shtetlekh* of Eastern Europe) and the sites which were built or repurposed by the Nazis for the annihilation of the Jews (ghettos, concentration and death camps).[25] Whereas in *Journey to Poland* I had a specific focus on the Holocaust, in *Film, Hot War Traces and Cold War Spaces* I aim at using film to explore the locations of the broader range of historical events introduced in the previous pages.

The chapters which follow are based on the idea that history is inscribed in place and that filmic space embodies history; the process of capturing the Short Twentieth Century has thus led me to map its wars by digging through history and visual representation. I have built this approach to film on that recognition of the importance of the spatiality of human life in relation to history, which has also been discussed by Philip J. Ethington:

> Histories representing the past represent the places (*topoi*) of human action. History is not an account of change over time, as the cliché goes, but rather, change through space. Knowledge of the past, therefore, is literally cartographic: a mapping of the places of history indexed to the coordinates of space-time.[26]

In his commentary on Ethington's article, Edward S. Casey explains that the notion of mapping 'needs to be liberated from its alliance with modern cartography so that it can resume its original sense of charting one's way in a given place or region.'[27] Casey's words echo Ethington's attempt to make a case for the expansion of the meaning of mapping as a way of deciphering the relationship among *topoi*, 'be they points, lines, polygons, or actions, events, experiences, and ideas.'[28] Accordingly, I aim at exploring the past by mapping the connections between a range of *topoi* including geographical locations, filmic spaces, and testimonies.

Film, Hot War Traces and Cold War Spaces is about war in its most inflamed, bloodied, unfaltering and cruel forms. It is about the events which, in Hobsbawm's evocative words, saw 'the great edifice of nineteenth-century civilization crumpled in the flames of world war, as its pillars collapsed.'[29] This book is also about a century which was shaped less by the technological advancements which brought mankind to Mare Tranquillitatis and more by the catastrophes which unfolded on unprecedented scale across the world. It is about the anxieties of the Cold War and the fears of incidents which had the potential to ignite a thermonuclear war just as Gavrilo Princip's gun shots in Sarajevo led to the First World War.

Notes

1. Roger D. Launius, *Apollo's Legacy: Perspectives on the Moon Landings*, Washington, DC: Smithsonian Institution, 2019, p. 1.
2. George Orwell, *Nineteen Eighty-Four*, London: Penguin, 2000, pp. 191–226 (196) [first published in 1949 by Martin Secker & Warburg]. In the novel, *The Theory and Practice of Oligarchical Collectivism* was allegedly written by Emmanuel Goldstein, a former top member of the ruling Party who broke away early in the movement and started an organisation dedicated to the fall of the Party or, perhaps, a scapegoat fabricated by the Party itself.
3. Eric Hobsbawm, *Age of Extremes: the Short Twentieth Century 1914–1991*, London: Abacus, 1995, p. 13.
4. Hobsbawm, p. 6.
5. Hobsbawm, p. 22.
6. Hobsbawm, p. 22.
7. Hobsbawm, p. 83.
8. Marcia Landy, *Cinematic Uses of the Past*, Minneapolis: University of Minnesota Press, 1996, p. 1.
9. Marcia Landy, 'Introduction', in *The Historical Film: History and Memory in Media*, Marcia Landy (ed.), London: A. & C. Black, 2001, pp. 1–24 (5).
10. Ian C. Jarvie, 'Seeing Through Movies', *Philosophy of the Social Sciences*, Vol. 8, No. 4, 1978, pp. 374–97 (378).
11. Richard C. Raack, 'Historiography as Cinematography: A Prolegomenon to Film Work for Historians', *Journal of Contemporary History*, Vol. 18, No. 3, 1983, pp. 411–38 (416).

12. Robert A. Rosenstone, 'History in Images/History in Words: Reflections on the Possibility of Really Putting History onto Film', *The American Historical Review*, Vol. 93, No. 5, 1988, pp. 1173–85 (1181).
13. Raack, p. 416; Rosenstone, p. 1181.
14. *Film, Hot War Traces and Cold War Spaces* is based on my research on archival films held in the collections of Pathé News (London), Istituto Luce (Rome), National Film Archive (Warsaw), RCC Broadcasting Company (Hiroshima), United States Holocaust Memorial Museum (Washington), RAI (Rome), and BBC Archive (London).
15. James Hay, 'Piecing Together What Remains of the Cinematic City', in *The Cinematic City*, Clarke David (ed.), New York and London: Routledge, 1997, pp. 209–29 (219).
16. François Penz and Andong Lu, 'Introduction: What is Urban Cinematics?', in *Urban Cinematics: Understanding Urban Phenomena Through the Moving Image*, François Penz and Andong Lu (eds), Bristol: Intellect Books, 2011, pp. 7–19 (9).
17. Penz and Lu, p. 12.
18. Penz and Lu, p. 14.
19. Pierre Nora, 'Between Memory and History: *Les Lieux de Mémoire*', *Representations. Special Issue: Memory and Counter-Memory*, No. 26 (1989), pp. 7–24 (7).
20. Pierre Nora, 'Entre Mémoire et Histoire', in *Les lieux de mémoire: La République*, Nora (ed.), 2.ª ed., París: Gallimard (Bibliothèque illustrée des histoires), 2001, pp. 23–43.
21. Edward W. Soja, *Thirdspace: Journeys to Los Angeles and Other Real-and-Imagined Places*, Malden: Blackwell, 1996, p. 1.
22. Soja, p. 2.
23. Soja, p. 3.
24. Soja, p. 16.
25. Maurizio Cinquegrani, *Journey to Poland: Documentary Landscapes of the Holocaust*, Edinburgh: Edinburgh University Press, 2018.
26. Philip J. Ethington, 'Placing the Past: "Groundwork" for a Spatial Theory of History', *Rethinking History*, Vol. 11, No. 4, 2007, pp. 465–93 (466).
27. Edward S. Casey, 'Boundary, Place, and Event in the Spatiality of History', *Rethinking History*, Vol. 11, No. 4, 2007, pp. 507–12 (512).
28. Ethington, p. 485.
29. Hobsbawm, p. 22.

Part 1

Hot War Traces

CHAPTER 1

Latin Bridge, Sarajevo, Austria-Hungary, 28 June 1914, 11:00 a.m.

> *A nineteen-year-old man from Obljaj, Austria-Hungary, steps onto the footboard of a Gräf & Stift Double Phaeton car and shoots Archduke Franz Ferdinand of Austria and his wife Sophie, Duchess of Hohenberg. His name is Gavrilo Princip and this happens on the morning of 28 June 1914 in Sarajevo.*

Made in 1918, the newsreel *L'esercito americano in Italia durante la Prima Guerra Mondiale* (*The American Army in Italy during the First World War*) includes several scenes filmed in the regions of Veneto and Friuli-Venezia Giulia and shows American soldiers and officials at work in the supply and support lines of the front or walking in local towns and villages.[1] Among other locations, a sequence from this newsreel was filmed on the trenches along the Piave River near the village of Varago, the theatre of the Second Battle of the Piave River, which was fought in June 1918 and resulted in over 20,000 deaths and 100,000 wounded. *The American Army in Italy during the First World War* also provides an evocative visual record of the landscape of the battles which took place on the Italian front of the First World War and which would later be sketched by Ernest Hemingway in *A Farewell to Arms*. This novel was based on the writer's recollection of the time he spent in Italy in 1917 and 1918 as a volunteer ambulance driver and in its opening paragraph Hemingway describes the unfolding of military action taking place across the spectacular scenery of the region:

> In the late summer of that year we lived in a house in a village that looked across the river and the plain to the mountains. In the bed of the river there were pebbles and boulders, dry and white in the sun, and the water was clear and swiftly moving and blue in the channels. Troops went by the house and down the road and the dust they raised powdered the leaves of the trees. The trunks of the trees too were dusty and the leaves fell early that year and saw the troops marching along the road and the dust rising and leaves, stirred by the breeze, falling and soldiers marching and afterward the road bare and white except for the leaves.[2]

As Laura Gruber Godfrey suggests, in the opening pages of *A Farewell to Arms* the 'implicit feeling of remembered experience is evoked primarily by means of definite, familiarizing articles [...] and also by occasional deictic language that gives readers the illusion of a shared experiential perspective.'[3] Hemingway thus summons the experience of war by means of a detailed recollection of time and place.

Published in 1929, the story of a love affair between an American paramedic serving in the Italian Army, Frederic Henry, and an English nurse, Catherine Barkley, was adapted for the cinema by Frank Borzage in 1932 and, twenty-five years later, by King Vidor. Borzage's adaptation was filmed in the Paramount studio and ranch in California whereas Vidor's film was partly shot on location in the municipality of Venzone, in the Friuli-Venezia Giulia region, and the Italian Dolomites, and it opens with a series of establishing shots of the mountains and of the picturesque villages dotting the Alps.[4] There is little trace of Hemingway's reflection on war and pacifism in the Hollywood adaptations of *A Farewell to Arms*; Borzage and Vidor hardly engage with Hemingway's attention to the devastating effects of war on people and instead focus on the melodramatic love story unfolding between Frederic and Catherine. The Alpine landscapes vividly described by Hemingway, as I hope to demonstrate in this chapter, would later be used as locations in a greatly diverse range of cinematic depictions of war which reflected the politics of the time of their making and often broached the anti-militarism pervading *A Farewell to Arms*.

Italy's declaration of war on Austria-Hungary on 23 May 1915 was precipitated by the Austria-Hungarian declaration of war on Serbia, and this event was itself triggered by the assassination of Archduke Franz Ferdinand of Austria at the hands of Gavrilo Princip.[5] The incident of 28 June 1914 in Sarajevo thus led to the outbreak of the First World War, and the war which was supposed to end all wars eventually led to two tumultuous decades and to the Second World War, an event whose outcome sparked the flare-up of the Cold War in the second half of the century. Princip, whose actions spurred this chain of occurrences, would die from tuberculosis on 28 April 1918 in Terezín, the fortress in North Bohemia which in 1940 would be turned into a ghetto and concentration camp by the Gestapo, and which would be used by the Czechoslovak Socialist Republic for military purposes during the Cold War. Terezín is thus one of countless locations reflecting the intertwining of the major historical events of the Short Twentieth Century.

While Princip was imprisoned in Terezín, the war triggered by his actions raged across Europe and beyond, and unfolded across the Western Front, the Eastern Front and the campaigns in Italy, Macedonia, Romania, Caucasus, Serbia, Gallipoli, Sinai and Palestine, Mesopotamia and south-west Africa. The complex topography of the First World War has been narrated in a wide range of newsreels, documentary and fiction films framing the war within patriotic and heroic narratives, melodrama and comedy, military propaganda and pacifism. In what follows I investigate the sites of memory and the cinematic space of one of the most treacherous campaigns of the First World War, the trench warfare in the north-eastern landscapes of Italy captured by Hemingway in *A Farewell to Arms*; the films discussed in this chapter are mainly set in Veneto and Friuli Venezia Giulia and, in particular, in the locations of the theatre of war such as the banks of the Piave River and the Altopiano di Asiago (Asiago Plateau).[6] With a focus on these places, I aim to explore patriotic and heroic narratives of war as well as stories rooted in anti-militarism, pacifism and humanism. Later fiction films are also discussed with a focus on narratives of class division and regional diversity built in opposition to the myth of unity emerging from films made from the beginning of the First World War to the end of the 1950s.

In 1915 the Kingdom of Italy was just over fifty years old, and the multitude of dialects used by the soldiers who fought in the northeast of Italy was a barrier to the ideal of unity celebrated by the militarist propaganda. The use of a range of dialects at the front is made explicit in several war dramas; for example, in a scene from *La Sciantosa* (Alfredo Gianetti, 1971) where the words 'Ciao Tosa' (*tosa* meaning girl in the Venetian dialect) can be read on the side of one of the carriages taking the soldiers to battle, while the main male character, Tonino (Massimo Ranieri), has a pronounced Neapolitan accent.[7] In *La Grande Guerra* (*The Great War*, Mario Monicelli, 1959), the contrast between the Milanese accent of Giovanni (Vittori Gassman) and the Roman accent of Oreste (Alberto Sordi) is employed to emphasise differences between the two men and used here for comedic purposes; for example, Giovanni claims that all Italians coming from south of Parma are *romani* as he is unable to recognise any of the regional accents of fellow soldiers from Tuscany, Apulia or Sicily. Monicelli's film, as Luca Barattoni argues, juxtaposes these diverse regional identities to articulate an image of the conflict which can be described as 'quietly patriotic without excesses in nationalistic or chauvinistic pride or pacifist rhetoric.'[8]

Films such as *The Great War* and *La Sciantosa* also share the idea of war understood as a recurring event unfolding against social justice and the common good; in this chapter these films are made to dialogue with earlier fiction films, newsreels and documentaries, as well as with the memoirs written by those who survived the carnage of the battlefields. What emerges from this comparative study is a fragmented image of Italy where the specific territory of the front in the northeast encapsulates class and regional division. This is made explicit in Bernardo Bertolucci's *Novecento* (*1900*, 1976), an epic drama where the First World War occupies a relatively small fraction of the narrative and yet one that reflects the perception of the war at the time of *cinema d'impegno*, the Italian political cinema of the 1960s and 1970s. In *1900*, peasant Olmo (Gérard Depardieu) enlists with the Italian army while landowning Alfredo (Robert De Niro) evades the draft and spends the war years running his family's business and plantation. This is the first drift in the lives of two friends whose class identity would eventually lead Olmo to champion workers' rights and bring Alfredo to embrace his role as a wealthy landowner. This theme was also explored in *La Sciantosa*, where the slogan *Abbasso la Guerra* (Down with War) is misspelled on a wall graffiti as *Abbaso la guerra*; the film thus reveals an association between illiteracy and hostile feelings towards the war, a sentiment reiterated by several observations made by working-class characters throughout the film.

Both *La Sciantosa* and *1900* exemplify the class divisions which characterised the experience of the First World War in clear contrast to patriotic films made at the time of the conflict such as *Il Canto della Fede* (*Song of Faith*, Filippo Butera, 1917), a drama focusing on the home front and promoting an ideal of class unity and a fictitious sense of national solidarity while ignoring the fact that conscription affected social classes differently, or *Maciste Alpino* (*The Warrior*, Luigi Romano Borgnetto and Luigi Maggi, 1916), a farcical action film about the adventures of a soldier of extraordinary strength who defeats his enemies with his bare hands. The narrative of *The Warrior* anticipates fascist rhetoric and the hero of the film, strongman Maciste (Bartolomeo Pagano), was the protagonist of a long saga including twenty-seven films made between 1915 and 1927, well into the fascist era. As Stephen Gundle suggests, Maciste both inspired and adopted Benito Mussolini's gestures and poses while sharing with the dictator the belief that violence was always a legitimate course of action.[9] A long extract from *The Warrior* is included in the 1934 montage documentary *Il Piave mormorò* (*The Piave River Burbled*), a commemorative film largely made of newsreel material filmed in the period 1915–21.[10] *The Piave River Burbled* includes footage from various locations on the front and, in particular, the sites of memory of the Second Battle of Piave River; it also contains still photographs displaying swollen and disfigured corpses on the battlefields, images which were normally excluded from the newsreels. Edited in the second decade of fascist rule, this material is juxtaposed with a sequence from *The Warrior* where Maciste escapes from an Austrian prison and defeats three enemies; the result of this contiguity is the articulation of the theme of Italy's heroic victories in stark contrast with the emphasis on class and regional division later postulated in *La Sciantosa*, *The Great War* and *1900*.

In the years after the war, fiction films memorialised victory and at times reflected the anger aimed at the allies for what was perceived as the unfair treatment of the country in the negotiations which followed the conflict.

The term *vittoria mutilata* (mutilated victory), which was coined by the poet Gabriele D'Annunzio, captured the disappointment caused by the fact that the territorial gains promised in the Treaty of London, signed by Italy in 1915, were ultimately denied at the end of the war when the Treaty of Versailles of 1919 nullified the previous pact.[11] This outcome fuelled vexation and inflamed a nationalist rhetoric which became a key argument in fascist propaganda and which was reflected in a number of fiction films about the war released in the mid-thirties and until the ousting of Benito Mussolini in September 1943.[12] The nationalistic message of war dramas had a counterpart in newsreels from the fascist era covering events such as the tenth anniversary of the declaration of war on Austria-Hungary, an occasion during which veterans from several regions took part in a visit to the former battlefields and to other locations on an itinerary from Monte Grappa, in the Venetian Prealps in Veneto, to Trieste. The newsreel *Dal Grappa al mare; ricordi di guerra e scene dei campi di battaglia (From Monte Grappa to the Sea; War Memories and Battlefield Scenes*, 1925) follows war veterans on a route of sites of memory including Bassano del Grappa, Montello, Treviso, Possagno, San Donà del Piave, Meolo, Vittorio Veneto, Cividale del Friuli, Caporetto, Gorizia, Doberdò, the Redipuglia War Memorial and the Miramare Castle.[13] In *From Monte Grappa to the Sea*, the image of fascist officials standing next to the veterans, the presence of Blackshirts (members of the Voluntary Militia for National Security) and the frequent recurrence of the Roman salute reveals how the memorialisation of the First World War was by then inscribed into the nationalist and militarist mythology created by the fascist regime; this imagery was firmly chiselled on the landscapes of the battles for propaganda purposes and in order to serve the narrative of a mutilated victory.

After 1945, patriotic narratives of the First World War largely fell into oblivion and, until the release of the pivotal film *The Great War* in 1959, only a few titles, which had little success, were produced.[14] While the films made in the 1950s departed to some extent from the chauvinistic pride and propaganda of their fascist-era predecessors, they continued to articulate a simplistic image of the First World War in a patriotic attempt to memorialise a war fought and won to juxtapose with the defeat and humiliation suffered by the country in the Second World War. The jingoistic and largely romanticised image of the war unfolding in the films made before *The Great War* had its origin in misperceptions which were fuelled by illustrated magazines published at the time of the conflict. The First World War saw the use of caterpillar-tracked armoured vehicles and poison gas onto the battlefield, the first attempt to use air warfare and the submarine as a means to either kill civilians or starve them by stopping seaborne supplies.[15] And yet, the image of the battlefields emerging from the films made in the period 1915–59 is highly romanticised and largely neglects the deployment of advanced modern machine warfare. A similar incongruent representational strategy has been investigated by Jay Winter in regard to the romantic imagery produced in France after the outbreak of the war, and his argument can effectively be applied to the Italian context. In his investigation of the relationship between film and *Images d'Épinal*, a series of traditionalist and naïve prints on popular subjects, Winter argues that both media aimed to represent the war as a mythical or romantic adventure that did not correspond to the reality of the battlefields. Furthermore, as they carried on the tradition of *Images d'Épinal*, French films provided a popular iconography of the nation at war and explicitly aimed at an escape from a reality too hard to bear. In the darkness of the cinema, concludes Winter, the supernatural aura of the war emerged sanitised, magical and mundane.[16]

Similarly, Italian war newsreels produced in the period 1915–18 operate through a process of selection, omission and emphases in the treatment of their subject matter and exemplify the ways in which films can create meaning by what they leave out as much as by what they include. The newsreel *Tra le Nevi e i Ghiacci del Tonale* (*Amid Snow and Ice on Mount Tonale*), produced by the Cinematographic Section of the Italian Army, was filmed just before the Italian final offensive of June–July 1918 on a series of key battlegrounds including the Piave River, Camonica River, Mount Presena, Mount Tonale, and Ponte di Legno.[17] *Amid Snow and Ice on Mount Tonale* introduces the viewer to that wintry landscape, characterised by snow, mud and wind, which would become a recurring feature in later war films (Figure 1.1). This footage shows convoys of motorised and horse-drawn vehicles carrying food, fodder and equipment to Mount Tonale and the Piave River valley. The convoy follows a mountain road through small villages such as Ponte di Legno, a locality in Lombardy that had almost been razed to the ground by Austrian cannons in 1917. Alpine soldiers can be seen carrying dismantled Maxim machine guns up to their positions, reassembling the weapons and firing them against the enemy. In another sequence, stove-pipe mortars bombard the Austrian positions while Alpine soldiers capture the enemy's artillery. The film ends with images of Austrian prisoners escorted to the valley, where they are fed and eventually marched to the collecting station.

Amid Snow and Ice on Mount Tonale also shows the use of mule-drawn flat-cars, dog sledges and skis for transport. Like the traditionalist prints discussed by Winter, this film thus presents a sanitised image of a front haunted by the deaths of the Alpine soldiers, the Austrians, the civilians of Ponte di Legno, and yet deprived of its darkest features, the seriously injured, the disfigured, the fear that inhibits solidarity and, ultimately and unavoidably, those noises

Figure 1.1 The wintry landscape of *Tra le Nevi e i Ghiacci del Tonale* (*Amid Snow and Ice on Mount Tonale*, 1918).

which play an important role in war memoirs such as that written by Lucio Fabi:

> A hundred yards from us a cry, not human, but the cry of wounded beast breaks, heart-rending, the air. A few moments later I see a soldier coming down the path with one hand holding the leg hanging loosely to his body. No soldier offers his help, and only when he is very close to the rocks a pair of hands come to his aid.[18]

This extract from the diary of an Alpine soldier deployed in Carnia details how the Austrian mortars injured a soldier while his comrades were occupied playing a board-game. The gruesome image and the admission that others were too frightened to help the wounded soldier would have hardly been suitable subjects for reassuring war newsreels like *Amid Snow and Ice on Mount Tonale*. As Pierre Sorlin suggests, unlike war memoirs an ordinary newsreel 'hides neither the destruction nor the suffering of the soldiers but never reveals a corpse, a mutilated body or a wounded man.'[19] Similarly, fiction films made during the war hardly evoked the sense of annihilation that characterised the battlefields in favour of a romanticised imagery.[20]

The perspective of films like *Amid Snow and Ice on Mount Tonale* has been discussed by Gian Piero Brunetta by means of the definition of an 'inverted telescope' which relies on the categories of distance and absence rather than those of nearness and presence.[21] Brunetta has investigated the ways in which newsreels produced by the Ministries of Army, War or Navy provided an answer to the propagandistic aims of the Italian government and aimed to boost the morale of the public, and concluded that the action on the front-line trenches was not deemed a suitable subject for the newsreels. Films thus represented the supply, artillery and support lines, those auxiliary military actions depicted in *Amid Snow and Ice on Mount Tonale* or, alternatively and with great emphasis, they would focus on the celebrations following Italian victories. For example, *La guerra d'Italia a 3,000 metri sull'Adamello* (*The Italian War at 3,000 Meters on the Adamello*, Luca Comerio and Paolo Granata, 1916) contains no evidence of the mass deaths caused by poison gas, flamethrowers and hand grenades; on the contrary, *The Italian War at 3,000 Meters on the Adamello* details the activities of Italian soldiers on the supply lines.[22] A newsreel titled *Battaglia sulle colline italiane* (*Battle on the Italian Hills*, 1918) brings the viewer a little closer to the reality of war and to the frontline near Alano di Piave in the province of Belluno; the footage is unidentified and the title cards in English suggest this was a British production.[23] Title cards like 'Italian artillery keeps up a constant bombardment of the Austrian positions on Monte Tomba', 'The infantry rushes into action over ground swept by enemy shells' or 'With rifle and machine gun they carry on the grim task' introduce battle scenes where, while the dead and the injured are still invisible, the large clouds of smoke caused by heavy artillery clearly imply death and mass destruction.

Footage from newsreels produced during the Second Battle of the Piave River (1918) would be repurposed forty years later in the commemorative news report *Piave: Rievocata la Gloriosa Epopea* (*Piave River: Recalling the Glorious Epic*, 1958). The film juxtaposes footage of the battle with images taken in 1958 during a ceremony attended by veterans gathering on the sites of the battle and shots of a memorial monument to Italy's top fighter ace Francesco Baracca.[24] The tone of this celebratory newsreel is still pervaded by highly patriotic undertones which were at odds with the popular fiction film which was directed by Monicelli in the same year. *The Great War* follows soldiers Oreste and Giovanni, both of whom are characterised by their lack of patriotic idealism, their limited military valour and a strong desire to keep away from danger. Accustomed to the war imagery of films such as *Piave River*, the Italian press was prejudiced against the idea of a film like *The Great War*. On 10 January 1959, the newspaper *La Stampa* reported the news of a First World War film in pre-production to be presented by Dino De Laurentis, directed by Mario Monicelli and starring two of the most popular comic actors of the time, Alberto Sordi and Vittorio Gassman. Paolo Monelli, who signed the article as Simplicissimus, expressed his concern for the comic elements of a film dealing with events such as the defeat at Caporetto and, more specifically, for the presence of two actors identified with the comedy genre in the role of two Italian soldiers tempted to desert the battlefields; over the following four days other Italian newspapers, including *Il Giorno*, *Il Mattino* and *Il Giornale d'Italia*, wrote about the forthcoming film and, despite the director's reassurances, they all feared that the film would express contempt for the army and those who died in the trenches.[25]

In his study of Monicelli's film, Franco Calderoni argues that the First World War was interpreted by the Italian audiences in a jingoistic and largely inaccurate manner due to the country's tendency to forget, to conform, to over-celebrate its triumphs and hide its failures; between 1918 and 1959, the arts only sporadically addressed the events of the war and, Calderoni continues, Italian attitudes towards the conflict had been irremediably damaged by the unreliable treatment of the war in the newspapers of that time and by their failure to portray the conflict in an objective manner; they emphasised each victory, while ignoring major defeats.[26] A rejection of this patriotic image of war emerges vividly from *The Great War* in the scene where Giovanni reads an extract from *Domenica del Corriere*, a morale-bolstering illustrated magazine characterised by richly jingoistic undertones. While the cover of the magazine illustrated by Achille Beltrami shows soldiers celebrating Christmas in the trenches with a generous meal, one of the soldiers complains *Domenica del Corriere* should instead report on the poor quality of their food and on the limited supplies of general goods.

The Great War was filmed on location in the municipalities of Venzone and Nespoledo di Lestizza, the valley of Sella Sant'Agnese and the town of Palmanova in the Friuli-Venezia Giulia region; the use of the sites which had seen the bloodshed of 1915–18 in *The Great War* make its humanist message more poignant. *Uomini Contro* (*Many Wars Ago*, Francesco Rosi, 1970), on the contrary, could not be filmed on location because of its more radical antimilitarist views, the reputation of Rosi as a militant filmmaker and the consequent resistance by local authorities and political parties. The Italian front had to be creatively relocated at the Centralni Filmski Studio and a park-forest in Košutnjak, both in Belgrade, Serbia. On the background of this setting, *Many Wars Ago* reads the events of the First World War in line with Marxist political cinema of the 1960s and contains a more direct pacifist message than that of *The Great War* or *La Sciantosa*. Rosi's film was loosely based on Emilio Lusso's *Un anno sull'altipiano* (*A Year on the Plateau*, 1938), the memoir of an infantry captain which had also inspired *The Great War*. Lusso's book discusses how the Italian Army was under-equipped and as a result units lacked morale; in a memorable section of the book General

Figure 1.2 The Farina cuirasses in *Uomini Contro* (*Many Wars Ago*, Francesco Rosi, 1970).

Leone describes new equipment and explains that 'The enemy might have rifles, machine guns, artillery: with our Farina cuirasses we can break through their lines.'[27] The Farina cuirasses were composed of a helmet and frontal armoured plate for trench warfare and were in fact completely ineffective when opposed to modern machine guns (Figure 1.2). This episode is included in *Many Wars Ago*, in the sequence where Rosi stages a grotesque image of Italian soldiers wearing these cuirasses, advancing towards the enemy lines only to be killed by Austrian artillery. A long shot taken from the point of view of the sniper shows a small contingent of armoured Italian soldiers systematically executed, with the cuirasses clearly limiting their field of vision. Ironically, General Leone had told the soldiers that the Romans triumphed in battle thanks to their cuirasses and the most remarkable feature of this sequence lies in the anachronistic appearance of the Italian soldiers. These cuirasses seem to belong to distant past, to a long-gone era of forgotten warfare, to a Roman centurion or a mediaeval knight rather than to a technologically advanced war.[28]

As the comparison between the films hitherto discussed demonstrates, the memorialisation of the First World War, and the way in which it is reflected in film, is a changeable construct, an open-ended process determined by historical context. Memory works differently for those who lived through the war and for those who remember it by imagination and through mediated narratives and images. Accordingly, Jay Winter has defined film as one of a series of collective languages of mourning and remembrance searching for some redemptive meaning.[29] Film, according to Winter, has the power to affect the ways in which viewers think and remember the past and 'while film mediates the construction of individual and group memories, and in particular memories of war, it does so in ways which are never mechanical and which, in their variety and subtle power, reach different collectives in different ways.'[30] Winter focuses here on the ways in which shared mediators, including films, do not correspond to shared memories; different cohorts cannot simply be added to a vague concept of collective experience, and thus both film and memory are difficult to relate to a political contestation about ideas of nation and community.

Many Wars Ago reflects this reading inasmuch as the film was made at a time of great political turmoil in Italy and, rather than presenting an answer to the nation's need to cling nostalgically to its history, it reconstructs the past in relation to the events and the political battles of the present. For example, *Many Wars Ago* addressed desertion and self-harm on the front while, at the time of its making, conscientious objectors in Italy were campaigning for the right to refuse to perform military service, a right which would be recognised by Parliament two years after the release of the film.[31] Rosi's narrative of the First World War is informed by later events – fascism, the Second World War, the Cold War – and departs from a purely historical understanding of the conflict to use the trenches of the Italian front as a social and political reflection on the history of the country in the Short Twentieth Century. In *Many Wars Ago*, Rosi interprets Lusso's work through a Marxist perspective in line with his commitment to the *cinema d'impegno* and thus the film distances itself from previous glorifications of war through a radical attempt to find meaning in the shattering experience of the trenches and, paradoxically, in the meaningless mass slaughter. Rosi articulates a political discourse which was partly based on *A Year on the Plateau* and on the knowledge that the battles were fought by working-class men on both fronts, in Lusso's words: 'For the first time we realised that the war was only fought by countrymen, shepherds, workers and artisans. Where was everyone else? Another discovery: the Austrian army was also made of countrymen and workers.'[32]

Both Lusso and Rosi emphasise the ways in which the war affected social classes differently; specialised industrial workers, for example, were exempt from conscription and more than half of the 5 million men called into the army were peasants, often illiterate and with little understanding of the causes of the war.[33] However, whereas the book broadly reflected Lusso's sense of betrayal (in 1914 the writer had been in favour of Italy's intervention in the conflict) the film portrays its main character, Lieutenant Ottolenghi (Gian Maria Volonté), as a committed antimilitarist socialist standing against the military establishment. Ottolenghi's worldview can also be traced in other political memoirs of the war. On 28 August 1917, Giuseppe Garrone, commander of the sixth unit of the Battaglione Alpini Tolmezzo, wrote a letter to his father from the front in Carnia:

> Thank You! The codes have arrived! I had forgotten all about these books and was so happy to see them again! These days I am not the only one who has forgotten the codes. The world is a strange place. Even the ultimate social justice resulting from this war will be the consequence of a number of injustices, great or small.[34]

Garrone was killed by enemy fire on 16 December 1917. In his letter he anticipated and, like Ottolenghi in *Many Wars Ago*, hoped for social justice and for a fair society as the ultimate result of the conflict. Instead, the outcome of the conflict was a fascist dictatorship built on the myth of a mutilated victory; the films I discuss in this chapter regularly address a political discourse on illusions, disillusions and on the utter failure to build a better society. For example, Giannetti's *La Sciantosa* departs from any belief in a social justice brought about by the war, portraying instead a series of working-class individuals with little interest in the politics of war and a dubious attitude towards any potential benefit resulting from it. A similarly sceptical view is articulated by Oreste in *The Great War* in the scene where he explains that the only just war is the war against inequality and that the country needs reforms and not fallen soldiers. Oreste reads Russian anarchist Mikhail Bakunin and claims that nobody has the right to order a man to meet his death in the trenches. Whereas *La Sciantosa* and *The Great War* exemplify the disillusion of a generation, *Many Wars Ago* offers an alternative, the hope in a more just society emerging not from the conflict itself but from a socialist revolution. Rosi presents a reflection on war and men's behaviour when facing death in the trenches, and by doing so he introduces the audience to events that can be interpreted as the starting point of the political division which characterised twentieth-century Italy. After the war, fascism rapidly suffocated genuinely revolutionary forces, and fifty years later, when Rosi directed *Many Wars Ago*, the opposition between radical left- and right-wing groups was central to the wave of terrorism and political turmoil known as *Anni di Piombo* (Years of Lead), a period of time which I discuss in Chapter 7 in relation to film and the locations of the kidnapping of Aldo Moro.

In *Many Wars Ago*, Rosi re-imagines the First World War on account of the socio-political landscape of the Years of Lead. In the trenches of the First World War, in Rosi's view, one can see the emergence of the revolutionary forces and the reactionary powers whose opposition delineated historical events which took place later in the century. *Many Wars Ago* implicitly suggests that social justice might well still be a much-delayed result of the First World War; Rosi admitted that one of the main aims of *Many Wars Ago* and its representation of history as the product of class struggles was to understand the wars which followed and thus the present of the making of the film.[35] In *Many Wars Ago*, the image of a soldier dying on the barbed wire, shot and unable to move, echoes images of the barbed wire of the concentration and extermination camps of the Second World War. The relationship between the two world wars is also articulated by Ermanno Olmi in *I Recuperanti* (*The Scavengers*, 1970) with a focus on the same locations of Lusso's memoir and on the tangible evidence of war marking the landscape.

Filmed in 2013, the documentary *L'Albero tra le Trincee* (*The Tree in the Trenches*, Alessandro Scillitani) follows Italian journalist Paolo Rumiz to the sites of memory of the First World War, to the landscapes sketched by Hemingway in *A Farewell to Arms*; Rumiz searches for traces of the war as he walks on the Dolomites and on the Karst Plateau through tunnels and narrow trenches lined with grey stones and rusted metal remains. The landscapes of the First World War in the northeast of Italy are indeed still scattered with leftover war materials. A year after the making of *The Tree in the Trenches*, over 220 lbs of grenades from the First World War emerged from the Vedretta di Nardis glacier near Trento. Findings like this are rare but for several decades after the end of the war scavengers made a living by recovering noble metals from the trenches. This forgotten activity is portrayed by Olmi in *The Scavengers*, a film where a demobilised Alpine soldier named Gianni (Andreino Carli) returns to the Asiago Plateau from the Second World War and, unable to find decent employment, teams up with an old scavenger. The pair recover metal remains of weapons, including old, unexploded bombs, grenades, bullets, and pieces of guns and cannons, and other relics left behind from the First World War on the rocks and meadows of Asiago and in the hidden bunkers and depots of the plateau (Figure 1.3). Made at a time of increasing political tension and violence in Italy, *The Scavengers* addresses issues of memory and historicity in relation to the two world wars and illustrates social issues previously addressed by Neorealist filmmakers in the immediate post-war years, including unemployment and more broadly that 'crisis of self-esteem and self-identity' which, as Mark Shiel suggests, defined neorealist characters such as Antonio Ricci in Vittorio De Sica's *Ladri di biciclette* (*Bicycle Thieves*, 1948) and which 'indicated the crisis of an entire people at a unique moment in their history.'[36] In *The Scavengers*, Andreino Carli's character is unable to find a secure job, contemplates emigration to Australia, and experiences the failure of the woodcutter's cooperative; his crisis is that of an entire community and generation incapacitated by post-war dejection.

Olmi is not only concerned with the specific context of the setting of the late 1940s and his film aims at a profound multilayered historical engagement

Figure 1.3   Gianni and Du in *I Recuperanti* (*The Scavengers*, Ermanno Olmi, 1970).

with the impact of war on a community inhabiting a landscape which had often been a theatre of conflict. The Asiago Plateau, where both *Many Wars Ago* and *The Scavengers* are set, had already been one of the battlefields of the Italian wars of independence against the Austrian empire in the mid nineteenth century. In *Amore di Confine* ('Frontier Love', 1986), a collection of short autobiographical stories about the Second World War, Mario Rigoni Stern, one of the scriptwriters for *The Scavengers*, reminds the reader that Asiago had already been burnt to the ground by Sigismund, the Archduke of Austria, in 1446 and again by the Austrian artillery in 1916: 'Asiago was a mountain village; I say it was because in 1916 the war destroyed it and burnt it to the ground; it was rebuilt between 1919 and 1922, but it is no longer the same place.'[37] Later, between 10 and 25 June 1917, the Italian and Austro-Hungarian armies fought for possession of Mount Ortigara in the Asiago Plateau: over 31,000 soldiers were killed or seriously wounded. In 1945 the plateau town of Pedescala saw one of the most infamous massacres of civilians at the hands of the *Wehrmacht*, *Waffen-SS* and Italian fascists; eighty-two civilians were killed.

The concept of historical recurrence evoked by Stern and Olmi has been discussed by Garry W. Trompf, who has argued that the idea that history repeats itself 'is wider than its cyclical formulation' and includes 'notions such as retribution, rebirth, re-enactment, and even imitation.'[38] In Olmi's film, the words of old scavenger Du (Antonio Lunardi) echo the idea of historical recurrence and exemplify the world view of a generation that experienced two world wars and that came to see war as an inevitable and recurring event: 'War is a nasty beast – he explains – it goes around and around the world and never stops [...]. You build houses and war tears them down and here I come, looking for relics.'[39] Olmi's humanism is reminiscent of Lusso's work and of Monicelli's *The Great War*, where Oreste similarly argues that centuries of wars have not brought any greater good to peoples and nations. Du's words imply the concept of historic recurrence, wherein repetitive patterns in the history of a country, place or community exhibit the striking similarities of specific events as they converge and resonate in what is understood as a shared memory or dissipation of memory. Soon after their first encounter, Du invites Gianni to look at the landscape in the way he does, paying particular attention to the copper, brass, iron and lead remnants of the First World War and seeing and understanding the impact of the cyclical repetition of history on place, the cyclical process from which the wounds of war struggle to heal.

Central to the narrative of *The Scavengers* are the metal remains of the war, relics bearing witness to history while providing an unmediated impression of the past made available to the senses by their physicality. The film thus enacts that connection with the past and its inevitability which has been described by David Lowenthal as follows: 'Each scene and object is invested with a history of real or imagined involvements; their perceived identities stem from past acts and expectations. Without the past as tangible or remembered evidence we could not function.'[40] Olmi uses these relics to make the past live in the present and to illustrate the overlap between the time when the film is set, the war of 1915–18, and year when the film was made; in 1970 the Assiago Plateau was a peaceful landscape but the national context was political turmoil marked by both far-right and far-left acts of terrorism. The relationship between past and present articulated in *The Scavengers* can also be illustrated by the reflection on the passing of time and the persistence of memory articulated by Andreas Huyssen:

> A sense of historical continuity or, for that matter, discontinuity, both of which depend on a before and an after, gives way to the simultaneity of all times and spaces readily accessible in the present. The perception of distance, both spatial and temporal, is being erased.[41]

Accordingly, by means of simultaneity and erased distance, the temporal layers of the landscapes captured in *The Scavengers* reflect and evoke other images and narratives of war. This process is also exemplified in the first sequence of Gianetti's *La Sciantosa*, where Anna Magnani's character, Flora Torres, looks at an old leather-bound album of photographs of herself as a young woman.⁴² One of these photographs was taken in 1936 and portrays Magnani on the set of *Cavalleria* (*Chivalry*), a fascist-era patriotic film focusing on an air force pilot, directed by Goffredo Alessandrini. Both *La Sciantosa* and *Chivalry* are set during the First World War, and the intertexuality of this scene provides Magnani's character with a fictitious past emerging from a previous cinematic narrative of war. *La Sciantosa* thus establishes a relationship between past and present and, as Emiliano Morreale suggests, places Magnani at the juncture between the memorialisation of Neorealism and of the world of *café chantant* or *café-concert* and thus articulates a sublimation of Magnani's long-gone beginnings in the variety show.⁴³

With films such as *The Great War*, *Many Wars Ago*, *The Scavengers* or *La Sciantosa*, the First World War is no longer seen through the lens of an inverted telescope but rather through a magnifying lens challenging earlier representations of the conflict and their nationalist narratives. What emerges consistently across decades is the significance of place, the importance of the landscapes of war and the passing of time; the aftermath of the First World War is inscribed in its sites of memory, in the Asiago Plateau or the Piave River, in the act of returning to the locations of the war through film. Like the First World War, the historical events I discuss in the following chapters were captured in newsreels and eventually memorialised in documentaries and represented in fiction films. In Chapter 2 I address the cinematic image of specific sites of the Spanish Civil War and the shifting representation of that conflict during the war itself, the Francoist regime and Spain's return to democracy. While the Hollywood adaptations of *A Farewell to Arms* were the only notable non-Italian films set on the Italian front of the war, a group of international films of the Spanish Civil War provides a multilayered reading of the event through time and across space. Films of both bloodsheds, as we shall see, reveal the importance of site-specific memorialisation and the significance of tangible remnants of war.

Notes

1. *L'esercito americano in Italia durante la Prima Guerra Mondiale* (*The American Army in Italy during the First World War*), 1918, Archivio Storico Istituto Luce (Rome), Film ID: 111H1228/ D030401.
2. Ernest Hemingway, *A Farewell to Arms*, London: Vintage, 2005 [first published by Jonathan Cape, London, 1929], p. 3.
3. Laura Gruber Godfrey, *Hemingway's Geographies: Intimacy, Materiality, and Memory*, London and New York: Palgrave Macmillan, 2016, p. 59.

4. The fascist regime considered the anti-militarism overtones of the novel detrimental to the honour of the Armed Forces and the book would not be published in Italy until 1948.
5. Between 23 May 1915 and 28 August 1916 Italy declared war on Austria-Hungary, the Ottoman Empire, Bulgaria and the German Empire.
6. This investigation is partly based on my chapter 'Place, Time and Memory in Italian Cinema of the Great War' published in *The Great War in Post-Memory Literature and Film* (Martin Löschnigg and Marzena Sokolowska-Paryz, eds, Berlin: De Gruyter, 2014, pp. 321–34).
7. The term *sciantosa*, a misuse of the French word *chanteuse*, describes a female stock character that developed in Italian variety shows at the turn of the twentieth century. In Gianetti's film it refers to Anna Magnani's character, Flora Torres.
8. Luca Barattoni, *Italian Post-Neorealist Cinema*, Edinburgh: Edinburgh University Press, 2012, p. 208.
9. Stephen Gundle, *Mussolini's Dream Factory: Film Stardom in Fascist Italy*, New York and Oxford: Berghahn Books, 2013, p. 44.
10. *Il Piave mormorò* (*The Piave River Burbled*), 1934, Archivio Storico Istituto Luce (Rome), Film ID: D030401.
11. Gabriele D'Annunzio, 'Vittoria nostra, non sarai mutilata', in *Corriere della Sera*, 24 October 1918, p. 1.
12. Films of the First World War made during the fascist dictatorship include: *Le Scarpe al Sole* (*Shoes in the Sun*, Marco Elter, 1935), a heroic depiction of life in the trenches that was awarded a prize by the Ministry of Propaganda at the Venice Film Festival; *Tredici Uomini ed un Cannone* (*Thirteen Men and a Gun*, Giovacchino Forzano, 1936), a whodunit narrative focusing on thirteen soldiers guarding a long-barrelled cannon; *Passaporto Rosso* (*Red Passport*, Guido Brignone, 1936), a story of Italian immigrants in South America returning to Italy to fight for king and country; *Piccolo Alpino* (*Little Alpine Soldier*, Oreste Biancoli, 1940), a film about a child who is taken prisoner by the Austrians during the occupation of the north-eastern territories of Italy and who escapes, thus proving himself as courageous as an Alpine soldier. In 1943, Marcello Albani directed *Redenzione* (*Redemption*), a film in which the First World War is used as a narrative device to deliver a clear propaganda message about the Second World War: an Italian communist who had deserted the front in 1915 finally embraces the nationalist cause, fights and dies for Mussolini in the new war.
13. *Dal Grappa al mare; ricordi di guerra e scene dei campi di battaglia* (*From Monte Grappa to the Sea; War Memories and Battlefield Scenes*), 1925, Istituto Nazionale Luce, Film ID: M014801.
14. Films of the First World War made soon after the end of the Second World War include: *Senza Bandiera* (*Without Flag*, Lionello De Felice, 1951), a spy story on the background of the First World War; *La Leggenda del Piave* (*The Legend of Piave River*, Riccardo Freda, 1952), a film about the conflict between a patriotic woman and a husband who is engaged in criminal activities during the war; *Fratelli d'Italia* (*Brothers of Italy*, Fausto Saraceni, 1952), the biopic of Austrian-born Italian

irredentist and sailor Nazario Sauro; *Bella Non Piangere* (*Bella, Don't Cry*, Davide Carbonari, 1954), a film about a disabled man working as a postman on the front; *I Cinque dell'Adamello* (*The Adamello Five*, Pino Mercanti, 1954), the story of an heroic mission to recover the bodies of five Alpine soldiers killed by a landslide in 1918.

15. See Hobsbawm, pp. 27–30.
16. Jay Winter, *Sites of Memory, Sites of Mourning: the Great War in European Cultural History*, Cambridge: Cambridge University Press, 1998 [first published in 1995], pp. 119–44.
17. *Tra le Nevi e i Ghiacci del Tonale* (*Amid Snow and Ice on Mount Tonale*), 1918, Cinematographic Section of the Italian Army, Imperial War Museum (London), Film ID: IWM 459.
18. 'Un urlo non umano ma di belva ferita rompe, staziante l'aria a cento metri da noi. Pochi istanti dopo vedo un soldato che a salti segue il sentiero mentre tiene con una mano a la gamba penzoloni. Nessun soldato gli offre aiuto, soltanto quando egli è vicinissimo alle rocce delle mani lo soccorrono.' Lucio Fabi, *Gente di Trincea: la Grande Guerra sul Carso e sull'Isonzo*, Milano: Mursia, 2009, p. 274.
19. Pierre Sorlin, 'Cinema and the Memory of the Great War', in *The First World War and Popular Cinema: 1914 to the Present*, Michael Paris (ed.), Edinburgh: Edinburgh University Press, 1999, pp. 5–26 (11).
20. An example of this narrative is given by *Mariute* (Eduardo Bencivenga, 1918), a war melodrama with silent-era diva Francesca Bertini. There is a significant intertextual relationship between Bencivenga's film and *The Great War*: a photograph of Bertini from the poster of *Mariute* is revered by Sicilian soldier Rosario (Tiberio Murgia) in one of several hints to the popular culture of the First World War used by Monicelli.
21. Gian Piero Brunetta, 'L'immagine della Prima Guerra Mondiale attraverso il cinema', in *Operai e Contadini nella Grande Guerra*, Mario Isnenghi (ed.), Bologna: Cappelli Editore, 1982, pp. 273–82.
22. *La guerra d'Italia a 3,000 metri sull'Adamello* (*The Italian War at 3,000 Metres on the Adamello*, Luca Comerio and Paolo Granata), Comerio Milano Cinematografia, 1916, Archivio Storico Istituto Luce (Rome), Film ID: CF00302.
23. *Battaglia sulle colline italiane* (*Battle on the Italian Hills*), 1918, Archivio Storico Istituto Luce (Rome), Film ID: RW55201.
24. *Piave. Rievocata la Gloriosa Epopea* (*Piave River. Recalling the Glorious Epic*), 1958, Settimanale CIAC/SC497, CIAC, Compagnia Italiana Attualità Cinematografiche, Archivio Storico Istituto Luce (Rome), Film ID: KB049701.
25. The newspaper articles are included in Franco Calderoni, *La Grande Guerra: dal Soggetto al Film*, Bologna: Cappelli, 1959, pp. 72–9.
26. Calderoni, pp. 17–19.
27. 'Il nemico può avere fucili, mitragliatrici, cannoni: con le corazze Farina si passa dappertutto.' Emilio Lusso, *Un anno sull'altopiano*, Torino: Einaudi, 2005 [first published by Edizioni Italiane di Cultura in 1938], p. 92.

28. In the silent film *La Guerra e il Sogno di Momi* (*The War and the Dream of Momi*, Giovanni Pastrone, 1917), an old man reads to his grandchild, Momi, a letter written by the boy's father at the front and including adventurous tales of war and courage. Momi later falls asleep and dreams of tin soldiers and trenches in a series of sequences that presents one of the earliest sophisticated uses of stop-motion animation in Italian cinema. These tin figurines evoke the image of Italian soldiers wearing the Farina cuirasses; in 1917 only the fantasy of a child and the misjudgement of the high-ranking military officials could have contemplated a war of armoured knights facing the new pneumatic trench mortars.
29. Jay Winter, *Remembering War: the Great War between Memory and History in the 20th Century*, New Haven: Yale University Press, 2006, pp. 183–200.
30. Winter, 2006, p. 185.
31. Self-harm was a common recurrence in the Italian trenches, with over 10,000 soldiers found guilty of this practice in 1916 alone (see Callisto Cosulich, *Uomini Contro: dal Soggetto al Film*, Bologna: Cappelli, 1970, p. 37).
32. 'Per la prima volta si rendevano conto che la guerra la facevano solo i contadini, i pastori, gli operai, gli artigiani. E gli altri dov'erano? Altra scoperta: anche dall'altra parte, la guerra la facevano i contadini e gli operai.' (Emilio Lusso, 'La Brigata Sassari e il Partito Sardo D'Azione', *Il Ponte*, No. 9–10, 1951).
33. See David Nicolle, *The Italian Army of World War One*, Botley, Oxford: Osprey Publishing, 2012.
34. 'Grazie! Anche i codici sono arrivati! Che effetto mi ha fatto rivedere questi libricini che da più di due anni avevo persino dimenticato che esistessero. E non ero il solo ad averli dimenticati in questi tempi. Com'è strano il mondo. Anche la somma giustizia sociale che scaturirà dalla Guerra, sarà l'effetto, sia pure parziale, di tante piccolo e flagranti ingiustizie.' Giuseppe and Eugenio Garrone, *Lettere e Diari di Guerra 1914–1918*, Milano: Garzanti, 1974, p. 394.
35. See Cosulich, p. 60.
36. Mark Shiel, *Italian Neorealism: Rebuilding the Cinematic City*, London: Wallflower Press, 2006, p. 98.
37. 'Era un paese di montagna, dico era perché nel 1916 la guerra lo ha prima incendiato e poi distrutto e raso al suolo; e anche se tra il 1919 e il 1922 è stato ricostruito, ora non è più quello.' Mario Rigoni Stern, *Amore di Confine*, Torino: Einaudi, 1986, p. 6.
38. Garry W. Trompf, *The Idea of Historical Recurrence in Western Thought: from Antiquity to the Reformation*, Berkeley: University of California Press, 1992, p. 1.
39. 'La guerra e una brutta bestia, gira e gira il mondo e non si ferma mai. [...] Tiri su case che poi la guerra le buttera giu e io verro qui a trovare bombe.'
40. David Lowenthal, 'Past Time, Present Place: Landscape and Memory', *Geographical Review*, Vol. 65, No. 1, 1975, pp. 1–36 (5–6).
41. Andreas Huyssen, 'Monument and Memory in a Postmodern Age', *The Yale Journal of Criticism,* Vol. 6, No. 2, 1993, pp. 24–261 (253–4).
42. In Gianetti's film, Flora, an aging diva whose career has dramatically declined, receives an invitation to visit the supply and support lines behind the front and

to sing for the army, and decides to sing a jingoistic military march. She appears on stage wearing an Italian flag over her dress and a crown resembling that of the House of Savoy. Flora realises that she was not invited to sing for the frontline soldiers but for the wounded, and is profoundly moved by the sight of the young men who have been severely injured and disfigured on the battlefields. She interrupts the band, removes her crown and the flag – thus revealing a black dress evoking the process of mourning – and sings 'O *surdato 'nnammurato*, a Neapolitan song written by Enrico Cannio in 1915 about a young soldier who is fighting at the front. Her performance is later interrupted by Austrian artillery. The contrast between the patriotic images of Flora wrapped in the Italian flag and the image of the tearful singer performing a moving interpretation of a popular song reveals the conflicting vision of a war of heroes and patriotism coexisting with a humanist understanding of the shattering violence and pointlessness of war.

43. Emiliano Morreale, *L'invenzione della nostalgia. Il vintage nel cinema italiano e dintorni*, Roma: Donzelli, 2009, p. 113.

CHAPTER 2

Huesca, Aragón, Spain, 20 May 1937, 5:00 a.m.

> *A thirty-three-year-old man born in Motihari, Bihar, is wounded in the throat by a bullet shot by a sniper. He is carried on a stretcher and then in an ambulance to a hospital in Lérida. His name is Eric Arthur Blair, better known as George Orwell, and this happens on the morning of 20 May 1937 in Huesca.*

Set in the eighteenth century against the background of an unnamed city besieged by an Ottoman army, the fantasy film *The Adventures of Baron Munchausen* (Terry Gilliam, 1988) includes an imaginative sequence where Baron Munchausen (John Neville) fires himself through the sky by using a mortar and then returns to the city walls by riding a cannonball; the Angel of Death flies above him as he approaches a group of the crumbling buildings. Smoke, fire and havoc characterise the city under siege and its sixteenth-century church bell tower seemingly ready to collapse. In a later and equally preposterous sequence, the Baron escapes in a hot air balloon made from women's underwear and rises next to the heavily damaged church (Figure 2.1). These scenes from *The Adventures of Baron Munchausen* were filmed on location in the ruins of the old town of Belchite, in the province of Zaragozza (Aragón region), and the old church used in the film is that of San Martín de Tours. Belchite, like the unnamed city of *The Adventures of Baron Munchausen*, was also under siege during an offensive led by Republican forces against the Nationalists in the Spanish Civil War (1936–9). The village was almost entirely destroyed during what is known as the Battle of Belchite in the summer of 1937 and its ruins, untouched since the end of that battle, have been filmed in several war newsreels as well as in later documentaries.[1]

Made a year after the offensive, the newsreel *Franco Push: End Near?* (British Paramount, 1938) shows a panoramic shot of the ruins of Belchite, including the church of San Martín de Tours, aerial views and various shots of Nationalist troops entering the town. Footage from this newsreel was later repurposed in order to illustrate the final phases of the conflict in two episodes of the Granada Television documentary series *The Spanish Civil War* (1983). The first episode of this documentary series, *Prelude to Tragedy: 1931–1936* (David Hart, 1983), opens with various present-day shots taken

Figure 2.1 The ruins of the old town of Belchite in *The Adventures of Baron Munchausen* (Terry Gilliam, 1988).

in Belchite and with shots following a local farmer herding a flock of goats and sheep through the ruins.² *Inside the Revolution* (David Hart, 1983), the fifth episode of the series, returns to this location and incorporates archival footage of the battle, including shots of the church tower hit by mortar fire during the Republican offensive. As an archival image of the church fades into a present-day view of the same building, *Inside the Revolution* continues with the testimony of Bill Bailey, an Irish-American communist activist who volunteered in the International Brigades during the war. Bailey returns to Belchite and stands in one of the crumbling buildings and, later, on what used to be Calle Mayor. Here he continues his account in front of the gate known as El Arco de la Villa or Portal-capilla de Santa María. This sequence then bridges the gap between past and present as the shot fades into archival footage from the 1930s filmed from the exact same place on Calle Mayor. This use of the ruins of Belchite in film exemplifies the intertwining of archival footage, present-day testimonies and fictional accounts which characterises the cinematic image of the sites of memory of the Spanish Civil War.

Newsreels like *Franco Push: End Near?* have also been repurposed in fiction films; Ken Loach's *Land and Freedom* (1995), for example, offers a meaningful example of the connection between factual and fictional footage of the war. The film begins in Liverpool in the mid 1990s and sees David Carr (Ian Hart) dying at an old age and his granddaughter (Suzanne Maddock) discovering a stack of old letters from which she learns about her grandfather's time in Spain with the International Brigades during the war. This scene is followed by a non-diegetic insert made of archival footage of the Second Spanish

Republic and expository title cards summarising the events which led to the war. This footage is accompanied by the anarchist song *A las Barricadas* (To the Barricades, 1936), written by poet and trade unionist Valeriano Orobón Fernández; when the music stops the expository use of newsreels becomes diegetic as the footage of the Republican militias heading to the Aragón front is projected on a screen in order to illustrate the account of the war given by a recruiter at a 1936 meeting of the Communist Party in Liverpool. The following sequences are also set in the 1930s and were mainly filmed in the towns of Mirambel and Morella, respectively in the Teruel and Castelló provinces of Aragón, a region which was one of the main fronts of the war.

The cinematic topography of the Spanish Civil War, which is exemplified in the use of the ruins of Belchite or in the archival footage and location shooting of *Land and Freedom*, sees battles, sieges, the bombing of civilians and the destruction of cities and villages unfolding across the entire country.[3] In a process which evokes the ways in which films of the Italian front in the First World War immortalised incidents like the Second Battle of Piave River, countless newsreels and reconstructions of the events which took place during the Spanish Civil War have contributed to the memorialisation of a key accident in the history of the Short Twentieth Century and one which anticipated the events of the Second World War.[4] Both in the case of the First World War and in that of the Spanish Civil War, the places where the battles unfolded bear witness to the bloodshed and display the physical marks of the fighting; film has captured or re-enacted these events from different perspectives. In the case of the Italian campaign in the First World War, film reflects a split between militarist and patriotic narrative on the one hand and pacifist and humanist readings of the event on the other. In the instance of the Spanish Civil War, the rupture is between films which embraced the Republican cause and those which supported the Nationalist side. Both wars had long-term repercussions on Spanish and Italian history in the Short Twentieth Century. In this chapter, I investigate the relationship between past and present and I travel to the spaces traversing the cinema of the Spanish Civil War with a focus on a selected number of locations where the action unfolded. These sites include the towns of Gernika (Guernica) in the Basque County, Lérida (Lleida) in north-eastern Catalonia, Badajoz in Extremadura, Ciudad Universitaria (University City) in Madrid, the municipal cemetery in Guadalajara and the Alcázar of Toledo in the Castile-La Mancha region.

The aerial bombing of Guernica which took place on 26 April 1937 at the hands of Francisco Franco's allies, the Condor Legion of the German Luftwaffe and the Legionary Aviation of Italy, was one of the most dramatic episodes in the Spanish Civil War and cost hundreds of deaths and untold damage. While the ruins of Belchite were left untouched by order of Franco, who could ascribe the destruction of that place to Republican forces, the bombed-out buildings of Guernica were not preserved and the town was eventually rebuilt on the same site. Despite Franco's early attempt to blame the Basques for the destruction of Guernica, the involvement of Italian and German forces in the bombing of civilians on Spanish soil was ascertained in and outside the country; and so, the memorialisation of Guernica by means of preserving its ruins could not fit the propaganda narrative articulated by the regime after the war. Photographs and archival footage bear witness to the destruction and to the ways in which the civilians of Guernica were targeted by the bombing in a manner which anticipated the air raids of the Second World War. A newsreel such as *Guernica Wiped out by Air-Raid* (Gaumont British News, 1937), for example, provides a visual record of the impact of the bombing on the people and buildings of the town and reveals the extent of the damage done by the incendiary bombs dropped from German and Italian planes: few buildings are still standing, and all seem irreparably damaged. The brutality of the attack would later inspire *Guernica* (1950), a short essayistic film directed by Alain Resnais which was narrated by artist Jacques Pruvost, and which included a poem written by Paul Eluard and recited by María Casares, with music by Guy Bernard. This film uses photographs of Guernica taken after the bombing and paintings, drawings and sculptures by Pablo Picasso in order to articulate a reflection on the horror and meaninglessness of war. Resnais thus anticipated his anti-war argument about the annihilation of civilians which he would later bring to fruition in *Hiroshima Mon Amour* (1959), a film which I discuss in Chapter 4.[5]

During the dictatorship, the bombing of the Basque town was largely ignored in Spanish Cinema and it was only in international films such as *Guernica*, which would not be distributed in Spain until well after the death of Franco and the return to democracy, that the brutality of the attack and the condemnation of the use of civilians as targets could be fully articulated. The Italian-French production *L'arbre de Guernica* (*The Tree of Guernica*, Fernando Arrabal) was made in 1975 and only released in Spain in 1982. This surrealist take on the events of the civil war engages with the symbolic meaning evoked by the name of the bombed out town. The film is set in the fictional town of Villa Ramiro and filmed in Matera, Italy. The bombing of Guernica is evoked in the title of the film: the *Gernikako Arbola* (Tree of Gernika) is an oak tree that symbolises the identity of the Basque people, and which survived the war and did not die until 2004. In the absence of ruins, the tree becomes here an emblem of peace and resilience which stands in for Guernica, the Spanish Civil War and the later repression of the Basques at the hands of Franco's regime.

The anti-war symbolic nature of the bombing of Guernica was famously exemplified in the nightmarish scene of human and animal figures in flames created by Pablo Picasso in *Guernica* (1937). This painting, with its horrifying greyscale, is used in the opening sequence of *Battleground for Idealists* (John Blake, 1983), the third episode of the television series *The Spanish Civil War*. Manoli and Koni Aguirre, two sisters who witnessed the destruction of Guernica a few hours after the attack had taken place, visit Museo Reina Sofía in Madrid and stand in front of Picasso's painting. As Manoli remembers the dead animals and the victims, the film juxtaposes close-up shots of details from the painting, archival material, photographs of Guernica taken soon after the bombing and present-day footage of the new town.[6] This intertwining of images evokes the attack and the symbolic nature of Guernica as an episode defining twentieth-century warfare. As the camera reveals one of the main figures in the painting, Manoli explains how she is always been filled with emotions in front of that image of a woman burning on a balcony with her arms outstretched, and explains how she feels that could have been her grandmother. For these two women, the visit to the museum thus acts as a return to Guernica and Picasso's painting effectively becomes a site of memory on its own account; one of the figures painted by Picasso is re-imagined as a lost relative and Manoli's thought exemplifies the ways in which the painting can conjure personal memory while evoking a collective tragedy.

Battleground for Idealists also uses the photographs of Guernica taken by Florence 'Fifi' Roberts, a Welsh woman who sailed with her father, Captain William Roberts, from Wales to Spain in 1937 at the age of twenty. Their ship, named *Seven Seas Spray*, delivered a large cargo of supplies to the Basques who were starved by the Nationalist blockade of Bilbao. The *Seven Seas Spray* was then seized by Franco's forces and kept for two months in the port of Santona, in Cantabria. On 3 November 1937, following the Roberts' return to Wales, the *Daily Mail* published the woman's account of her time in Spain:

> Going to sea is great fun. Running blockades and being captured is greater fun still. I had plenty of thrills. When we entered the port it was in the hands of the Reds. Just as we were preparing to leave, General Franco's forces swept up to the coast and seized the port. We were called on to surrender and to remain in port.[7]

During her time in Spain, Roberts also visited the ruins of Guernica soon after the bombing and took the photographs, which were later used in *Battleground for Idealists*.

The documentary also follows the return journey of Roberts to Guernica in the early 1980s; thus, Manoli and Koni Aguirre's return to Guernica by means of Picasso's painting is juxtaposed in the film with a more conventional return to the physical site of memory of Guernica. On the background of a street in the new town, Roberts gives an account of her visit to the place and describes the destruction she witnessed firsthand, and which echoes the words spoken by Manoli in front of Picasso's work. Her account is accompanied by the photographs she took in 1937, and which are now juxtaposed with present-day shots of the same locations (Figure 2.2). A photograph of Guernica in ruins taken by Roberts from the top of a hill shows the heavily damaged Iglesia Santa María (St Mary's Church) in the middle of the frame; this is followed by a present-day extreme long shot taken from the same location and by a medium shot of Roberts as she stands on that same hill and gives her account on the background of Guernica, with the refurbished St Mary's Church visible in the middle of the frame. Both Roberts' return to Guernica and that of the Aguirre sisters, mediated by Picasso's painting, serve the purpose of anchoring the historical event to individual experience and thus memorialise the site of the fascist bombing. While in Belchite the untouched ruins of its buildings bear witness to the trauma of war, in the case of Guernica archival photographs, paintings and testimonies such as those used in *Battleground for Idealists* can unlock the memorialisation of the site in place of the missing ruins.

Figure 2.2 Florence 'Fifi' Roberts returns to Guernica in *Battleground for Idealists* (John Blake, 1983).

The Guernica sequences of *Battleground for Idealists* also use footage from a Nationalist newsreel with a propaganda message conveyed by a voice-over narrator claiming that Basques forces were responsible for the attempt to burn their own city to the ground. A month after the bombing, *The Illustrated London News* published two photographs of the city in ruins and commented: 'In ravaged Guernica: a typical scene of destruction, caused, according to the Basques, by aerial bombardment, but according to their opponents by petrol fires started by "red" elements.'[8] The attempt to deceive public opinion in Spain and abroad failed and the role of Franco's Nazi and fascist allies became clear soon after the publication of that article; and yet, in Spain the truth about Guernica was largely repressed until after the death of the dictator in 1975 at a time when many voices that had been silenced for nearly forty years began to re-emerge. On 3 July 1977, for example, thousands of anarchists assembled for the first time since the end of the Spanish Civil War in front of the Palau Nacional (National Palace) on the hill of Montjuïc in Barcelona; the crowd listened to a very critical speech about the Communist Party leadership of Santiago Carrillo delivered by Federica Montseny, an anarchist and former Minister of Health during the Spanish Revolution of 1936 who had recently returned from exile after the death of Franco.

The newsreel titled *Spain: A Rally by 100,000 Anarchists, Meeting In Barcelona For The First Time In 40 Years* (Reuters, 1977) captures Montseny's speech and the red and black flags of the anarchist union Confederación Nacional del Trabajo (CNT) waved by the anarchists gathering on Avinguda de la Reina Maria Cristina. The flags joining diagonally the red colour of the labour movement and the black colour of anarchism, along with other political flags, had dominated the cityscape of Barcelona, a resolutely Republican city during the civil war, and regularly appeared in later dramatic reconstructions of the events which took place in those days. In *Libertarias* (*Libertarians*, Vicente Aranda, Spain, 1996), a drama about a young nun (Ariadna Gil) who is recruited by an older woman (Ana Belén) into an anarchist militia, there is a long sequence filmed in Plaça Reial in the Gothic Quarter of Barcelona and set in July 1937; these scenes include various shots of men and women waving a large number of anarchist flags while parading on the square. This sequence from *Libertarians* stages an image whose main symbol, the anarchist flag, was soon to disappear from Franco's Spain only to resurface after the death of the dictator as revealed in the newsreel *Spain: a Rally by 100,000 Anarchists*.

The abundance of anarchist flags in Barcelona was witnessed by George Orwell in 1936, when he arrived in Spain to fight against fascism; in *Homage to Catalonia*, the English writer recalls that 'practically every building of any size had been seized by the workers and was draped with red flags or with the red and black flag of the anarchists' and remembers how, as he marched down

La Rambla (the street connecting Plaça de Catalunya with Port Vell) with his comrades from the *Partit Obrer d'Unificació Marxista* (Workers Party of Marxist Unification), he could see 'red flags and red and black flags everywhere, friendly crowds thronging the pavement to have a look at us, women waving from the windows.'[9] Soon after his days in a city on the verge of revolution and while fighting in the Huesca area of the Aragón front, Orwell was wounded in the throat by a bullet shot by a sniper and taken to a hospital in Lérida, in the west of Catalonia; in *Homage to Catalonia* he remembers the place fondly:

> And in Lérida there were old crumbling buildings upon whose cornices thousands upon thousands of swallows had built their nests, so that at a little distance the crusted pattern of nests was like some florid moulding of the rococo period. It was queer how for nearly six months past I had had no eyes for such things. With my discharge papers in my pocket I felt like a human being again, and also a little like a tourist. For almost the first time I felt that I was really in Spain, in a country that I had longed all my life to visit. In the quiet back streets of Lérida and Barbastro I seemed to catch a momentary glimpse, a sort of far-off rumour of the Spain that dwells in everyone's imagination. White sierras, goatherds, dungeons of the Inquisition, Moorish palaces, black winding trains of mules, grey olive trees and groves of lemons, girls in black mantillas, the wines of Malaga and Alicante, cathedrals, cardinals, bull-fights, gypsies, serenades – in short, Spain.[10]

Evocatively described here by Orwell, Lérida was bombed by the Legion Condor air forces from Nazi Germany and eventually conquered by the Nationalists. During the dictatorship, the city was used as a location in *La fiel infantería* (*The Faithful Infantry*, Pedro Lazaga, 1960), a civil war drama which follows the imaginary Nationalist Battalion Barletta in the offensive to capture Cerro Quemado, an equally imaginary location, from Republican forces. The film was shot in the Estudios Cinematográficos Chamartín of Madrid and on the grounds of the former Catedral de Santa María de la Seu Vella (Cathedral of St. Mary of La Seu Vella) located on top of the Lérida hill; a site of both military and religious significance, the cathedral was turned into a military citadel at the beginning of the eighteenth century and in *The Faithful Infantry* provides the background for scenes of military manoeuvre in preparation for the battalion's mission.

Both in Orwell's words provoking a nostalgia for a Spanish landscapes lingering in the imagination and in a Francoist film like *The Faithful Infantry*, the streets and landmarks of Lérida emerge as sites of memory of a war which, as David Archibald suggests, has become a 'touchstone in the Western political imaginary' and whose cinematic depictions have accommodated 'varying political positions in numerous cinematic forms' including Republican and Nationalist perspectives originating in diverse contexts and expressed through a variety of media.¹¹ Similarly, Peter Monteath has argued that films of the Spanish Civil War 'express unambiguously the political sympathies of their creators' and yet their 'political commitment tends to evaporate as the war recedes into the past.'¹² During the dictatorship, Spanish cinema was unequivocally embracing a Nationalist view of the civil war. In this context, newsreels from the 1930s were repurposed for propaganda aims in films such as *El camino de la paz* (*The Way to Peace*, Rafael G. Garzón, 1961), a documentary produced by state-controlled *Noticiarios y Documentales* (News and Documentaries) and presented to the public as an objective summary of the events of the 1930s while effectively embracing a Nationalist mythic retelling of the years of the Republic and of the war itself. Described in the titles as the 'Cinematographic highlights of the war of Spanish liberation',¹³ *The Way to Peace* emphasises Republican violence while Nationalist war crimes are omitted; furthermore, Franco's connections with the regimes in Italy and Germany are entirely absent from the film.

Rafael De España has observed that films made during the dictatorship expose a common trait of Francoist propaganda, the tendency to frame the war as an internal affair which saw the interference of the USSR.¹⁴ Additionally, Joxean Fernández has argued that, as a result of the defeat of fascism in the Second World War, films made during Franco's dictatorship, like *The Way to Peace*, ignored the most controversial aspects of the Spanish Civil War and, in particular, they omitted the involvement of Nazi Germany in the aerial bombing of the Basque Country.¹⁵ A rare exception to this pattern was provided by *La Caza* (Carlos Saura, *The Hunt*, 1966), a film which, as Archibald puts it, employs symbolism in order to articulate a 'fierce critique of the celebration of machismo and the military in previous pro-Franco civil war films.'¹⁶ After the death of Franco and the return to democracy in the following decades, Spanish cinema witnessed, in a manner which mimics the slow re-emergence of Jewish memory in post-war Polish cinema which I discuss in the next chapter, the return of what had been repressed in earlier films, a Republican view of the conflict.¹⁷ And yet, the ways in which memory resurfaced after the transition to democracy was, and to some extent still is, highly problematic.

In 1942, over thirty years before the death of Franco, Orwell looked back at his experience in Spain and speculated on the ways in which the Spanish Civil War would be memorialised after the end of the dictatorship. He anticipated some of the most controversial and long-lasting facets of how the events of the 1930s have been remembered in democratic Spain:

> How will the history of the Spanish war be written? If Franco remains in power his nominees will write the history books, and (to stick to my chosen

point) that Russian army which never existed will become historical fact, and schoolchildren will learn about it generations hence. But suppose Fascism is finally defeated and some kind of democratic government restored in Spain in the fairly near future; even then, how is the history of the war to be written? What kind of records will Franco have left behind him? Suppose even that the records kept on the Government side are recoverable – even so, how is a true history of the war to be written?[18]

The main obstacle to the writing of that true history of the war evoked by Orwell has been the organised act of forgetting enabled by a political deal agreed by both left-wing and right-wing forces two years after the death of Franco, when the Spanish Parliament promulgated an amnesty law based on the so-called *Pacto del olvido* (Pact of Forgetting). The Spanish 1977 Amnesty Law freed political prisoners while guaranteeing impunity for those who participated in human rights violations during the Spanish Civil War and, across four decades, in Francoist Spain; as a result, thousands of men and women who were unlawfully imprisoned during the dictatorship and the relatives of those who were murdered by the regime have struggled to find justice.[19]

The documentary *El silencio de otros* (*The Silence of Others*, Robert Bahar and Almudena Carracedo, 2018) addresses the ways in which the war and the persecutions of political opponents which took place in the years of the dictatorship have left profound scars on the social fabric of the country. The film is centred on a group of men and women whose parents were executed during the war as they seek the human remains of their loved ones, and also focuses on a group of women whose children were victims of state-sanctioned kidnappings during the dictatorship. Additionally, *The Silence of Others* follows a group of survivors who were imprisoned and tortured by Franco's police and who are now seeking justice by filing a lawsuit in Argentina on the basis of the principle of universal jurisdiction for crimes against humanity. In the opening sequences of the film, José María 'Chato' Galante, a pro-democracy activist who had been a political prisoner during the Franco years, leads the cameraman to the address of Antonio González Pacheco, the man who tortured him when he was in prison.[20] The fact that victim and perpetrator inhabit the same places evokes the incidence of Holocaust survivors living close to their former tormentors in Latin America; I address this paradox in Chapter 5 in relation to the cinematic landscapes of Latin America and argue that the memory of the Holocaust can inform the history of the dictatorships in Argentina. The Spanish Civil War and the dictatorships in post-war Latin America are intertwined in a memorialisation evolving in multiple directions and finding a reflection on film. Accordingly, Chato's pursuit of justice in Argentina establishes political and historical parallels between the ways in which that country has successfully persecuted members of its former military junta which controlled the country during the Dirty War and the ways in which Spain has failed to obtain justice for the political crimes committed during the dictatorship; in doing so, *The Silence of Others* evokes an alternative to the amnesty law of 1977 and the necessity to find personal and collective closure for the civil war and its aftermath.

Largely filmed in Madrid, *The Silence of Others* engages with the sites of memory of a persecution which unfolded during the dictatorship and which had its roots in the events of the 1930s. One of the most significant locations of the film is the Real Casa de Correos (Royal House of the Post Office) in Puerta del Sol, today the office of the President of the Community of Madrid. A recurring presence in newsreels and documentaries of the Spanish Civil War, during the dictatorship this building was the headquarters of the Dirección General de Seguridad (General Security Directorate) and one of the places where political opponents of the regime were detained, tortured and killed.[21] *The Silence of Others* includes various street scenes filmed near the building as well as interviews with a group of young men and women who display a very limited knowledge of the events of the war and the dictatorship. These scenes are followed by a sequence where the survivors and civil rights campaigners who were detained in the General Security Directorate in the 1960s and 1970s are demonstrating in front of the Royal House of the Post Office for the persecution and indictment of their oppressors. The return to a site of memory and oppression enables the survivors to make a case for justice amidst the challenge given by the continuity of the past into the present, by the sense of being in a city and a country which has not dealt with its recent history; this is exemplified by the fact that the Royal House of the Post Office, the place where these men and women were imprisoned and tortured, is still in use as a public building.

Apart from the Royal House of the Post Office, in *The Silence of Others* one of the most significant sites of memory bridging the gap between past and present is the municipal cemetery in Guadalajara. On 16 November 1939, socialist unionist Timoteo Mendieta Alcala was lined up with many other supporters of the Republic against its wall, shot by a nationalist firing squad and dumped into a mass grave located within the cemetery. Seventy-eight years later his daughter, Ascensión Mendieta, located his remains and had them exhumed and buried in Madrid (Figure 2.3). The conditions for this type of exhumation, as Francisco Ferrándiz has argued, are 'deeply embedded in the fabric of Spain's civil society, where they had been kept alive despite the dictatorship and its mandatory historiographical construction of victory, and despite the political pacts that paved the way for Spain's transition to democracy in the 1970s.'[22] In the same vein, Jo Labanyi has argued these exhumations have 'a major therapeutic value for the relatives concerned, in

Figure 2.3 Exhumation at the municipal cemetery in Guadalajara in *El silencio de otros* (*The Silence of Others*, Robert Bahar and Almudena Carracedo, 2018).

addition to fulfilling an ethical obligation to honour the victims of injustice.'[23] As I have argued in Chapter 1, Olmi's *The Scavengers* used metal relics of the First World War in order to provide an unmediated impression of the tangible past; in *The Silence of Others*, human remains are used for the same purpose as remembered evidence. A long sequence from the film illustrates the therapeutic process described by Ferrándiz and Labanyi as it follows Ascensión Mendieta to the cemetery in Guadalajara while she witnesses the exhumation of her father's remains across several days; the film thus inscribes the memory of the killings which immediately followed the civil war to a specific site of memory where the tangible evidence of history materialises in the form of human bones emerging from the ground. The exhumation is the result of a laborious process evoking the equally complex way in which what was first suppressed and later overridden by the infamous amnesty of 1977 is re-emerging in present-day Spain.

The Silence of Others articulates the process of anchoring the memories of the war to specific sites such as the cemetery in Guadalajara and the Royal House of the Post Office in Puerta del Sol. This documentary also reveals the ways in which the memory of the Spanish Civil War is literally inscribed onto the streets of Madrid named after Franco's generals and captains and including officers whose names are associated with some of the locations which I discuss elsewhere in this chapter, namely Badajoz, Toledo and Belchite. The film reveals how Madrid streets were named after General Juan Yagüe, who was also known as *el Carnicero de Badajoz* (the Butcher of Badajoz) and who ordered the execution of over 4,000 prisoners in the town's bullfighting ring; General José Moscardó and General José Enrique Varela, who defended and held the Alcázar of Toledo against Republican forces; Captain Carlos de Haya González, who supplied the defenders with medicines and ammunition during the Battle of Belchite. *The Silence of Others* also includes a shot of Arco de la Victoria, the triumphal arch which, completed in 1956, commemorates the victory of Francoist troops against Republican defenders in the *Batalla de la Ciudad Universitaria* (Battle of the University City) in Madrid on 23 November 1936.[24] On that day, the campus of the Complutense University of Madrid was severely damaged in the battle and, after the war, as Alfredo González-Ruibal explains, the regime made plans to 'preserve the ruins of the University City (Ciudad Universitaria) in Madrid as they stood at the end of the war and make them into a place of *memory* where one could take tours guided by wounded veterans.'[25] Unlike the case of Belchite though, the regime eventually decided to restore or reconstruct the buildings of a site with great symbolic significance. *Revolution, Counter-Revolution & Terror* (John Blake, 1983), the second episode of the television documentary series *The Spanish Civil War*, addresses in detail the battle which took place on the university campus and returns to the site of the action. In this film, Willie Forrest, who had been the *Daily Express* correspondent from Spain during the war, walks in the vicinity of the Facultad de Filosofía y Letras (Faculty of Humanities) and stands outside the building; here he remembers and provides an account of his visit to the same place in 1936 and describes how he saw several bodies lying across the ground. Forrest explains that those men were most likely Nationalists murdered by communist or anarchist forces in the indiscriminate terror which characterised the early days of the war. The gap between past and present is bridged by Forrest's account and by the juxtaposition of these scenes to archival footage used as a tangible trace of the battle and showing the dead bodies lying on the ground later filmed in *Revolution, Counter-Revolution & Terror*.[26]

At a time when the war was still raging, film had already dealt what took place in and around the Complutense University. The documentary *The Spanish Earth* (Joris Ivens) was released in 1937 and provides a visual record of the events and yet, as Archibald has argued, in this film the identity of the opposition to the Republican cause is vague and 'there is no attempt to explain the civil war's complex political background, with Hemingway describing the "enemy" simply as "they".'[27] Nevertheless, *The Spanish Earth* contributes to understanding the events which took place in Madrid during the war by including a map of the university district and various panoramic views of its buildings. These shots reveal the frontline of the Battle of Ciudad Universitaria running through the university campus and the public park Casa de Campo, including a French School called Casa de Velázquez and the university hospital building. This is followed by footage of the battle between Republican and Nationalist forces as it unfolded on the grounds of the university and Casa de Campo. Both *The Spanish Earth* and, forty-six years later, *Revolution, Counter-Revolution & Terror* thus use editing to inscribe the memorialisation of the events onto the topography of Madrid.

On the day of that battle, Badajoz, in the autonomous community of Extremadura, had already seen the sheer violence and destruction brought by the civil war. The town was taken by the Nationalist forces on 14 August 1936 and, in the following days, thousands of civilians and soldiers affiliated with the Republic were executed by firing squad or machine-gunned across several locations including Badajoz's Plaza de Toros (Bull Ring) and the Cementerio de San Juan. Filmed by René Brut, *Troubled Spain: Fierce Fighting near the Portuguese Border* (Pathé Gazette, 1936) incorporates various scenes displaying the bombed-out buildings of Badajoz, comprising shots of the Moorish citadel called Alcazaba of Badajoz; excluded by the final edit of the gazette, the footage filmed by Brut in Badajoz also included shots of a number of charred corpses of people executed by the Nationalists and dead bodies lying in the rubble of the city's buildings.[28] This footage would later be used extensively in *Revolution, Counter-Revolution & Terror*, a documentary which introduces the Battle of Badajoz with a panoramic view of the city and a map of the Iberian Peninsula showing the location of the town at the border with Portugal. This is followed by an interview with Mário Neves, a Portuguese journalist who covered the war for the evening newspaper *Diário de Lisboa* and witnessed the mass executions in the city, recorded on the background of Alcazaba. Accompanied by the sound of gunfire and edited with archival footage, various present-day shots of the wall of the Alcazaba, including the Torre de Espantaperros, still reveal the damage caused by bullets. The archival footage included in the film shows Franco's troops celebrating in the streets of Badajoz and a panoramic view of the city which fades into a present-day long shot of the same location. In the process of memorialising the events which took place after the fall of Badajoz, Neves gives an account of the arrests which were made by the Nationalists. The camera zooms out from a medium shot of Neves and reveals the entrance to the bull ring. Images of the stands and of the ground of the bull ring, by then a car park, accompany the journalist's report of the executions and are juxtaposed with footage of the corpses from *Troubled Spain*. The testimony continues at the other significant site of memory of the Badajoz massacre, the Cementerio de San Juan; present-day footage of the cemetery, including close-up shots of the damage caused by the bullets which could also be seen in the archival films, is here juxtaposed with other harrowing images of the burnt bodies from *Troubled Spain*.

In *Revolution, Counter-Revolution & Terror*, the account of the massacre shifts from the journalistic take of Neves' words to an individual dimension with the testimony given by Teresa Villalobos, the widow of one of the victims; her husband, she explains, was taken by the Nationalists to the bull ring. The testimony accompanies present-day footage of the place, including the exact window through which Villalobos saw her husband alive for the last time. The widow explains how she would later see his dead body at the cemetery and the film again uses footage of dead bodies from *Troubled Spain* in order to provide a visual referent to the dramatic testimony given by the woman. Badajoz's bull ring thus becomes a site of memory where the intertwining of testimony, archival material and present-day footage memorialises the massacre and bridges the gap between past and present. Like the ruins of Belchite, this location contains traces of the conflict and embodies the single perpetual fabric of places where the ongoing effects of war on people can be retrospectively articulated in documentary film.

While the Alcazaba of Badajoz is seen as a symbol of Nationalist aggression, the topography of the Spanish Civil War also includes a fortress whose siege was used by Franco's propaganda in order to celebrate the resilience of his forces. Located on the highest hill of Toledo, in the autonomous community of Castile-La Mancha and on the site of a third-century Roman palace, the Alcázar of Toledo is a sixteenth-century stone fortification which was largely rebuilt after the siege of 1936. The Alcázar had been held by Nationalist forces under the attack of Republican militia since 21 July 1936 when Franco's *Ejército de África* (Army of Africa) ended the siege on 27 of September of the same year. The documentary *Revolution, Counter-Revolution & Terror* includes footage of Franco's visit to the ruins of the fortress and a present-day scene where Willie Forrest from the *Daily Express* gives his testimony as he sits outdoors with the city of Toledo and its rebuilt fortress in the background. Forrest explains that the failure of the siege was due to the disorganised offensive of the Republican forces which allowed the fortress to become a celebrated symbol of victory for Franco's Spain. The ruins of the building were promoted as a patriotic tourist destination during the war at a time when Franco's propaganda, as Miriam Basilio has argued, had already found in the Alcázar a 'powerful combination of commemoration, tourism and religious pilgrimage.'[29] After the war, Basilio continues, 'the Alcázar became central to the new regime's mythic retelling of history. It was promoted as a tourist destination – a site of memory that linked Spanish military and imperial history with Franco's Civil War victory.'[30]

The mythic retelling of the siege migrated onto the screen with the Italian fascist propaganda film *L'Assedio dell'Alcazar* (*The Siege of the Alcazar*, Augusto Genina, 1940).[31] Largely filmed in the Cinecittà Studios (Rome), Genina's film opens with a panoramic view of the Alcázar and ends with a similar panoramic view of the building in ruins. Despite the ultimate destruction of the Alcázar, these shots exemplify the attempt to raise the image of the building and its ruins to a legendary story of resilience and victory.[32] A sequence from *The Siege of Alcazar* shows the bombardment of the outlying buildings, which took place in September 1936, and includes various staged shots of the cameramen who were filming the siege.[33] This sequence from *The Siege of the Alcazar* exemplifies the relationship between fiction and factual footage of the Spanish Civil War and between past and present. This is an intersection where locations such as the fortresses of Toledo and Lérida, the ruins of Belchite and Guernica, the municipal cemetery in Guadalajara, the bull ring of Badajoz, the university city of Madrid emerge through film as the sites of memory of the Spanish Civil War. These locations were either re-appropriated by the regime in its mythic retelling of the war or identified as sites of persecution by the Republican side and by those who, in later years, opposed the dictatorship. Both documentary and fiction films have contributed to evoking the discordant memories of the civil war in a deeply divided country and, in the case of more recent films, amidst the act of organised forgetting embedded in the amnesty of 1977. Film has enhanced the powerful symbolic meaning emerging from the ruins of bombed-out places and from the iconography of flags and uniforms, from artwork such as Picasso's *Guernica* and from the testimonies of those who were there and did not forget.

During Franco's regime the Nationalist narrative of the war was unchallenged in the use of cinema as a propaganda tool. Newsreels from the 1930s were first repurposed by Franco's cinematographers in order to celebrate the victory of the Nationalists and put the blame on the Republican forces; later they were used in documentaries such as the series *The Spanish Civil War* in order to evoke the war crimes committed by the Nationalists during the conflict. This tension is a reflection of the complexities enabling the past to be recalled in a country where political and regional sectarianism is still strong and where even street names bear witness to the divide between different factions. The aftermath of war thus sees processes of memorialisation shaped by politics and by a narrative established by social forces. In Chapter 1, I argued that the ever-changing memorialisation of war through film also characterises the ways in which Italy has remembered the unfolding of the First World War. In Chapter 3, I want to build on the ideas discussed so far and explore the ways in which post-war Poland struggled to address the specificity of the genocide of the Jews; I thus use the cinematic landscapes of the Holocaust in occupied Poland during the Second World War, and more specifically in the city of Lublin and the camps of Majdanek and Sobibór, in order to articulate a reflection on the ambivalent memorialisation of the Jewish genocide in Polish cinema and in international films.

Notes

1. The ruins of Belchite have also been used as a location in *El laberinto del fauno* (*Pan's Labyrinth*, Guillermo del Toro, 2006), a horror film set against the background of the Spanish Civil War, and *Spider-Man: Far From Home* (Jon Watts, 2019), a film where Belchite plays the role of an unnamed Mexican town.
2. *Prelude to Tragedy: 1931–1936* also anchors the memorialisation of the Spanish Civil War to a specific address – 11 Calle de Augusto Figueroa in Madrid. On 12 July 1936, Republican police officer José Castillo, who lived at that address, was killed by four Falangist gunmen as he walked from his home to Calle de Fuencarral. His assassination led to a sequence of events, starting with the killing of monarchist leader José Calvo Sotelo at the hands of leftist gunmen, which contributed to the ignition of the war. *Prelude to Tragedy: 1931–1936* includes a scene taken along the final itinerary which took Castillo from Calle de Augusto Figueroa to Calle de Fuencarral.
3. Hollywood films about the Spanish Civil War made during and soon after the conflict, on the other hand, created vague Spanish settings in studios. *For Whom the Bell Tolls* (Sam Wood, 1943) and *Blockade* (William Dieterle, 1938), for example, were entirely filmed in studio. As Archibald suggests, *For Whom the Bell Tolls* 'is an individualised, romanticised narrative that can be watched easily without worrying about historical or political specificity. Although set in Spain during a civil war there is little attempt to explain the details of the conflict; indeed in some ways this could be any war' (Archibald, p. 40, see ft. 10). *The Last Train from Madrid* (James P. Hogan, 1937) was filmed in studio with some establishing shots and background filmed in Palencia, a city in northern Spain; the film also uses factual footage of fighting and war damage in Madrid in its opening sequence.
4. For a discussion on the use of newsreels of the Spanish Civil War as a primary source see Anthony Aldgate, *Cinema and History: British Newsreels and the Spanish Civil War*, London: Scolar Press, 1979.
5. Resnais also developed his anti-war cinematic reflection in *Nuit et brouillard* (*Night and Fog*, 1956) with a focus on the unfolding of the Holocaust in the camps of Auschwitz II-Birkenau and Majdanek. In Chapter 3 I discuss how Majdanek was used as a location in newsreels from the 1940s and 1950s and in later fiction films.
6. *Battleground for Idealists* also includes interviews with Guernica witnesses Ignacia Ozamiz, and Condor Legion pilot Karl Von Knauer.
7. Fifi Roberts, 'Girl Reveals Full Story of Seized British Ship', *Daily Mail*, Issue Number 12957, London, 3 November 1937, p. 13.
8. 'Books of the Day', *The Illustrated London News*, Vol. 190, Issue 5118, 22 May 1937, p. 962.

9. George Orwell, *Homage to Catalonia*, London: Penguin, 2000, p. 13 [first published by Secker and Warburg in 1938].
10. Orwell, 2000, p. 164.
11. David Archibald, *The War That Won't Die: The Spanish Civil War in Cinema*, Manchester: Manchester University Press, 2014, pp. 187, 184.
12. Peter Monteath, 'Introduction', in *The Spanish Civil War in Literature, Film, and Art: An International Bibliography of Secondary Literature*, Santa Barbara: ABC-CLIO, 1994, pp. ix–xxx (xxi–xxii).
13. Síntesis cinematográfica de la Guerra de liberación Española.
14. Rafael De España, 'Images of the Spanish Civil War in Spanish feature films, 1939–1985', *Historical Journal of Film, Radio and Television*, Vol. 6, No. 2, 1986, pp. 223–36 (227).
15. Joxean Fernández, 'La memoria cinematográfica franquista de la Guerra Civil en el País Vasco', *Amnis. Revue de Civilisation Contemporaine*, No. 2, October 2011 (last accessed 17 April 2021, http://journals.openedition.org/amnis/1496). There was a shift in the propaganda message after the Second World War dictated by the outcome of the conflict and exemplified by the re-release of Francoist drama *Raza* (*Race*, José Luis Sáenz de Heredia, 1942) in 1950 under the title of *Espíritu de una raza*; in this version of the film all references to fascism and to anti-American feelings were eliminated as the dictator presented himself as one of Europe's foremost anti-communist leaders and sought the support of North Atlantic Treaty Organization (NATO).
16. Archibald, p. 84.
17. See, for example, *Huidos* (Sancho Gracia, 1993), a film which focuses on a group of resistance fighters during the civil war, and *Guernica* (Koldo Serra, 2016). During the dictatorship, the only films which were supportive of the Republican cause were made in other countries. Beside international documentaries about the civil war, non-Spanish fiction films also addressed the events while embracing the Republican side. For example, *Fünf Patronenhülsen* (*Five Cartridges*, Frank Beyer,1960), a film made in the German Democratic Republic and focusing on the contribution of members of the International Brigades to a major Republican offensive, depicted, in Archibald's words, 'the events that took place in Spain between 1936 and 1939 in a manner that fitted with the East German state leadership's view of the conflict: not as a war between democracy and fascism [...] but as the "National Revolutionary War of the Spanish People" or the "War of Fascist Intervention"' (Archibald, p. 48).
18. George Orwell, 'Looking Back on the Spanish Civil War', in *The Collected Essays, Journalism and Letters of George Orwell: Volume II My Country Left or Right, 1940–1943* (eds Sonia Orwell and Ian Angus), London: Secker and Warburg, 1968, pp. 249–67 (257).
19. See Javier Tusell, *Spain: From Dictatorship to Democracy*, Hoboken: John Wiley, 2011.
20. Both Galante and Pacheco died in the COVID-19 pandemic during the spring of 2020.

21. The Royal House of the Post Office appears in the Nazi newsreel *Francos Streitkräfte betreten Madrid* (*Franco's Forces Enter Madrid*, Deutsche Monatsschau, 1939, British Pathé Film ID: 520.15), in a shot portraying a large crowd welcoming Nationalist forces and chanting Franco's name. This building also appears in the final scenes of Soviet documentary *Ispaniya* (*Spain*, Esfir Shub, 1939).
22. Francisco Ferrándiz, 'The Return of Civil War Ghosts: the Ethnography of Exhumations in Contemporary Spain', *Anthropology Today*, Vol. 22, No. 3, 2006, pp. 7–12 (8).
23. Jo Labanyi, 'The Politics of Memory in Contemporary Spain', *Journal of Spanish Cultural Studies*, Vol. 9, No. 2, 2008, pp. 119–25 (121).
24. Additionally, *The Silence of Others* reveals other places associated with Francoist Spain: Plaza del Caudillo, the sight of Franco's coat of arms on a building, and Plaza de Arriba España (Hail Spain Square). The city of Madrid has only recently begun to rename streets and squares honouring Franco's regime.
25. Alfredo González-Ruibal, 'Museums and Material Memories of the Spanish Civil War: An Archaeological Critique', in *Public Humanities and the Spanish Civil War: Connected and Contested Histories*, Alison Ribeiro de Menezes, Antonio Cazorla-Sánchez and Adrian Shubert (eds), Berlin: Springer, 2018, pp. 93–114 (96–7).
26. The series titled *The Spanish Civil War* uses a large number of newsreels from the 1930s providing a vivid record of the impact of the war on Madrid, including *Bombing Madrid* (British Pathé, 1937, Film ID: 524.07) and *In Defence of Madrid* (British Pathé, 1937, Film ID: 574.08), two films juxtaposing aerial views of the city centre of Madrid to various scenes of a Nationalist attack and its aftermath, with images of civilian men, women and children lying dead on streets and pavements and the massive destruction of buildings of the inner districts of the city. *In the Firing Line in Madrid* (British Pathé, 1937, Film ID: 1903.01), a newsreel which was also used in the documentary series *The Spanish Civil War*, shows a group of young men building barricades out of bricks and debris from bombed-out buildings.
27. Archibald, p. 32. *The Spanish Earth* was written by Ernest Hemingway and John Dos Passos and narrated by Hemingway and Orson Welles. Jean Renoir narrated the French version of the film.
28. The gazette is catalogued under *Troubled Spain* (British Pathé, 1936, Film ID: 895.0) while the additional silent footage is archived as *Spanish Civil War* (British Pathé, 1936, Film ID: 512.02).
29. Miriam Basilio, 'A Pilgrimage to the Alcázar of Toledo: Ritual, Tourism and Propaganda in Franco's Spain', in *Architecture and Tourism: Perception, Performance and Place*, D. Medina Lasansky and Brian D. McLaren (eds), Oxford: Berg, 2004, pp. 93–107 (105).
30. Basilio, p. 95.
31. In *The Siege of Alcazar*, General José Moscardó, after whom one of the streets of Madrid shown in *The Silence of Others* was named, is played by Rafael Calvo.

32. The Spanish Civil War was a popular subject in Italian cinema of the fascist era and other titles included *Carmen fra i rossi* (*Carmen Among the Reds*, 1939, Edgar Neville), *L'uomo della legione* (*The Man of the Legion*, 1940, Romolo Marcellini), *L'ebbrezza del cielo* (*The Thrill of the Skies*, 1940, Giorgio Ferroni), and *Inviati speciali* (*Special Correspondents*, 1943, Romolo Marcellini).
33. Newsreels had indeed covered the unfolding of the events from the beginning of the action to the retreat of the Republican forces; *Civil War in Spain: Troops in Action* (Pathé Gazette, 1936, Film ID: 891.04), for example, was filmed on location in August, at a time when the Alcázar was still standing, while *Spain from Both Sides: Front-line Despatches from Government and Rebel* (Gaumont British News, 1936) shows the ruins of the building soon after the end of the siege.

CHAPTER 3

Sobibór, Generalgouvernement, Occupied Poland, 14 October 1943, 4:00 p.m.

> *A seventeen-year-old Jewish boy from Warsaw swings an axe and splits open the skull of a Schutzstaffel officer killing him instantly; with the help of a Soviet POW, he hides the body, cleans up the blood and waits for the next guard. His name is Yehuda Lerner and this happens on the afternoon of 14 October 1943 in Sobibór.*

In May 1924 a formal ceremony at 85 Ulica Lubartowska, Lublin, marked the laying of the cornerstone of what would become one of the most important Talmudic academies in Eastern Europe. Chachmei Lublin Yeshiva would open in 1930; ten years later the Nazis ransacked the building, burnt the library and established the headquarters of the military police there. In the following months and years the entire Jewish community of Lublin was annihilated in the Holocaust. The *Judenrat* of Lublin was established in the winter of 1940 and one year later, on 24 March 1941, the ghetto was created in a designated area of the city.[1] It was sealed with a barbed-wire fence at the end of that year and, despite the high mortality rate, its population continued to grow as a result of the continuous relocation of Jews from other regions of Poland.[2] Sixty-three years after the liquidation of the ghetto in spring 1942 the building in Ulica Lubartowska was returned to the Jewish community of Poland and the former yeshiva was filmed by Leszek Wiśniewski in *Uczniowie Widzącego z Lublina* (*Students of the Seer of Lublin*, 2005). This documentary on the history of Polish Hasidism focuses on the figure of Hassidic Rabbi Yaakov Yitzchak HaLevi Horowitz (1745–1815), the seer or visionary of Lublin, and bears witness to a void impossible to fill, to the catastrophe of Lublin's Jews. In *Students of the Seer of Lublin*, representatives of Hasidic communities from around the world and mainly from the United States and Western Europe, visit and pray in Lublin, the city which hosted one of the administrative headquarters of the *Generalgouvernement* (General Governorate for the Occupied Polish Region) and which was central to the plans of the Nazis both in relation to the extermination of the Jews and to the conquest of a *Lebensraum* (living space) in the East.[3] It was from a building at 1 Ulica Spokojna that *SS Gruppenführer* Odilo Globocnik ran the death camps of Treblinka, Sobibór and Bełżec. Additionally, the concentration and death camp Majdanek was built and operated by the *Schutzstaffel* (SS) on the outskirts of the city.[4] In this chapter I investigate the cinematic landscapes of three key locations of the Holocaust in the Lublin district, including Stare Miasto (the Old Town of Lublin) and Majdanek.[5] Located 60 miles east of Lublin, the third place I discuss in this chapter is the site of the death camp in Sobibór, a location which I address with a focus on the uprising of 14 October 1943; on that day a seventeen-year-old Jewish boy from Warsaw named Yehuda Lerner swung an axe against one of his captors and escaped with 300 other inmates. The group of prisoners which was deported from Warsaw to Sobibór with Lerner stopped in Lublin and Majdanek before arriving at the death camp, and this chapter thus follows his journey across the region.

As I have explained in Chapter 2, Spanish cinema of the Francoist era contributed to building a propaganda narrative of the Spanish Civil War which naturally embraced the Nationalist side and vilified the Republican cause. In a manner akin to that of the memorialisation of the civil war in the years of Franco's dictatorship, in Poland the Second World War was narrated in film through the lens of Polish nationalism; Jewish identity was largely relegated to the margins. In his study of the relationship between Poles and Jews, Michael C. Steinlauf has argued that the struggle to integrate the image of the murdered Jews into Polish national memory is crucial to an understanding of the history and culture of post-war Poland.[6] A similar conclusion has been reached by Marek Haltof in his discussion of Polish cinema from the immediate post-war period and the years he describes as characterised by 'organised forgetting' (1965–80) to the more recent and still reluctant re-emergence of the memories and events which had been repressed in earlier films; the Holocaust, Haltof has argued, was first neglected and later framed by narratives emphasising Polish opposition to the Holocaust.[7] The image of the Lublin region in Polish films reflects the arguments articulated by Steinlauf and Haltof and thus mirrors the ways in which the Holocaust was incorporated in the broader notion of the martyrdom of the Polish nation. During the communist time, Polish cinema operated by omissions and emphases in order to build a unifying image of the country at war against the Nazi occupiers. In this context, war-time Lublin has often been portrayed in film with a selective gaze that emphasised the Polish suffering and neglecting the specificity of the destruction of its Jews. Early newsreels of Majdanek follow a similar pattern while more recent international films have established a connection between Lublin, Majdanek and the Holocaust. As I hope to demonstrate in the third section of this chapter, films about Sobibór have also reflected the ambiguity embedded in the memorialisation of the sites of the Holocaust in Poland.

Lublin

Before the Nazi invasion of Poland, Lublin had a number of Jewish-owned factories, free-loan societies and savings-and-loan associations, Jewish trade unions, charitable and welfare associations, a Jewish hostel and summer camp, clinics, a hospital, an orphanage, religious schools and branches of Jewish parties such as Bund and Agudath Israel.[8] This world ceased to exist with the Holocaust. After the liquidation of the Lublin Ghetto in 1942, 4,000 Jews were deported to Majdanek and another 30,000 were gassed in the Bełżec death camp. The 34,000 Jews persecuted by the Nazis had amounted to one third of the overall population of Lublin in the 1930s and only 200 of them survived the war. The Holocaust has also played a significant role in the cinematic image of the city; in what follows, I address processes of memorialisation of the Holocaust and investigate the ways in which war-time Lublin has been used as a film location both in a geographically-creative way, based on loose connections to the real identity and function of the sites, and in a coherent manner, where the use of streets and buildings is topographically accurate.

This section of the chapter looks at the complexities of a spatial reading of Lublin in film and compares the ways in which Zamek Lubelski, the medieval Lublin Castle, has been portrayed in Pathé's war-time newsreel *The Tragic City of Lublin* (1944),[9] in the four-part Soviet TV drama *Żołnierze Wolności* (*Soldiers of Freedom*, Jurij Ozierov, 1977), and in the British-American film *The Aryan Couple* (John Daly, 2004). Pathé's newsreel and Ozierov's film make a topographically coherent use of this location as both the films contain sequences filmed and set at Lublin Castle and portray events which took place there in 1944. However, they neglect to address the role played by the castle as a site of memory in the specific context of the persecution of the Jews. In contrast, *The Aryan Couple* articulates a creative geography of the city where Lublin is called to play the role of an unnamed Hungarian city. The events portrayed here are fictional and only loosely based on the life of Jewish industrialist Manfred Weiss, and yet Daly's film establishes a connection between the castle and the Holocaust while *The Tragic City of Lublin* and *Soldiers of Freedom* used the building, under whose shadow the Jews of Lublin lived and were killed, exclusively as a site of Polish martyrdom.

On 23 July 1944, the Nazis massacred 300 Polish prisoners in Lublin Castle in the hours preceding their retreat from the city. *The Tragic City of Lublin*, an edited version of original Soviet footage of Lublin and part of the series *The Voice of Britain*, opens with a panoramic panning shot of the city in ruins and shots of several tanks advancing through the streets of the inner districts of Lublin. A rapid montage sequence shows a number of mortars being fired against the Nazis and Red Army soldiers who were firing towards the windows of the surviving buildings of the city. The viewer is then introduced to images of the castle, while the voice-over explains the use the Nazis had made of this building (Figure 3.1). A series of shots filmed inside the castle reveals a large number of corpses, victims of a final massacre perpetrated by the Nazis. The Soviet footage used in *The Tragic City of Lublin* records the aftermath of the massacre and shows the victims in the courtyard of the castle and the people of Lublin mourning their losses. The following scenes focus on the Roman Catholic memorial service held outside the castle to commemorate the victims and show the priests and nuns attending the service. In the courtyard there is a large cross, erected next to the walls of the castle.

The footage incorporated in *The Tragic City of Lublin* anticipates the consistent absence of the extermination of the Jews in post-war Polish cinema. A demonstration of the ways in which texts can signify by what they leave out as much as by what they include, *The Tragic City of Lublin* erases all traces of pre-war Jewish life and later persecution near and in Lublin Castle. It does not reveal the fact that the area around the castle had been Jewish and does not make reference to the fact that the ghetto had been established there nor

Figure 3.1 Lublin Castle in *The Tragic City Of Lublin* (British Pathé, 1944).

to the conspicuous absence of the Great Lublin Synagogue, which had stood at the foot of the castle and was demolished soon after the liquidation of the ghetto. The Soviet footage included in this newsreel thus inscribes the castle in the cinematic image of post-war Lublin and anticipates two consistent narratives of post-war Soviet and Polish cinema: the heroism of the Red Army and the Roman Catholic identity of the country.

According to Henri Lefebvre in his discussion of the spatialisation of history, the impact of the events taking place at a particular location becomes inscribed in space. And yet, although the past leaves its traces in specific locations, space is always a present space, whole and complete, at once product and part of the production process of historical events. The location, continues Lefebvre, is never owned by the past and is continuously processed through the connection between past events and their actuality.[10] Accordingly, the historical events of 1944 are inscribed in Lublin Castle and processed in post-war films by means of their juxtaposition with the present. The scene of the memorial service for the victims of the 1944 massacre included in *The Tragic City of Lublin* was recreated on location thirty-three years later in *Soldiers of Freedom*. This Soviet narrative covers the history of Poland from the capitulation in 1939 to the creation of a national government in Lublin and reflects the post-war sovietisation of Poland and its persisting actuality. The castle sequence sees an actor playing Bolesław Bierut, a former President of Poland, speaking over the coffins aligned in the courtyard, while a religious service is held and a large crowd is shown outside the castle. The film focuses on Polish resistance and defines the events of 1944 in Lublin as key to the birth of the People's Republic of Poland; and yet, despite the topographical coherence of its use of locations, it largely evades the crucial question of the fate of Lublin's Jews. *Soldiers of Freedom* thus reiterates the narrative established in the Soviet footage used in *The Tragic City of Lublin*, and its structured absences mirror the ways in which history was reshaped by the communist regime in a patriotic re-appropriation of the fight against Nazism.

Lublin Castle can be understood in terms of representational space, a site defined by Lefebvre as a place that has its source in the history of people and individuals belonging to that site.[11] Conflicts can occur between representational spaces and their symbolic systems, in particular where two or more people claim an ownership of their past. In Chapter 2, I have argued that the Alcazaba of Badajoz can be read as a symbol of Nationalist aggression while the Alcázar of Toledo was key to Franco's propaganda celebrating the resilience of the Nationalist forces; in both instances the symbolic systems of these fortresses emerge from a group of films where two parties claim ownership of the overall narrative of the Spanish Civil War. As with Alcazaba and the Alcázar, Lublin Castle embodies a past where multiple historical viewpoints coexist; while *The Tragic City of Lublin* and *Soldiers of Freedom* inscribed Polish and Christian identity onto this space, a more recent British-American production has returned the site to Jewish history. *The Aryan Couple* tells the story of a rich Jewish Hungarian industrialist (Martin Landau) who, in order to ensure his family's passage to Switzerland, is forced to hand over his business and estate to the Nazis. Despite the fact the film is not set in Lublin, the use of the castle as a location establishes a coherent connection with the history of the eradication of the Jews of the city. Joseph Krauzenberg, Landau's character, meets a member of the SS in the castle and can be seen walking through the courtyard previously filmed by Ozierov. Krauzenberg is wearing the Star of David on his coat and his frail figure is surrounded by threatening elements, including swastikas, weapons and German soldiers, and this sequence thus identifies the castle as a site, or representational space, of Jewish martyrdom. Nevertheless, administrative offices of the occupation forces were located a mile away from the castle in Litewski Square and thus Krauzenberg's visit only loosely reflects the role of this site on the map of Nazi-occupied Lublin.

The Aryan Couple uses other locations with a creative approach to the specificity of the city's historical topography. Located at 1 Rynek, Lublin's market square, the building known as Trybunał Koronny (The Crown Court) was used in this film as the location of Krauzenberg's residence. In a long sequence, Krauzenberg observes from the balcony a large group of Jewish men, women and children being escorted by the Gestapo towards Brama Grodzka (Grodzka Gate), the city gate that historically separated the Old Town from the Jewish Quarter. The Crown Court was never a private residence and no Jews lived in this part of the city. Also, this would have been an unlikely route for the resettlement of Jews from other regions to the main ghetto and again the film is not following a coherent topography of the city. The narrow alleys leading to the Rynek are also used in Uri Barbash's *Spring 1941* (2007), the first Israeli film to use Lublin as a location. *Spring 1941* focuses on a Jewish family seeking shelter from Nazi persecution and includes scenes filmed in Ulica Archidiakońska, Ulica Jezuicka and Ulica Dominikańska behind the market square. However, Lublin is not named in the film and the city plays the more generic role of an unnamed Eastern European place. The scene of mass deportation of the Jews through the streets of Lublin resembles the scene observed by Krauzenberg from the balcony of the Crown Court in *The Aryan Couple*. Several buildings are decorated with swastikas and three Jewish men executed by the SS can be seen hanging from the balconies of the old houses of the city. This implies that the Jews were made to march through the streets of the ghetto, while the scene is filmed on streets that never belonged to the Jewish district nor the ghetto. Both *Spring 1941* and *The*

Aryan Couple use the market square and adjacent streets in a creative manner than is not consistent with its historical topography and with the unfolding of the eradication of Lublin's Jewry.

As in *Spring 1941* and *The Aryan Couple*, cinematic Lublin has often played the role of other cities, including Warsaw, Moscow, Paris and Rivne.[12] Andrzej Wajda's *Kronika Wypadków Miłosnych* (*A Chronicle of Amorous Accidents*, 1985) is set in Vilnius, in modern Lithuania, and includes a sequence filmed at Grodska Gate.[13] However, Wajda's film presents the same strategy seen in *The Aryan Couple* as it inscribes Jewish heritage in the cinematic topography of Lublin despite being set in another city. *A Chronicle of Amorous Accidents* looks at the years that preceded the annihilation of the Jews and is a nostalgic view of the summer of 1939, just before the German invasion of Poland. The two young Polish protagonists can be seen walking through Grodska Gate, surrounded by Ashkenazi Jews engaged in their trades. The sequence filmed at Grodzka Gate presents the Jewish quarter of this cinematic version of Vilnius in accordance with the pre-war topography of Lublin. Anti-Semitism is largely absent from this image of inter-war Poland and the issue of the problematic coexistence of Poles and Jews in Lublin or Vilnius is avoided. *A Chronicle of Amorous Accidents*, *The Aryan Couple* and *Spring 1941* use various locations in Lublin in a way which reflects what James Hay has described as the intrinsic value of the cinematic city, its capacity to produce or reproduce a past articulated on the basis of a series of relations between memory, history and environment.[14]

Majdanek

Cinematic Lublin is made of what Penz and Lu have discussed in terms of 'narrative geographies where urban fragments are collaged into spatial episodes.'[15] A similar pattern of omissions and emphasis as well as a creative use of topography can also be observed in regard to the cinematic image of the concentration and death camp of Majdanek. While 59,000 victims out of a total of 79,000 were Jewish, the image of the camp in post-war Polish and Soviet films largely focused on Majdanek as a site of Polish suffering.[16] When the camp was liberated on 24 July 1944 Soviet cameramen turned their attention to the discovery of this site of murder on an industrial scale at the outskirts of Lublin, and filmed the barracks, gas chambers, human remains and survivors for the newsreels. In *Majdanek: Cmentarzysko Europy* (*Majdanek: Burial Ground in Europe*, Aleksander Ford, 1944) the role of the camp in the extermination of the Jews was not made explicit. Ford's film, as Jeremy Hicks suggests, illustrates the crimes committed by the Nazis against the Polish people and Soviet POWs and does not address the real extent of the genocide perpetrated against the Jews.[17] Similarly, Irina Setkina's newsreel *Majdanek* (1944) can be read in terms of what Hicks has called a 'sovietised' interpretation of the events resulting from a tendency in Polish and Soviet cinema of the liberation to suggest that the victims belonged to the same group as the spectator, the Polish and Russian people.[18] These films, Hicks continues, were largely neglected and in Western Europe they were seen primarily as an example of Soviet propaganda.[19]

The selective gaze of the footage filmed by Soviet cameramen migrated into later Polish newsreels such as Ludwik Perski and Jerzy Bossak's *Lublin. Uroczystości na Majdanku* (*Lublin: Commemoration at Majdanek*, 1948), a reportage made for *Polska Kronika Filmowa* (Polish Film Chronicle) which failed to address the role of the camp in the Holocaust. Shown in Poland's cinemas prior to feature films, *Lublin: Commemoration at Majdanek* includes various shots of the population of the city visiting the camp and laying flowers on the site of the crematorium; Supreme Court judge Wacław Barcikowski can be seen delivering a speech (Figure 3.2). A number of close-up shots show the people of Lublin weeping and mourning the victims of the Nazis at Majdanek; a large cross can be seen in the background and a Catholic service is taking place in the grounds of the former camp. In 1948 the association between Majdanek and the Holocaust was again largely ignored and the camp was presented as a site of martyrdom for Soviet POWs and Poles; in a manner akin to the image of Lublin Castle, Majdanek can be read as a contested representational site where the destruction of the Jews unfolded, only to be eventually inscribed through film in the broader idea of Polish national martyrdom.[20] Early newsreels of Majdanek did what *The Tragic City of Lublin* had done for the castle and paved the way to a persistent tendency to underestimate the role of the camp in the destruction of the Jews. Similarly, Polish fiction films have primarily used the camp in Majdanek to portray the suffering and courage of the Poles and have used the location creatively. For example, Leszek Wosiewicz's *Kornblumenblau* (*Cornflower Blue*, 1989) is based on Kazimierz Tyminski's memoir *Uspokic Sen* (*Calm My Dreams*, 1985) and focuses on the experience of a Polish Catholic who was arrested in 1941 under suspicion of hiding stolen guns and sent to Auschwitz and to the Montelupich Prison in Kraków.[21] The film is set in Auschwitz and it was filmed both in Field III in Majdanek and in Auschwitz II-Birkenau. Tyminski was never taken to the Lublin district and in *Cornflower Blue* Majdanek merely plays the role of the most notorious death camp.

According to Pierre Nora the absolute nature of memory is constantly challenged by the relative nature of history and, on this basis, the cinematic image of Majdanek can be seen as the result of a process of memorialisation which 'proceeds by strategic highlighting, selecting samples and multiplying

Figure 3.2 The site of the Majdanek camp in Lublin. *Uroczystości na Majdanku* (*Lublin: Commemoration at Majdanek*, Ludwik Perski and Jerzy Bossak, 1948).

examples.'[22] While the memorialisation of Majdanek in Polish film has emphasised a narrative of national martyrdom, more recently the role of the camp in the Holocaust has emerged in a German-American production, Stephen Daldry's *The Reader* (2008). This is an adaptation of Bernhard Schlink's novel of the same title (1995) and it focuses on the post-war affair between young Michael Berg (David Kross) and Hannah Schmitz (Kate Winslet), a former German female SS guard at Auschwitz accused of letting over 300 Jewish women die in a burning church after the evacuation of the camp. Following the revelation about the woman's past, Michael visits the ground, barracks, gas chamber and crematorium of Majdanek (Figure 3.3). In the sequence introduced by the iconic sight of the barbed wire fence, he enters the camp through the former SS sector and goes to the barracks in Field I. Michael then enters one of the buildings and silently observes the bunk beds. He continues his visit with the shower room in Barrack 41 and makes his way to the gas chamber at the back of the barrack; Prussian blue residues which resulted from exposure to Zyklon B can be seen on the walls.

As recorded in Setkina's *Majdanek*, thousands of shoes and other items were found by the Red Army when they liberated the camp.[23] In *The Reader*, the protagonist visits the display in Barrack 45, possibly containing the

Figure 3.3 The site of the Majdanek camp in *The Reader* (Stephen Daldry, 2008).

same shoes filmed by Soviet cameramen sixty-four years earlier in *Majdanek*. Finally, Michael visits the crematorium and stands by the ovens. No dialogue or narration accompanies the camp sequence and there is a lack of topographical specificity. None of the sights which could facilitate the identification of Majdanek as the location of this sequence – such as the mausoleum and Wiktor Tołkin's *Pomnik Walki i Męczeństwa na Majdanku* (Majdanek Fight and Martyrdom monument, 1963) – are included in the film. In *The Reader*, Majdanek is finally presented as a site of racial extermination; and yet, Auschwitz II-Birkenau was the camp where Hannah worked during the war, and it is implied that Michael is visiting the camp in the south-west of Poland rather than Majdanek. Nevertheless, *The Reader*'s narrative rings true to history. For German guards, who were often trained in the Reich territory's concentration camps, the experience of 'going' east, as Elissa M. Koslov suggests, often increased their violent behaviour.[24] Both Auschwitz and Majdanek are thus suitable locations for *The Reader*, a narrative that focuses on the darkest experience of the Nazis' system of extermination, one where apparently ordinary individuals like Hannah could be transformed into perpetrators. Daldry uses Majdanek in a symbolic way by means of a cinematic creative geography where, as in *Cornflower Blue*, the camp plays the role of Auschwitz; the lack of topographical coherence in *The Reader* ultimately allows the scenes filmed in Majdanek to stand for the Holocaust as a whole.

The re-elaboration of history, place and images in the representational space of Majdanek is taken further in Micha Wald's *Simon Konianski* (2009), a drama where the former camp is finally acknowledged as a site of extermination of the Jews and also recognised for its regional specificity, with recognisable images of its barracks and of the Fight and Martyrdom monument. Landmarks can be used in the cinematic space to define and reveal the specific geographical coordinates of the location, and thus its history and significance in the plot of the film. The inclusion of the memorial, which had been avoided by Daldry in *The Reader*, thus provides the film with a specific location and, arguably for the first time, here Majdanek finally plays itself. Filmed on several locations in Eastern Europe, *Simon Konianski* is a Franco-Belgian road movie where the title character aims to fulfil his father's last request to be buried in the Ukrainian village where he was born. Members of the Konianski family were murdered by the Nazis and during the trip Simon (Jonathan Zaccaï) and his six-year-old son Hadrien (Nassim Ben Abdelmoumen) decide to visit Majdanek. As they approach the camp in their car, the Fight and Martyrdom monument appears in the background. Father and son park the car near the barracks of Field III and enter the camp from the gate near the replica of the original Kolumna Trzech Orłów (Column of Three Eagles), another iconic site specific to Majdanek.[25] Hadrien runs through the field and briefly disappears; Simon looks for his son inside one of the barracks and is visited by the ghost of his dead father. He eventually finds Hadrien outside the barracks. In *Simon Konianski* we do not see the gas chambers or the crematorium, and yet Hadrien's disappearance is reminiscent of what happened in the death camps during the war, when families were separated at the moment of arrival and loved ones were last seen as they vanished in the extermination process. This is what happened in all death camps and yet *Simon Konianski* inscribes this pre-existing narrative in the specific representational space of Majdanek by revealing iconic landmarks of the camp. In particular, the presence of the Fight and Martyrdom monument and the Column of Three Eagles places *Simon Konianski* in a specific geographical space and emancipates Majdanek from a location hitherto devoted to playing the role of Auschwitz to an identifiable place with its own specific history.

Sobibór

On 3 November 1943, over 10,000 Jews were killed in Majdanek as part of Aktion Erntefest (Operation Harvest Festival), the mass murder of at least 43,000 Jews in the *Generalgouvernement* ordered by Heinrich Himmler and executed by the SS, the *Ordnungspolizei* (Order Police battalions), and the Ukrainian *Sonderdienst*. The decision to annihilate the Jews who were still forced to work for the Nazis in the Lublin district came as a result of the uprisings in Treblinka and Sobibór, which had taken place in the summer and autumn of that year, with the hope of avoiding similar incidents in Trawniki, Poniatowa, Majdanek and other smaller camps.[26] It was the uprising in Sobibór, the most successful rebellion ever to take place in a death camp, and the killing of eleven members of the SS during the escape in particular, which came as a shock to the Nazis. Among those who died on that day, *SS Untersturmführer* Johann Nieman was killed by Jewish Red Army soldier Alexander Shubayev with an axe in the barracks. In 2015, Nieman's grandson handed over to the educational organisation Bildungswerk Stanislaw Hantz fifty photographs taken by his grandfather in Sobibór and showing, for the first time, SS leaders and their auxiliaries in the death camp.[27] These photographs are among a small number of existing images of Sobibór during the Holocaust; unlike the events which took place in Italy and Spain and which I have discussed in the previous chapters, no tangible record of the extermination process and no photographs or footage of the uprising exist. However, the killing process and the unfolding of the revolt in Sobibór have been addressed in a number of documentaries and a smaller group of fictional reconstructions based on the testimonies of survivors who took part in the uprising.

Sobibór's documentaries have also included survivors' journeys to the site of the death camp. For them, the spatial experience of the sites of the Holocaust during return journeys is always challenged by the ways in which the sites of concentration and death camps have changed in the years which followed the war. In Auschwitz II-Birkenau, for example, the present-day tranquillity of the place is difficult to connect to the survivors' vivid memories of chaos, of dogs barking and people screaming, and of the smell and smoke coming from the crematoria. In Sobibór, as in the case of the death camps in Treblinka and Bełżec, the total disappearance of traces poses an even more significant challenge to the spatial experience of the site of memory. After the uprising the SS tried to conceal the evidence of the genocide, demolished the camp and planted pine trees on its site.[28] The typical disorientation of the survivors is thus exacerbated by the total disappearance of physical remnants of the past. Tim Cole has discussed this type of disorientation in regard to Auschwitz II-Birkenau as it emerges from survivors' testimonies based on return journeys to the camps; Cole has argued that the space of the camps is experienced by survivors as 'a series of interconnected micro-sites rather than a homogenous memorial landscape' and has advocated the necessity to understand the survivors' experience by means of a 'dynamic relationship between landscape and memory'.[29] This relationship leads to an understanding of the space of Auschwitz II-Birkenau as a series of heterogeneous micro-sites; similarly, in the case of Sobibór, the memorialisation of the uprising emerges through the topography of the camp and by means of the discernment of the specificity of the places visited or staged by filmmakers.

Led by *SS Obersturmführer* Richard Thomalla from the Lublin SS Headquarters, the construction of the Sobibór death camp near the rural town of Włodawa took place in the spring of 1942 and the first transports of deportees arrived in May. In the seventeen months leading to the uprising 170,000 to 250,000 Jews, mainly from Poland and the Netherlands, were murdered there. Situated west of Sobibór station and near farms and living quarters of railway workers, Sobibór was divided into four camps, including the *Vorlager* (Forward Camp) and three camps numbered from I to III.[30] The Forward Camp included the unloading platform, a dentist, a guard house, the SS quarters, kitchen, canteen, barber shop, showers and clothing store, a laundry, a well, a garage, the living quarters of the camp commanders, an armoury, a bakery and the barracks of the Ukrainians guards. *Lager I* (Camp I) contained the barracks for both male and female Jewish prisoners, a dispensary, a tailor, shoemakers, saddler, workshops for blacksmiths, carpentry and painting, latrines and kitchen for the prisoners, and a water ditch. *Lager II* (Camp II) contained the undressing yard and barracks, storage barracks for clothing, luggage, food and silverware and other valuables, an electrical generator, stables and barns, an incinerator, a latrine, the SS ironing room, a garden, the barrack where women's hair was cut, and the administration building. A path surrounded by barbed wire called the *Himmelfahrtstrasse* or *der Schlauch* (Road to Heaven or the Tube) led to *Lager III* (Camp III) where the victims were killed and which included the barracks of the *Sonderkommando* (squads composed of Jewish prisoners forced to perform a variety of duties in the killing process), the gas chambers, the engine room next to the chambers, mass graves and outdoor crematoria. Beside the foundations of the gas chambers, which were only identified in 2014, there are no traces of the buildings which occupied these four camps. Documentaries have thus used maps of the camp drawn by survivors in order to identify the specific locations of the extermination process and of the uprising and have employed various narrative techniques to place their testimonies on the site of the death camp; meanwhile, fiction films have recreated the camps elsewhere on the basis of the accounts given by the survivors. The intertwining of factual accounts and fictional reconstructions can thus provide a spatial experience of Sobibór in spite of the demolition of its buildings, watchtowers and barbed wire entanglements.

Claude Lanzmann was one of the first filmmakers to visit the site of the death camp and the sequences of *Shoah* (1985) filmed in Sobibór exemplify his geographical approach to the comprehension of how the Holocaust unfolded which underlines the film; in Lanzmann's words:

> I did not make an idealist film; it is not a film with grand metaphysical or theological reflections about why all this happened to the Jews, why they killed them. This is a film from the ground up, a topographical film, a geographical film. (2007: 38–9)[31]

The topographical nature of the film is revealed in the sequences containing Lanzmann's interview with former assistant switchman at Sobibór railway station Jan Piwonski. In these sequences Lanzmann attempts to understand, with the guidance of Piwonski, the topography of Sobibór as he faces the disappearance of all traces. The conversation between Lanzmann and the Polish bystander begins by the local railway station and continues while, along with the translator, the two men walk in the direction of the Forward Camp and more specifically to the exact site of the unloading ramp. Here Piwonski performs his testimony on the site which saw the unloading of hundreds of thousands of Jews destined for the gas chambers. Lanzmann and Piwoski also walk through the forest and to the clearing where Camp III and its gas chambers once stood; this is a micro-site of the camp which would have been excluded from Piwonski's experience of the place in the 1940s and whose knowledge belongs to those who were killed there and to the members of the *Sonderkommandos* who were forced to work in Camp III.

While the scenes with Piwonski are filmed on a sunny day, Lanzmann also includes scenes filmed on a separate visit to Sobibór on a snowy winter day, including a tracking shot which follows the itinerary from the uploading ramp to the site of Camp II and, along the Road to Heaven, to that of Camp III and the gas chambers. This footage reveals the memorialisation and monumentalisation of the camp with the presence of Mieczysław Welter's cast-iron statue of a woman with a child on the Road to Heaven and the mausoleum with the mound of ashes and crushed bones of the victims. In a manner which evokes the Fight and Martyrdom monument and the Column of Three Eagles in Majdanek, these landmarks testify to the monumentalisation of the site of the death camp as the disappearance of barracks and gas chambers has given monuments, as sites of mourning, the task of providing a visual referent to the name of Sobibór. *Shoah* captures this process through its slow and meditative tracking shots of the site; in these scenes the testimony performed by Piwonski is replaced by silence as the film intertwines past and present, history and memory.

During the making of *Shoah*, Lanzmann also filmed a long interview with Sobibór survivor and insurgent Yehuda Lerner. The interview was not included in the final cut of the film and it was later used in Lanzmann's *Sobibór, October 14, 1943, 4 p.m.* (2001). In this documentary Lanzmann incorporates footage of Sobibór filmed fifteen years after the release of *Shoah* in order to establish a connection between the testimony given by Lerner in his apartment in Jerusalem and the site of memory in Sobibór. This is a recurring characteristic of Lanzmann's techniques leading to the memorialisation of the sites by juxtaposing remote testimony and location shooting. Beside

Chełmno survivor Szymon Srebnik in *Shoah*, Lanzmann's witnesses regularly give their testimony in mundane locations distant from the sites of memory and, accordingly, the interview with Lerner took place in the private space of the survivor's apartment. And yet, as Gary Weissman suggests, all testimonies in *Shoah* are located on the sites of the death camps 'through the use of voice-over narration and images of present-day sites which, through skilful editing, are made to coincide with the events being narrated.'[32] The same argument can be applied to *Sobibór, October 14, 1943, 4 p.m.*, where the interview recorded in Jerusalem twenty years earlier is placed in Sobibór by means of its juxtaposition to footage filmed on location and at the sites of memory which brought Lerner from the Warsaw Ghetto to the death camp.[33] The first half of the film combines the recording of the interview with Lerner with footage filmed by Lanzmann during a journey to Poland and Belarus, thus following the itinerary of Lerner's journey from Warsaw to Sobibór via Minsk, Chelm, Lublin and Majdanek. Lerner's account of his arrival at Majdanek, where he only spent a few hours before being sent to Sobibór, is accompanied by a series of panning shots revealing the surviving barracks and the rebuilt crematorium of the camp. The account of the uprising is accompanied by panoramic views of the sites of the events, the land which was occupied by camps I and II and the Forward Camp.

Whereas Lanzmann uses the technique discussed above in order to place Lerner's testimony in Sobibór, the documentary *Z królestwa śmierci* (*From the Realm of Death*, Urszula Hasiec and Grzegorz Michalec, 2008) follows the return journeys of survivors to the micro-sites of the death camp, and places them on meaningful locations interconnected with the testimonies they perform in front of the camera. *From the Realm of Death* directly positions testimonial performances in Sobibór with survivors Jules Schelvis, Philip Bialowitz, Thomas 'Toivi' Blatt, Symcha Bialowitz and Regina Zielinski standing on the sites of the unloading ramp in the Forward Camp, on Camp II and along the Road to Heaven, and on Camp IV next to the mound of ashes; this group of survivors gives testimonies bound to the specific locations of the camp, following the process of extermination from the arrival of transports to the execution in the gas chambers. Thomas Blatt had already appeared in a short documentary produced by the Simon Wiesenthal Centre and titled *Past and Present, History Falsified* (Thomas and Dena Blatt, 1987); in this film the survivor returns to his *shtetl* Izbica, 37 miles south-east of Lublin, and then to Sobibór. Here Blatt gives an account of the arrival and selection process on the site of the unloading ramp in the Forward Camp. He then visits a section of the camp which he did not experience during his captivity, the site of the gas chambers and cremation pits now occupied by a mound of ashes and crushed bones shaped into a pyramid.

Blatt also stops by the area where the Nazis had planned unsuccessfully to build a fourth camp. Here he witnesses the construction of a church just 300 feet from the site of the gas chambers and reads a memorial plaque explaining that 250,000 POWs, Jews, Poles and Romani people were killed in Sobibór. Blatt explains that the POWs were all Jewish and that there were no Romani in this death camp; he engages a Capuchin monk and Leo Kuchar, an Austrian priest, in the debate on the falsification of history which provides the title of the film; he thus accuses the clergymen of colluding in the attempt to deny the specific nature of Sobibór as a site built for the annihilation of the Jews. The construction of the church and the text contained in the memorial plaque reflect the failure to address the specificity of the Holocaust and, as in the case of the Polish newsreels and dramas set in Lublin and Majdanek, this incident exemplifies the attempt to absorb the Jewish genocide into the broader notion of Nazi war crimes in Eastern Europe. The church and the plaque thus function like the Christian crosses erected near Lublin Castle and in Majdanek during the post-war commemorations and revealed in newsreels such as *The Tragic City of Lublin* and *Lublin: Commemoration at Majdanek*; these symbols falsify the way in which the events unfolded and deny the specificity of the camp as a site of extermination of the Jews.

During the conversation with Blatt, Kuchar explains that his knowledge of Sobibór comes from the television series *Holocaust* (Gerald Green, 1978). One of the final sequences of this series stages the uprising in Sobibór and includes a version of the barracks and workshops in Camp I as well as the main gate to the camp with its *Arbeit Macht Frei* inscription. Here the fictional character of football player Rudi Weiss (Joseph Bottoms) interacts with the historical figures such as uprising leader Alexander 'Sasha' Pechersky and Polish resistance fighter Leon Feldhendler. The sequence consists of a loose reconstruction of the uprising as it unfolded in Camp I and the Forward Camp. In *Past and Present, History Falsified*, Blatt acknowledges that that sequence reflects the events of 14 October 1943; the result is a paradoxical intertwining of fiction and documentary where the actual site of the uprising and the testimony of one of its survivors are validated for Kuchar by recalling the events as they were represented in a fictional television series.

Testimonies given by survivors such as Blatt and Lerner have provided the basis for other fictional reconstructions of the events. Beside the sequence from Green's *Holocaust*, the story of the uprising has been told in a film whose narrative unfolds in camps I and II, *Escape from Sobibór* (Jack Gold, 1987).[34] Gold's film is set by the unloading ramp in the Forward Camp, the living quarters of the SS in Camp I, and the various workshops and barracks in Camp II. *Escape from Sobibór* also includes a sequence set in one of the micro-sites of Sobibór which was excluded from the experience of Lerner and most other survivors, and which strictly belonged to the ordeal of those who were murdered and to that of the *Sonderkommandos*. In this sequence, *SS-Stabsscharführer* Bauer (Klaus Grünberg) commissions a golden decoration for the handle of his whip. This is delivered by prisoner Moses Szmajzner (Eli Nathenson) to Bauer in Camp III. Szmajzner walks through the gate in Camp II and along the Road to Heaven; a point-of-view long take of his walk filmed with a hand-held camera is followed by a reverse shot were the prisoner walks towards the camera. Szmajzner reaches Camp III and stands by the gate witnessing the unfolding of the execution of a group of Jewish women and children. The juxtaposition of the fictional recreation of the camp and the testimonies performed in the documentaries thus contribute to the exhumation of the events which took place in Sobibór in a way which defies the Nazis' attempt to conceal all traces of their crimes. The intertwining of testimonies, location shooting and fictional reconstruction of Sobibór make up for the lack of tangible traces of the camp and places Sobibór in a filmic topography of the landscapes of the Holocaust in occupied Poland.

The Lublin district of the *Generalgouvernement* saw many of the darkest events in the extermination of the Jews of Europe. The sites of memory in Lublin, Majdanek and Sobibór bear witness to the genocide and tell stories of oppression and resilience while documentary and fiction films set in these locations have aimed to unlock the memories inscribed on the old buildings of Lublin, the surviving barracks of Majdanek and the monumentalised emptiness of Sobibór. The study of the diverse group of films I have investigated in this chapter reveals the profoundly geographical nature of the Holocaust and has been inspired by Lanzmann's spatial reading of destruction of the European Jews. Film has also reflected the problematic ways in which the Holocaust was absorbed into a post-war narrative of Polish victimhood neglecting the fact that these sites are primarily associated with the extermination of the Jews. Most Holocaust survivors left Poland after the war. Many went to Israel, others to North America and a smaller number of survivors chose to settle in Latin America. One of them, Stanisław Szmajzner, had escaped from Sobibór on 14 October 1943 and eventually left his hometown Puławy, in the Lublin district, and moved to Brazil. He was joined by other survivors as well as by many of the perpetrators, including the commander of the Sobibór camp. In Chapter 5, I investigate the topographical connections between the war in Europe and the post-war years in Latin America through the study of newsreels, amateur footage, documentary and fiction films addressing the unlikely aftermath of the Holocaust in the tropical landscapes and the cityscapes of Argentina, Brazil and Chile. But before I do that, the journey unravelling in this book takes us to the final phases of the Second World War on the Pacific Front. On the day of the escape from Sobibór the resolution of the conflict was not yet in sight and it would only be achieved two years later with that watershed event which would mark the end of the Age of Catastrophe and which led to the Cold War and a threat of mutual assured destruction: the atomic bombing of Hiroshima by the American forces. The next chapter investigates the ways in which the atomic bombing is embedded in the symbolic meaning of a very specific building and focuses on how this emerges through film.

Notes

1. The ghetto of Lublin was filmed in 1940 by Fritz Hippler for his anti-Semitic propaganda documentary *Der ewige Jude* (*The Eternal Jew*).
2. See Guy Miron, *The Yad Vashem Encyclopaedia of the Ghettos during the Holocaust*, Jerusalem: Yad Vashem, 2010, pp. 422–5.
3. See Peter R. Black, 'Rehearsal for "Reinhard"? Odilo Globocnik and the Lublin Selbstschutz', *Central European History*, Vol. 25, No. 2, 1992, pp. 194–226.
4. 1.5 million Jews were murdered at these death camps between 1942 and 1943. See Yitzhak Arad, *Belzec, Sobibor, Treblinka: The Operation Reinhard Death Camps*, Bloomington: Indiana University Press, 1999.
5. The first two sections of this chapter are partly based on my article 'The cinematic city and the destruction of Lublin's Jews' (*Holocaust Studies: A Journal of Culture and History*, Vol. 22, No. 2–3, 2016, pp. 244–55).
6. See, Michael C. Steinlauf, *Bondage to the Dead: Poland and the Memory of the Holocaust*, New York and Syracuse: Syracuse University Press, 1997.
7. See, Marek Haltof, *Polish Film and the Holocaust: Politics and Memory*, New York and Oxford: Berghahn Books, 2012, pp.118–39.
8. Miron, p. 421.
9. *The Tragic City Of Lublin* (British Pathé, 1944, Film ID: 1370.22). The castle was built in the twelfth century, demolished in 1655–7 and rebuilt in 1826–28.
10. Henri Lefebvre, *The Production of Space*, trans. by Donald Nicholson-Smith, Oxford: Blackwell, 1991 [first published as *La production de l'espace* by Anthropos in 1974], p. 37.
11. Lefebvre, p. 41.
12. The area near Grodzka Gate can also be seen in Andrzej Konic's *Czarne Chmury* (*Black Clouds*, 1973), a costume drama made for Telewizja Polska, as the set for a street in seventeenth-century Warsaw. In Jerzy Antczak's biopic *Chopin, Pragnienie miłości* (*Chopin – Desire for Love*, 2002), Lublin plays both Warsaw and Paris, with several scenes filmed near Brama Grodzka. Lublin is Vilnius in Antoni Bohdziewicz's *Rzeczywistość* (*Reality*, 1960). In Adek Drabiński's *Kryptonim <Puch>* (*Codename 'Down'*, 2005) Lublin is Rivne, Ukraine. Lublin is Warsaw again in Adek Drabiński's *Tajna Sprawa* (*A Matter of Secrecy*, 2005), where it also plays Moscow.
13. Vilnius was located in Wilno Voivodeship, a region of Poland between 1926 and 1939. The Jews of Vilnius shared the same fate as the Jews of Lublin and during

the Nazi occupation at least 70,000 Jews from that city were executed in the forests of Ponary.
14. Hay, p. 229.
15. Penz and Lu, p. 14.
16. The death toll for the Majdanek camp has been difficult to estimate and ranges from early overestimations suggesting that over 1 million people died in the camp to a more realistic estimate of 79,000 victims (See, Tomasz Kranz, *The Extermination of Jews at Majdanek Concentration Camp*, Lublin: Państwowe Muzeum na Majdanku, 2010, pp. 70–77).
17. Jeremy Hicks, *First Films of the Holocaust: Soviet Cinema and the Genocide of Jews 1938–1946*, Pittsburgh: University of Pittsburgh Press, 2012, p. 253.
18. Hicks, pp. 158–66.
19. Hicks, p. 165.
20. Alain Resnais' documentary *Nuit et Brouillard* (*Night and Fog*, 1955) was partly filmed in the grounds and ruins of Majdanek, the entire film uses the word 'Jew' on only one occasion and Nazi crimes are portrayed as perpetrated equally against a range of victims from different national, political and religious backgrounds.
21. Other Polish films used the spaces of Majdanek in order to present narrative largely focused on Polish resilience and bravery during the Nazi occupation. In 1979, for example, the camp at Majdanek was used as a location for Roman Wionczek's *Sekret Enigmy* (*The Secret Enigma*), the story of Henryk Zygalski and Jerzy Różycki and Marian Rejewski, the three Polish mathematicians who cracked the Enigma code used by the Germans during the war.
22. Nora, 1989, p. 19.
23. During the war Majdanek was also used as a storage facility for the belongings of the victims killed at Treblinka, Sobibór and Bełżec.
24. See, Elissa M. Koslov, '"Going east": colonial experiences and practices of violence among female and male Majdanek camp guards (1941–44)', *Journal of Genocide Research*, Vol. 10, No. 4, 2008, pp. 563–82.
25. The Column of Three Eagles was based on Albin Maria Boniecki's design and made by Polish prisoners in 1943 on the occasion of a visit by the International Red Cross. Prisoners were demanded to decorate the camp in order to create an impression of order and attractiveness (Maria Wiśnioch, *Majdanek: a Guide to the Historical Buildings*, Lublin: Państwowe Muzeum na Majdanku, 2012. p. 42).
26. Arad, pp. 366–9.
27. The United States Holocaust Memorial Museum later bought these photographs from the Bildungswerk Stanislaw Hantz. The collection, originally owned by Niemann's widow, includes 361 photographs taken at Sobibór, Bełżec, Sachsenhausen and other locations in Germany and Occupied Poland.
28. Arad, pp. 370–76.
29. Tim Cole, 'Crematoria, barracks, gateways. Survivors' return visits to the memory landscapes of Auschwitz', *History and Memory*, Vol. 25, No. 2, 2013, pp. 102–31 (102).

30. Lager IV (Camp IV) was still under construction at the time of the uprising and, located in an area to the north of the other camps, included a wooden chapel which had been built in 1926 and where the Nazis killed those who were ill at arrival to the camp. It was later demolished and a Roman Catholic Church was built on the same site in 1986. On the planning of Sobibór, see Arad, pp. 30–36.
31. Claude Lanzmann, 'Site and Speech: An Interview with Claude Lanzmann about *Shoah*', with Marc Chevrie and Hervé Le Roux, in *Claude Lanzmann's* Shoah*: Key Essays*, Stuart Liebman (ed.), Oxford and New York: Oxford University Press, 2007, pp. 37-49 (38–9).
32. Gary Weissman, *Fantasies of Witnessing: Post-war Efforts to Experience the Holocaust*, Ithaca, New York: Cornell University Press, 2004, p. 192.
33. Similarly, *Sobibór: the Plan, the Revolt, the Escape* (Karen Lynne and Richard Bloom, 2010) is a short documentary consisting of several talking-head interviews with survivors (Philip Bialowitz Thomas Blatt, Chaim Engel, Selma Engel, Samuel Lerer, Esther Raab, Kurt Thomas, Regina Zielinski), recorded remotely and edited with archival photographs of the Forward Camp and Camp I.
34. More recently, Russian war drama *Sobibór* (Собибор, Konstantin Khabensky, 2018) has also focused on the uprising. Additionally, the docudrama *Escape from a Nazi Death Camp* (Hereward Pelling, 2014) combines a dramatic reconstruction of the uprising with remote testimonies from survivors Thomas Blatt, Philip Bialowitz, Selma Engel-Wijnberg and Semjon Rozenfeld.

CHAPTER 4

Hiroshima, Chūgoku Region, Japan, 6 August 1945, 8:15 a.m.

> *A thirty-year-old pilot from Quincy, Illinois, departs from an airfield on Tinian in the Mariana Islands and reaches his target after several hours. There he drops a bomb which creates a tall mushroom cloud. His name is Paul Tibbets and this happens on the morning of 6 August 1945 in Hiroshima.*

The scene portrays a street in the city of Hiroshima where wounded soldiers are wearing bandages wrapped around their limbs, hands or heads. A small group of local women provide assistance while the national flag of Japan, the *Nisshōki* or *Hinomaru*, is flying in the background from a traditional wooden building (Figure 4.1). This street scene was illustrated in 1904 by Melton Prior, a renowned English artist and war correspondent for *The Illustrated London News* who was reporting on Japan's victory in the Russo-Japanese War (1904–5). The drawing, titled 'Back from the Wars: A Street Scene in Hiroshima', is described in Prior's handwriting on the sketch published on *The Illustrated London News* as the 'arrival home of sick and wounded fighting the battle over again'.[1] The image depicts a familiar view of the home front of a war including severely injured soldiers returning to their homes and receiving care and support from their people. Forty-one years later, on the day when Paul Tibbets flew to Hiroshima in the Boeing B-29 Superfortress bomber *Enola Gay*, a noiseless flash followed by a firestorm and by black rain erased most of the city and signalled the beginning of the atomic age in warfare. The bombing of Hiroshima and, one week later, Nagasaki were, as Michael J. Hogan suggests, 'the final acts in an Asian war that had its origins in the 1930s, specifically in Japan's effort to forge an empire in East Asia and the Western Pacific.'[2] This was a point of no return in the application of advanced science and technology to armaments; it was the event which captured with the greatest clarity the process which I have discussed in the introduction of this book and which saw that technological advancement which had first promised a century of peace and progress applied to the annihilation of an entire city. On 6 August 1945, there was no one there, in what was left of Hiroshima, to help out the wounded men, women and children who, unlike the soldiers depicted by Prior in 1904, had no bandages wrapping their bodies but rather, in the

Figure 4.1 Illustration by Melton Prior titled 'Back from the Wars: A Street Scene in Hiroshima' (*The Illustrated London News*, 13 August 1904).

vivid and horrific description written by American journalist John Hersey in 1946, skin hanging 'from their faces and hands' or 'the shapes of the flowers they had had on their kimonos' burnt on their flesh.³

The extraordinary destruction inflicted on the city by a single atomic bomb codenamed Little Boy was of a scale until then unseen in modern warfare; and yet the skeletal steel frame of a domed building located almost directly below the hypocentre, as well as the building's vertical columns and parts of the concrete and brick outer walls, were still standing after the blast. Located on the bank of the Motoyasu River, the *Hiroshima-ken Sangyo Shourei-kan* (Hiroshima Prefectural Industrial Promotion Hall) was known as the Prefectural Commercial Exhibition until 1921 and as the Prefectural Products Exhibition Hall until 1933. The building was completed in 1915 and it opened to the public in the summer of that year as a venue for industrial, commercial, cultural and educational events. Now known at the *Genbaku Dome* (Atomic Bomb Dome), the ruins of the building stand between the 'T'-shaped three-way *Aioi Hashi* (Aioi Bridge), which was constructed in 1932 and later chosen by the Americans as the aiming point for the atomic bomb, and the two-storey brick building of the *Shima byōin* (Shima Hospital), the actual hypocentre of the explosion.

The Prefectural Industrial Promotion Hall was used as a location in amateur films made in the 1920s and 1930s by local people and by visitors to the city, as well as in later animated films set in Hiroshima before the morning of 6 August 1945. Its ruins feature in a number of post-war newsreels and from 1952, following its inclusion in the *Hiroshima Heiwa Kinen Kōen* (Hiroshima Peace Memorial Park), they appear as the Atomic Bomb Dome in live-action and animated films focusing on the bombing and the struggle for survival which followed the end of the war. The multitude of uses and meanings embodied in this specific site of memory of the city of Hiroshima and symbol of the atomic age, as they emerge from a diverse range of films signalling the irreversible break marked by the bombing, is the main theme I address in this chapter. As N. A. J. Taylor and Robert Jacobs have suggested, Hiroshima is 'the name given to our changed relationship to both nature and human technological culture' and our long-term relationship to radiation thus demands that we 'engage in a process of experiencing and re-imagining Hiroshima again-and-again.'[4] Like the ruins of Belchite or the dilapidated barracks of Majdanek, the debris and remnants of the Prefectural Industrial Promotion Hall are at the core of a process of memorialisation of a space where past events are embedded into its built environment and its relics. Accordingly, in this chapter I investigate the ways in which the district now occupied by the Hiroshima Peace Memorial Park, and in particular the Atomic Bomb Dome and its immediate surroundings, have been used in a group of films articulating the memorialisation of the atomic bombing by means of narratives of commemoration and via an aesthetic of ruins bearing witness to the event.[5]

The use of the Atomic Bomb Dome as a film location immediately evokes the nuclear attack and the events which led to and followed the bombing; its presence on film defines Hiroshima as a cinematic city and serves as a constant reminder of the suffering which continued for several decades after the end of the war. For example, the ruins of the Prefectural Industrial Promotion Hall and the nearby district of Motomachi are constant presences in *Jingi Naki Tatakai* (*Battles Without Honour and Humanity*, 1974–6), a popular series of five *yakuza* films directed by Kinji Fukasaku and starring Bunta Sugawara. Motomachi is an area originally occupied by military facilities and after the war by an atomic bomb slum with houses and unauthorised shacks inhabited by the *hibakusha* (the Japanese term for the survivors of the atomic bombing). In *Battles Without Honour and Humanity*, Fukasaku uses both the Atomic Bomb Dome and Motomachi as locations defined by a significant connection between the war and post-war criminality; this interrelation is articulated by presenting urban violence as a phenomenon stemming from the experience of the soldiers coming back from the battlefields and from that of the civilians who survived the atomic bombing. As Kate E. Taylor-Jones suggests, Fukasaku uses the *yakuza* genre to chart 'the development of Hiroshima from a ravaged city to the sleek modern environment it has now become' and yet, by setting the action near the Atomic Bomb Dome, the director's work 'constantly reminds us that not all the people have benefited from this – many of the *hibakusha* still live in sub-standard conditions, an embarrassing living reminder of the war that the society would rather forget.'[6] As we shall see, the discrimination suffered by the *hibakusha* emerges as a theme from several fiction films in opposition to the image of national unity emerging from the official commemorations of the bombing recorded in post-war newsreels.

Between 1915 and 1945 the Prefectural Industrial Promotion Hall had been one of the main attractions of the city and its domed roof dominated the low-rise skyline of Hiroshima between the two world wars. The windows of the second and third floors of the hall offered beautiful views of the city and the image of the elegant building would often be reflected in the Motoyasu River. As Lisa Yoneyama explains:

> Designed by an architect from Czechoslovakia, Jan Letzel, this continental Secession-style building, crowned with a distinctive dome-shaped roof, was completed in 1915. It served as a public space where crafts and commodities from Hiroshima's environs, as well as from different regions throughout the empire, were brought in and displayed.[7]

Visitors from other cities and other countries would stop over at the hall and walk through its galleries in awe of its exhibits. They would also capture the building in their photographs and, in some instances, in amateur footage. Several films made by visitors to Hiroshima during the 1920s and 1930s have survived and are now preserved by the RCC (Kabushiki Gaisha Chugoku Hoso), a broadcasting company which serves the Hiroshima region. On 23 October 1925, Shuichi Fujii visited Hiroshima with his family and dined at a Western-style restaurant in the Nakajima Honmachi; the footage he filmed during on that day includes scenes taken at Motoyasu Bridge and across the river looking at what was to become the Atomic Bomb Dome.[8] Three years later, Kannosuke Kaminishi filmed similar shots of the building including people walking and fishing on the river bank.[9] In April 1936, Genjiro Kawasaki filmed the city during the cherry blossom season. This footage shows the ornamental cherry trees lining the riverbank near the Aioi Bridge and the bustling commercial district of Shintenchi; it also includes images of people fishing on the Motoyasu River and a panning shot revealing the

Prefectural Industrial Promotion Hall in the background.[10] These amateur films also show the electric trams representing the efficient public transport of Hiroshima, and display a lively and vibrant city with the Prefectural Industrial Promotion Hall emerging as its most distinctive and popular landmark. As I explain later in this chapter, the trams filmed by amateur filmmakers before the war would become a constant presence in post-war films set in the 1930s and staging the interwar city as a successful urban environment with the hall as its crown jewel. As Yoneyama has observed, the Prefectural Industrial Promotion Hall was a 'quintessential sign of Japan's early-twentieth-century imperial modernity'.[11] The character of Hiroshima emerging from the amateur films made by Fujii, Kaminishi, Kawasaki and others exemplifies this sense of imperial modernity. Even more prominently though, the image of the hall emerging from their films is one of entrepreneurship and civic pride; the amateur footage described above captured a building which embodied a thriving urban economy and which had been created to enhance the role of the city within the increasingly competitive domestic trade of the interwar years.

The locations filmed by amateur filmmakers in the 1920s and 1930s were captured in October 1945 for the *World News in Review* (British Pathé), a news report including various aerial and ground shots of the destruction in Hiroshima and Nagasaki and several images of the crumbling ruins of the Prefectural Industrial Promotion Hall.[12] The vibrant district which emerged from those amateur films had become a wasteland of rubble where only two figures can be seen walking in the rain under two large umbrellas, their feet partly exposed in two pairs of *geta*.[13] The archives of British Pathé also include unreleased Japanese footage showing the effects of the atomic bombing and titled *Nagasaki and Hiroshima* (British Pathé, 1945).[14] In this film the camera zooms on an aerial view of the city in the direction of the hypocentre over the Shima Hospital, and includes footage of what used to be the district surrounding the Prefectural Industrial Promotion Hall. This panoramic view is juxtaposed with harrowing footage of Japanese doctors dressing the wounds of atomic bomb casualties, including a child's hand with no flesh remaining on the fingers. The use of the aerial view of the city in the newsreel *Nagasaki and Hiroshima* inscribes into the post-atomic urban landscape of Hiroshima the horrors which were witnessed by the cameramen in the improvised hospitals of the city; in these images the lively crowds and the civic pride emerging from earlier amateur footage are replaced by death, destruction, suffering and emptiness.

A further transformation of this district and its most iconic building occurred when the ruins of the Prefectural Industrial Promotion Hall, instead of being completely demolished, were monumentalised and became what is now known as the Atomic Bomb Dome. Created in 1952 with the inauguration of the Memorial Cenotaph, the Hiroshima Peace Memorial Park, as Michael Lucken suggests, is a space based on an engagement with pain and memory through conservation, documentation and exhibitions.[15] An essential part of this project, the Atomic Bomb Dome embodies the memorialisation of an event which at once defined, locally, the history of the city and later, on the global stage, the arrival of the Atomic Age. In the years which followed the inauguration of the park, the new identity of what had previously been the Prefectural Industrial Promotion Hall was consistently used in the newsreels. For example, nocturnal footage showing 10,000 lighted paper lanterns floating down the Motoyasu river in memory of the victims and floating on the water in front of the Atomic Bomb Dome is included in the newsreel *Japan: Hiroshima Marks 22nd Anniversary Of Atom Bomb* (Gaumont British Newsreel, 1967); this newsreel captures the commemorative function of a building preserved in the state in which it appeared right after the atomic bombing and whose purpose, meaning and place in the urban fabric of the city had shifted from the embodiment of civic pride to that of collective mourning.[16]

The architectural plan for the Hiroshima Peace Memorial Park, of which the Dome is an integral and defining part, has been criticised for failing to contextualise the atomic bombing in relation to the culture of Japan in its age of empire. Yoneyama, for example, has argued that within both mainstream national historiography and the more universalistic narrative of the bombing, the memorialisation of what happened in Hiroshima in the summer of 1945 has been 'predicated on the grave obfuscation of the pre-war Japanese Empire, its colonial practices, and their consequences.'[17] Newsreels of the Peace Memorial Park embody this ambiguity and reflect what Yoneyama has called the 'unproblematized transition of Hiroshima's central commemorative space from celebrating imperial Japan to honouring the post-war peaceful nation' as well as the complexities of 'the persistence of pre-war social and cultural elements, even at the iconic site that supposedly symbolizes the nation's rebirth and departure from the past.'[18] Post-war newsreels intervene in this contested memorialisation of the atomic bombing while leaving pre-war imperial practices at the margins; their narrative is that of a city captured in the process of prolonged mourning and yet taking pride in the display of its rebirth. *Hiroshima, Six Years After* (British Pathé, 1951), for example, was filmed on the sixth anniversary of the bombing and shows men, women and children standing in silence and bowing their heads, near their houses, shrines and playgrounds. This footage focuses on individual and collective mourning while at the same time revealing a new city where crowds, brand new buildings and bustling traffic replace the dramatic emptiness which characterised the space captured in the newsreels filmed soon after the end of the war.[19]

Three years later, a news report titled *Hiroshima, Nine Years After A-Blast* (British Pathé, 1954) juxtaposed footage of the destruction which followed the attack to shots of the new buildings, parks and streets of the city; this newsreel also includes several low-angle medium shots of what used to be the Prefectural Industrial Promotion Hall, by then the memorialised embodiment of the atomic bombing or, as the voice-over suggests, a 'grim reminder' and a 'silent symbol' of the event.[20] This focus on the Atomic Bomb Dome thus characterised the newsreels made soon after the bombing as well as later newsreels reporting on the yearly commemorative ceremonies. The topographical focal point of the newsreels migrated into live-action fiction films depicting the aftermath of the destruction of the city and, as I explain later in this chapter, into animated films of Hiroshima. The cityscape emerging from the newsreels is evoked in an early fiction film about the atomic bombing commissioned by the Japanese Teachers' Union, *Genbaku no Ko* (*Children of Hiroshima*, Kaneto Shindo, 1952). Made soon after the end of the American occupation (1945–52) and released on the day of the seventh anniversary of the atomic bombing, *Children of Hiroshima* follows Takako Ishikawa (Nobuko Otowa), a teacher who lives on an island off the coast of Hiroshima and who goes back to the city to visit the graves of her parents and sister; here she observes the impact of the bombing on the lives of those who had survived the attack. The opening credits run on footage of the ruins of the Prefectural Industrial Promotion Hall: a series of panning shots capture details of the building, including its surviving walls and the piles of rubble surrounding its main structure and covering the ground which had once contained Western-style and Japanese gardens which included a pond and a large fountain. Takako's arrival in Hiroshima introduces the viewer to the city of the early 1950s: a long shot of the harbour includes a view of new buildings and is juxtaposed with a tracking shot of atomic bomb slums seen from the river. The proximity of urban redevelopment and *hibakusha* dwellings exemplifies how survivors were discriminated against and marginalised, and thus anticipates the main theme of the film.

In the following scenes, Takako walks to a derelict district where she visits the site of her family home and the burial place of her parents and sister. On this location a flashback takes Takako back to 6 August 1945 and includes harrowing images of the immediate impact of the atomic bombing on people and buildings. This flashback is followed by a non-narrative sequence including various shots of the Atomic Bomb Dome filmed from multiple angles in the manner of contemporary newsreels. Takako can then be seen standing on the opposite bank of the river as she observes carefully the ruins of the Prefectural Industrial Promotion Hall; a tracking shot follows her as she walks towards the Aioi Bridge and sees a disfigured and partially blind beggar whom she recognises as Iwakichi (Osamu Takizawa), a man who used to work for her parents. In the following sequences, Takako stays at Iwakichi's place, one of the unauthorised shacks inhabited by the *hibakusha*, and learns that the man's grandson, Tarō, is now living in an institution; following the death of Iwakichi, Takako takes the boy back with her to the island. Before departure and towards the end of the film, Takako and Tarō stand again in front of the ruins of the Prefectural Industrial Promotion Hall at dusk and this shot is followed by another montage sequence of images of the ruins standing against the sky at dawn (Figure 4.2). The Atomic Bomb Dome thus frames the narrative of *Children of Hiroshima* with two meditative scenes where Takako absorbs the long-term impact of the atomic bombing and remembers the city which was erased on 6 August 1945; as she stands by the bank of the river, she contemplates a site which, it is implied, she must remember as the remarkable building of the 1930s and as the epitome of the city's civic pride.

Between the two reflexive scenes of the Atomic Bomb Dome which frame the narrative of the film, *Children of Hiroshima* focuses on the lives of the *hibakusha* and the challenges they faced in the post-war years, a theme which is developed through the character of Iwakichi and already revealed in the early shots of the riverside slums inhabited by the *hibakusha*. As Robert Jay Lifton suggests, the discrimination against the *hibakusha* 'in both marriage and

Figure 4.2 Ruins of the Hiroshima Prefectural Industrial Promotion Hall at dusk in *Genbaku no Ko* (*Children of Hiroshima*, Kaneto Shindo, 1952).

employment was apparently greatest during the years immediately following the bomb; but it has left its mark, and has by no means entirely disappeared even now [2012].'[21] In *Children of Hiroshima*, the character of Iwakichi embodies this discrimination and is one of those *hibakusha* who, as Lifton suggests, tumbled down the social ladder and 'literally joined the ranks of the outcasts by moving into the special slum areas where they live and becoming virtually indistinguishable from them.'[22] *Children of Hiroshima* gives a voice to these *hibakusha* in a way which had not been encouraged during the occupation. Laura E. Hein and Mark Selden have argued that there is a symmetrical connection between the American response to the atom bombing and the memorialisation of the war in Japan:

> American commentators of the bombings leave out Japanese victims, whereas Japanese ones leave out the victims of Japanese aggression. The Americans falsified the arithmetic of suffering and loss by silencing the voices of *hibakusha*, while the Japanese silence on the larger issues of war preserved the image of a virtuous nation of innocent victims.[23]

With *Children of Hiroshima* the *hibakusha* are no longer silent and find a visual representation in the lives and struggle of Iwakichi and his son; the larger issues of war, the imperialist culture which fuelled Japan's aggressive war strategy and the atrocities committed in its name, on the other hand, are still absent.

Resentment towards the Americans and the struggle of the *hibakusha* became consolidated themes in other films from this period, including Hideo Sekigawa's *Hiroshima* (1953).[24] The first sequence of Hiroshima, a film which was also commissioned by the Japanese Teachers' Union, is set in 1953 in a middle-school classroom where students discuss and express their misconceptions about radiation exposure and leukaemia; one of the schoolgirls is traumatised by the discussion and, after school, relives the memory of the bombing. A flashback takes the narrative back to the day of the attack and scenes of wartime life in the city reveal a seemingly happy existence despite the hardship of war. Young men and women of Hiroshima, played by *hibakusha* as extras, look up at the sky as they hear the *Enola Gay* approaching the city. This is followed by scenes of the explosion and the destruction of the city. The following sequences show the chaos and the devastation which unfolded in the summer of 1945 and the impact of radiation sickness on people who were no longer able to work. As Reiko Tachibana has argued, 'the *hibakusha* were considered to be unreliable workers because many of them [...] were not physically robust and had to take a few days' rest after a period of hard labour.'[25] *Hiroshima* addresses this discrimination and the fact that a number of hibakusha appear as extras in the film establishes a significant collision between the cinematic city and the real space of Hiroshima.[26]

As they use a filmic space built on the lived experience of Hiroshima, *Children of Hiroshima* and *Hiroshima* capture the vision of 'the city as a phoenix', a symbolic ideal which has been described by Ran Zwigenberg as one of the main tropes of post-war Hiroshima,[27] and they also reveal that ambiguity of the memorialisation of the bombing. As Zwigenberg explains:

> While the city was rebuilding, well into the 1960s, many *hibakusha* still lived in the A-bomb slum (*genbaku suramu*) opposite the Peace Park. This glaring contrast between the peace park and the A-bomb slum symbolized the contradictions inherent in Hiroshima's modernization project. While the city looked into the future, the *hibakusha*, in whose name peace was proclaimed, were left behind with the bomb that had destroyed their bodies, killed their families and taken their livelihoods.[28]

Contemporary newsreels such as those I have discussed earlier in this chapter neglected to address the ways in which the *hibakusha* were left behind and used the Atomic Bomb Dome and other landmarks as silent witnesses of an event which was memorialised while its victims were being forgotten. Both *Children of Hiroshima* and *Hiroshima*, on the contrary, address the struggle imbedded in the rebirth of Hiroshima and use both the ruins of the Prefectural Industrial Promotion Hall and the slums inhabited by the *hibakusha* as meaningful locations. The result is a critical view of the process of post-war redevelopment of the city and an acknowledgment of the contradictions of a project built on inequality and neglecting to address discrimination.

Zwigenberg has discussed the necessity to articulate a balanced attempt to address the history and legacy of Hiroshima based on both the rejection of a reading of the event as unique, and thus the establishment of a hierarchy of tragedy, and the dismissal of a tendency to universalise and blur the line between fact and fiction when dealing with the suffering associated with the atomic bombing.[29] This argument evokes the tendency to read the atomic bombing as an incident whose legacy has been shaped less by the concern for those who suffered the consequences of exposure to radiation and more by vague ideas of national victimisation and universalised threat of atomic warfare. The complexities of this legacy as they emerge from the urban fabric of the city are at the core of *Hiroshima mon amour* (Alain Resnais, 1959). Written by Marguerite Duras and based on a series of conversations about memory and forgetfulness over a thirty-six-hour period, the film follows two nameless individuals, a French actress (Emmanuelle Riva) and a Japanese architect (Eiji Okada), after a brief sexual and romantic encounter. *Hiroshima mon amour* is ultimately about the relationship between memories by recall and memories by imagination; the trauma of the atomic bombing is addressed from the first sequence of the film as Riva's character tries to grasp a memory which is unavailable to those who were not in Hiroshima on 6 August 1945. The film opens with various shots of two interlaced bodies whose skin is covered in ashes, which evoke the nuclear fallout; as Cathy Caruth suggests, these images establish a connection between the 'dying bodies of the past' and the 'living bodies of the present'.[30] The following scenes affirm a further connection between bodies, memories and the built environment of Hiroshima: Riva's voice reconstructs the horror of the bombing by means of an account of her visit to one of the hospitals for the wounded, to the Hiroshima Peace Memorial Museum and the Peace Square. Contemporary images of these locations, including a panning shot from the Aioi Bridge to the Atomic Bomb Dome, are juxtaposed with newsreels from the 1940s as well as the atomic bombing sequence from Sekigawa's *Hiroshima*.[31] *Hiroshima mon amour* intertwines past and present, factual and fictional accounts of the atomic bombing, and builds a sequence where memories are connected by imagination to the post-war monumentalisation of the sites. Resnais thus returned, through the form of a feature length fiction film, to that cinematic use of a site of memory and conflict which, as I have explained in Chapter 2, he had articulated almost ten years earlier in *Guernica*.

Gary Weissman, whose work has been introduced in the previous chapter, has described an 'unspoken desire' to remember traumatic events expressed by individuals who have not experienced them directly, and has discussed the challenges posed by 'the post-war museumification of the site, the deterioration of what has been preserved, and the absence of the horrific past reality that, on some level, one anticipates encountering.'[32] In the opening sequence of *Hiroshima mon amour*, Riva's account of her visit to the sites of memory of the atomic bombing reflects a similar fantasy of witnessing a traumatic incident of which she has no direct experience. Riva's voice-over claims that she has 'seen everything in Hiroshima' and describes the reconstructions on display at the museum and what she has seen in the newsreels or in fiction films. Okada's voice-over regularly interrupts the account given by Riva and bluntly repeats that she has seen nothing in Hiroshima and hints to the impossibility of knowing or even truly speaking about what happened on the day when Little Boy detonated over the Shima Hospital. Riva's account thus reveals that unspoken yearning to remember traumatic events which has been discussed by Weissman, and the variety of images accompanying her words inscribes this desire onto the built environment of the city with a topographical precision embedded in the final shot of the sequence. This is an aerial view of the delta estuary of the Ōta River accompanied by the words written by Duras and recited by Riva:

> The seven branches of the delta estuary in the Ōta River empty and fill at the usual hours, with water that is fresh and rich with fish, gray or blue depending on the hour or the season. Along the muddy banks people no longer watch the tide rising slowly in the seven branches of the delta estuary of the Ōta River.[33]

At first, this looks like a reassuring view and commentary on a place where not even the atomic bomb could change the course of nature, the stream of the river and its branches, the richness of its water. And yet, with this shot *Hiroshima mon amour* also evokes the view seen by Colonel Paul Tibbets and his crew of twelve men from the *Enola Gay* and thus re-establishes Hiroshima and its environs as an aim for nuclear destruction.

The idea of Hiroshima as a target also emerges from similar aerial views of the delta estuary of the Ōta River which have been used in two popular *anime* films about the atomic bombing and its consequences, *Hadashi no Gen* (*Barefoot Gen*, Mori Masaki, 1983) and *Hadashi no Gen 2* (*Barefoot Gen 2*, Toshio Hirata, 1986). In these animated films, the ruins of the Prefectural Industrial Promotion Hall, as well as other sites of memory, play a defining role in a topography reminiscent of the cinematic cityscapes which unfolded in newsreels, fiction and amateur films. Loosely based on Keijij Nakazawa's own experience as a *hibakusha* and on his earlier work *Ore wa Mita* (*I Saw It*, 1972), and adapted from the manga series *Hadashi no Gen* (*Barefoot Gen*, 1973–87),[34] *Barefoot Gen* is set in 1945 and opens with a historical introduction to the events of the Second World War including references to the development of the atomic bomb and an aerial view of the delta area of Hiroshima.[35] This is followed by a short sequence introducing the character of Gen Nakaoka and his family. The opening titles are accompanied by various establishing shots, including a closer aerial view of the aiming point of the atom bombing, the Aioi Bridge. A long shot of the *Hiroshima-jō* (the Hiroshima Castle) is followed by two shots of the trams riding on the Aioi Bridge; the first one shows the Prefectural Industrial Promotion Hall in the background while the second is another aerial shot focusing on the 'T' junction of the bridge and panning from the Prefectural Industrial Promotion Hall to the Nakajima Honmachi district. Reminiscent of the amateur films I have discussed earlier in this chapter, this early sequence captures everyday life in Hiroshima before 6 August 1945 and anticipates the scenes of the atomic bombing.

The following sequences focus on Gen and his family as they struggle through food shortages and air raid warnings during the final weeks of the war and lead to the moment when the *Enola Gay* drops the atomic bomb aiming at the Aioi Bridge; Mori Masaki uses aerial views of the delta estuary of the Ōta River, of the city of Hiroshima and a shot of the trams riding on the Aioi

Bridge with the Prefectural Industrial Promotion Hall in the background. Little Boy is dropped and hits the target, the Aioi Bridge, whereas in reality the actual hypocentre of the attack was Shima Hospital, approximately 240 metres away from the intended aiming point.[36] *Barefoot Gen* recreates the silent explosion of the bomb and the flash of light; domestic settings and public places including the Aioi Bridge and the Prefectural Industrial Promotion Hall, turn to black and white in a series of shots anticipating a detailed representation of the damage inflicted on that building. This film thus captures the exact moment when the Prefectural Industrial Promotion Hall was turned into ruins and thus juxtaposes life and death, lived and experienced built environment and its destruction.

The new identity of the former Prefectural Industrial Promotion Hall as a crumbling site of memory is depicted in *Barefoot Gen 2*. Set in 1948, the film addresses radiation sickness and the predicament of the *hibakusha* while following Gen as he is scavenging for food and scrap metal to sell on the black market. A long nocturnal sequence set in the ruins of the Prefectural Industrial Promotion Hall sees Gen and his adopted brother Ryuta climbing to the top of the building to collect eggs from bird nests. The two boys observe the sun rising on the city as they stand on the skeletal steel frame of the dome. This sequence is reminiscent of a shot from *Children of Hiroshima* where local children are seen climbing and playing in the ruins of the hall. What used to be a space designed to display the civic and imperial pride of Hiroshima has become both a figurative ruin of that pride and a literal ruin of the built environment of the city reclaimed by two young *hibakusha* in an act of survival. This sequence is followed by a long shot of a tram travelling on the Aioi Bridge and then through the rubble to an atomic bomb slum and to the surviving building of Hiroshima Station. The scene evokes the opening of the first film and establishes a parallel between the lively space to which the viewer was introduced in *Barefoot Gen* and the devastation and emptiness which characterised the city in the immediate post-war years, thus reiterating the parallel between the lively scenes filmed by amateur filmmakers in the 1920s and 1930s and images of annihilation included in later newsreels.

Like the earlier films *Children of Hiroshima* and *Hiroshima*, *Barefoot Gen 2* focuses on the youngest survivors of the atomic bombing and also includes an episode set in a classroom in a local school. This sequence exemplifies what Hein and Selden have described as creative outputs which 'have repeatedly used the bomb as a vehicle for questioning not only Japanese colonialism, aggression, and atrocities but also the post-war Japanese political system, including rearmament, within the United States-Japan security relationship.'[37] Gen's teacher is talking about pacifism and about the mistakes committed in the past while observing the ruins of the Prefectural Industrial Promotion Hall from the widow; this scene is followed by a closer shot of the building which is thus made to symbolise both the suffering of the city and the image of a new and peaceful Japan that the teacher is trying to conjure.

An equally meaningful use of the ruins of the Prefectural Industrial Promotion Hall is made in a later animated drama titled *Kono Sekai no Katasumi ni* (Sunao Katabuchi, *In This Corner of the World*, 2016). Set in the years between 1933 and 1945, this is the story of a young woman named Suzu, her pre-war life in the seaside town of Eba, in the Hiroshima prefecture, and her time in Kure, a city situated on the Seto Inland Sea, with her husband Shūsaku and his family during the conflict. *In This Corner of the World* is an attempt to make sense of the atomic bomb and its impact on post-war culture and society in Japan in response to what is perceived as a widespread failure to come to terms with the event. As Donald Richie has argued:

> ... the Japanese failure to come to terms with Hiroshima is one which is shared by everyone in the world today. No one has come to terms with the bomb – least of all, perhaps, the people upon whom it was originally inflicted. When the thing itself has become the very epitome of chaos unleashed, it would be expecting too much that an ordered and directed reply could be instantly presented.[38]

Richie has also argued that Japanese cinema addressed 'the complexity of the associations which surround the word "Hiroshima" and the extent to which the bombed cities and the bomb itself have become symbols to the Japanese.'[39] *In This Corner of the World* addresses this symbolism in relation to traditional Japanese culture and its disappearance and pays particular attention to the recreation of its locations by means of research on old photographs, prints, documents and oral testimonies of pre-war Hiroshima.

Largely set in Kure, *In This Corner of the World* includes a prologue and an epilogue which take place in Hiroshima in 1933 and 1945 respectively. These sequences contain elements of magic realism and frame a story of wartime daily struggle with a fantastic retelling of the first encounter between Suzu and her husband-to-be Shūsaku. In the first sequence of the film, Suzu is delivering seaweed to a shop in the Nakajima Honmachi district of Hiroshima (now Nakajimacho), an area which would be erased by the bomb and is now part of the Hiroshima Peace Memorial Park. An aerial shot of Nakajima Honmachi, including the Honkawa and Motoyasugawa branches of the Ōta River, establishes the context of the following scenes. This aerial view includes three important locations in relation to the bombing: the Aioi Bridge, the two-storey brick building of the Shima Hospital and the Prefectural Industrial Promotion Hall. Suzu walks to a meticulously drawn Hondōri, an avenue made easily recognisable by the lanterns shaped like lily-of-the-valley flowers which were installed in 1931 in order to allow shops to stay open late at night. This was a very popular district of Hiroshima and it featured regularly in amateur films made in the late 1920s and 1930s. In 1927, Hiroshima-born migrant to Canada Kannosuke Kaminishi, who was spending two years in Japan, filmed Hondōri with its lily-of-the-valley street lamps and the Motoyasu Bridge.[40] In 1934, Shigeo Fukuichi filmed the celebrations for the birth of Crown Prince Akihito, Emperor Hirohito's first son, in a crowded Hondōri and at the Fukuya Department Store.[41] Three years later, Shinichi Yoshioka filmed bustling Hondōri, during one of Hiroshima's three festivals, *Ebisu Taisa*; the Mitsui Bank Hiroshima Branch (now the Hiroshima Andersen bakery) is clearly visible in this footage.[42] Between 1937 and 1940, local resident Nobuichi Yoshioka filmed market scenes in the Nakajima Honmachi and Kamiyacho districts on standard 8 mm film.[43] These amateur films show Hondōri, its lively shops and market stalls, the characteristic street lights and Ebisu Taisai decorations, and capture the bustling and lively Hiroshima cherished by locals and visitors. In an attempt to evoke this long-gone city, *In This Corner of the World* recreates Hondōri with great precision in a sequence which is reminiscent of these amateur films and where even individual shops are recognisable. In one of the shots, for example, Suzu is resting by the window of Taishoya Kimono, a shop housed in a 1929 building which survived the blast and is now a tourist information centre at 1–1 Nakajimacho, Naka Ward.

In a juxtaposition reminiscent of the sequences from *Barefoot Gen* and *Barefoot Gen 2* discussed above, the prologue of *In This Corner of the World* uses specific sites of memory in order to inscribe its narrative onto the urban space of Hiroshima; the epilogue returns to these locations in the process of articulating a sense of loss and regret for a past of which the ruins of the Prefectural Industrial Promotion Hall are amongst the few surviving traces. After the opening credits, Suzu returns to Eba and explains to her younger sister that she got lost in the city and there she met an ogre who gave her a telescope to help her find her way. In her fantastic flashback, point-of-view shots seen through the telescope include panoramic views of the Prefectural Industrial Promotion Hall and the Hiroshima Castle. Suzu explains that she then felt into the ogre's basket where she met an older boy who told her that they were being kidnapped. The ogre walks on the Aioi Bridge, exactly on the aiming point of the atomic bombing, in the direction of the Prefectural Industrial Promotion Hall, which is clearly visible in the background in the scene where the children manage to escape. This implausible story is told through words and by means of Suzu's drawings in a fantastic retelling of the first time Suzu met Shūsaku unfolding on the background of the sites of memory of Hiroshima.

In the final sequence of *In This Corner of the World*, Suzu returns to the central district of Hiroshima and stands in front of the ruins of the Prefectural Industrial Promotion Hall and meets Shūsaku (Figure 4.3). Followed by an aerial view of the city revealing the destruction caused by the nuclear bombing, this scene articulates a connection with the establishing shots of the thriving city of the 1930s included in the prologue of the film and is also reminiscent of the scene of Takako's return to Hiroshima in *Children of Hiroshima*. Suzu and Shūsaku stand on the Aioi Bridge on the exact spot where they escaped from the ogre's basket in her fantastic story. Shūsaku tells her that the bridge is the place where they first met and Suzu thanks him for coming to find her in that corner of the world; the ogre walks past them and waves goodbye. *In This Corner of the World* thus uses a fantastic narrative in juxtaposition to the landmarks of the city in ruins to introduce the final sequence of the film: a flashback goes back to the early morning of 6 August 1945, a short time before the detonation of the atomic bomb.[44]

Barefoot Gen, *Barefoot Gen 2* and *In This Corner of the World* all used the ruins of the Prefectural Industrial Promotion Hall as a location and recreated the building as it stood by the river until the early morning of 6 August 1945, in a series of shots reminiscent of the amateur footage of Hiroshima from the 1920s and 1930s. This building has told the story of Hiroshima in the twentieth century and is the most remarkable site of memory in the topography of the cinematic city. Tropes of the atomic bombing, including the rebirth of the city and the discrimination against the *hibakusha* have unravelled around this location in newsreels, live-action and animated dramas, and its crumbling stones have

Figure 4.3 Ruins of the Hiroshima Prefectural Industrial Promotion Hall in *Kono Sekai no Katasumi ni* (*In This Corner of the World*, Sunao Katabuchi, 2016).

fuelled memories by imagination such as those experienced by Riva's character and accounted for in the opening sequence of *Hiroshima Mon Amour*.

The bombing of Hiroshima soon became a point of reference in the revelation of the power of destruction of the nuclear weapons with which the world has had to live ever since. Its immediate legacy was the significant contribution, albeit not the sole reason, to the ending of the Second World War on the Pacific Front. Soon after the bombing of Hiroshima and Nagasaki, Japan signed the surrender documents at Tokyo Bay on the deck of the battleship USS Missouri and thus brought the war and the Age of Catastrophe to an end. Four years after the bombing of Hiroshima, the Soviet Union would conduct its first successful nuclear weapon test at the Semipalatinsk test site in Kazakhstan. The two superpowers which emerged from the Second World War could thus assure mutual destruction by means of full-scale use of nuclear weapons. In the meantime, and while Japan was occupied by American forces, those who had been responsible for the mass murder of the Jews in the Lublin district of the General Government, including the leaders of the Sobibór death camp, were seeking escape routes out of Europe. Many would sail across the Atlantic Ocean under fake names and would start a new life in Latin America. Meanwhile, a large number of Jews who survived the Holocaust also relocated to the cities and towns of Brazil, Argentina and other countries. While the Cold War between the USA and the USSR unfolded across the world, Latin America would see the aftermath of the Holocaust unravelling thousands of miles from Sobibór and the other sites of the extermination which I have discussed in the previous chapter.

Notes

1. 'Back from the Wars: A Street Scene in Hiroshima', *The Illustrated London News*, London, England, Vol. 125, Issue 3408, 13 August 1904, p. 226.
2. Michael J. Hogan, 'Hiroshima in History and Memory: an Introduction', in *Hiroshima in History and Memory*, Michael J. Hogan (ed.), Cambridge: Cambridge University Press, 1996, pp. 1–10 (1).
3. John Hersey, *Hiroshima*, London: Penguin Classics, 2001, pp. 39–40 (first published in *The New Yorker* in 1946).
4. N. A. J. Taylor and Robert Jacobs, 'Introduction: on Hiroshima becoming history', in *Reimagining Hiroshima and Nagasaki: Nuclear Humanities in the Post-Cold War*, N. A. J. Taylor and Robert Jacobs (eds), New York and London: Routledge, 2017, pp. 1–12 (2–3).
5. The Atomic Bomb Dome is also used in foreign films set in Hiroshima and filmed elsewhere; for example, an American film such as *Hiroshima: Out of the Ashes* (Peter Werner, 1990), which was otherwise entirely filmed in studio,

displays images of the ruins of the Prefectural Industrial Promotion Hall during the closing titles.
6. Kate E. Taylor-Jones, *Rising Sun, Divided Land: Japanese and South Korean Filmmakers*, New York: Columbia University Press, 2013, p. 58. On *Battles Without Honour and Humanity*, see also Isolde Standish, *A New History of Japanese Cinema*, London: Bloomsbury, 2006, pp. 305–06.
7. Lisa Yoneyama, *Hiroshima Traces: Time, Space, and the Dialectics of Memory*, Oakland: University of California Press, 1999, p. 2.
8. *At Restaurant Sushitoku, Hiroshima* (Shuichi Fujii, 1925), RCC Broadcasting Company (Hiroshima).
9. *Shokon-sai Festival* (Kannosuke Kaminishi, 1928), RCC Broadcasting Company (Hiroshima).
10. *Hiroshima City in the Spring of 1936* (Genjiro Kawasaki, 1936), RCC Broadcasting Company (Hiroshima).
11. Yoneyama, p. 2.
12. *World News in Review* (British Pathé, 04/10/1945, Film ID: 1165.21). This footage has been used widely in later documentaries; *Date With History: Hiroshima* (British Pathé, 1964, Film ID: 2733.01/2), for example, covers the technological and strategic process leading to the dropping of the first atomic bomb on Hiroshima and it uses from this earlier newsreel, including various views of the ruins of the Prefectural Industrial Promotion Hall.
13. The *geta* is a form of traditional Japanese footwear that resemble clogs.
14. *Nagasaki and Hiroshima* (British Pathé, 1945, Film ID: 2319.12).
15. Michael Lucken, 'The Peace Statue at Nagasaki', in *Japan's Postwar*, Michael Lucken, Anne Bayard-Sakai and Emmanuel Lozerand (eds), New York and London: Routledge, 2013 [translated by J. J. A. Stockwin], pp. 179–202 (187).
16. *Japan: Hiroshima Marks 22nd Anniversary Of Atom Bomb* (Gaumont British Newsreel, 08/08/1967).
17. Yoneyama, p. 3.
18. Yoneyama, p. 3.
19. *Hiroshima, Six Years After* (British Pathé, 1951, Film ID: 1469.36).
20. *Hiroshima, Nine Years After A-Blast* (Warner Pathé News/British Pathé, 1954, ID: 2490.19).
21. Robert Jay Lifton, *Death in Life: Survivors of Hiroshima*, Chapel Hill: University of North Carolina Press, 2012, p. 168.
22. Lifton, p. 170.
23. Laura E. Hein and Mark Selden, 'Commemoration and Silence: Fifty Years of Remembering the Bomb in America and Japan', in *Living with the Bomb: American and Japanese Cultural Conflicts in the Nuclear Age: American and Japanese Cultural Conflicts in the Nuclear Age*, Laura E. Hein and Mark Selden (eds), London and New York: Routledge, 2015, pp. 3–35 (7).
24. Similar themes emerged from films made in Nagasaki, the second Japanese city hit by an atom bomb in the summer of 1945. In this regard, Yūko Shibata has argued that early atom bomb films such as *Nagasaki No Uta Wa Wasureji* (*I will*

Not Forget the Song of Nagasaki, Tasaka Tomotaka, 1952) reflect a perception of warfare as intrinsically cruel and reveal how, only after the American occupation, criticism of the bombing could be made explicit. See: Yūko Shibata, 'Belated arrival in political transition: 1950s film on Hiroshima and Nagasaki', in *When the Tsunami Came to Shore: Culture and Disaster in Japan*, Roy Starrs (ed.), Leiden: Brill, 2014, pp. 231–48 (233). See also: Matthew Edwards, 'Suppression and Censorship: Japanese Cinema during the Occupation', in *The Atomic Bomb in Japanese Cinema: Critical Essays*, Matthew Edwards (ed.), Jefferson: McFarland, 2018, pp. 69–76.

25. Reiko Tachibana, *Narrative as Counter-Memory: A Half-Century of Postwar Writing in Germany and Japan*, Albany: State University of New York Press, 1998, p. 172.
26. These issues have been addressed in later films too. Mainly set in the Geiyo Islands in the Seto Inland Sea of the Hiroshima Prefecture, Shohei Imamura's *Kuroi ame* (*Black Rain*, 1989) is about the struggle of a Japanese family between 1945 and 1950 and it primarily deals with treatment of the *hibakusha* in post-war Japan. The film opens with an establishing shot of the day of the attack. A vivid representation of the atom bombing on the people of Hiroshima is followed by a focus on everyday life; as Inez Hedges has suggested: 'The photographic basis of film makes it uniquely suited for the portrayal of the everyday; at the same time filmmakers can resort to visual illusion to suggest almost any imagined reality. Imamura's film moves between these two poles, tracing the country life of the village on the one hand and offering re-enactments of the diary entries of August 6–15 (including Japan's decision to surrender and the radio address of the emperor acknowledging Japan's defeat) on the other' (Inez Hedges, *World Cinema and Cultural Memory*, Basingstoke: Palgrave Macmillan, 2015, p. 48).
27. Ran Zwigenberg, *Hiroshima: The Origins of Global Memory Culture*, Cambridge University Press, 2014, p. 65.
28. Zwigenberg, p. 65.
29. Zwigenberg, p. 22.
30. Cathy Caruth, *Unclaimed Experience: Trauma, Narrative and History*, Baltimore: Johns Hopkins University Press, 2010, p. 26.
31. The opening sequence of *Hiroshima mon amour* also includes footage of the rebuilt city of the 1950s. Contemporary newsreels such as *Hiroshima and Nagasaki Today* (British Pathé, 1964, Film ID: 3195.16), similarly, include busy street scenes, cinemas, parks and post-war buildings and bridges juxtaposed with several shots of the ruins of the Prefectural Industrial Promotion Hall filmed from across the Motoyasu River.
32. Weissman, pp. 4, 173.
33. 'Les sept branches de l'estuaire en delta de la rivière Ōta se vident et se remplissent à l'heure habituelle, tres précisément aux heures habituelles d'une eau fraiche et poissonneuse, grise ou bleue suivant l'heure et les saisons. Des gens en regardent plus le long des berges boueuses la lente montée de la marée dans les sept branches de l'estuaire en delta de la rivière Ōta.'

34. This manga was also adapted into three live action film in the 1970s and a later television drama: *Hadashi no Gen (Barefoot Gen 1976,* Tengo Yamada), *Hadashi no Gen: Namida no Bakuhatsu (Barefoot Gen: Explosion of Tears,* 1977, Tengo Yamada), *Barefoot Gen Part 3: Battle of Hiroshima (Hadashi no Gen Part 3: Hiroshima no Tatakai,* 1980 Tengo Yamada), and *Barefoot Gen (Hadashi no Gen,* 2007, Masaki Nishiura and Shosuke Murakami).
35. The opening sequence of HBO documentary *White Light/Black Rain: The Destruction of Hiroshima and Nagasaki* (Steven Okazaki, 2007) uses numerous interviews with *hibakusha* and includes a testimony given by Nakazawa, as well as extracts from both the manga and the anime film in order to illustrate his testimony and those of other *hibakusha*.
36. In *Barefoot Gen 2* what appears to be a mistake included in *Barefoot Gen* is corrected. The film opens with the atomic bombing of Hiroshima seen from the *Enola Gay* and the bomb can be seen detonating over the Shima Hospital and not over the intended aiming point at the Aioi Bridge.
37. Hein and Selden, p. 8. Akira Kurosawa, for example, has addressed the nuclear anxiety affecting the country in three films: *Hachigatsu no rapusodi (Rhapsody in August,* 1991) looks at the aftermath of the bombing of Nagasaki; *Ikimono no kiroku (I Live In Fear,* 1955) and *Yume (Dreams,* 1990) focus more broadly on the fear of atomic war in Japanese society.
38. Donald Richie, '"Mono no aware": Hiroshima in Film', in *Hibakusha Cinema: Hiroshima, Nagasaki and the Nuclear Image in Japanese Film*, Mick Broderick (ed.), New York and London: Routledge, 1996, pp. 20–37 (37).
39. Richie, p. 37.
40. *Motoyasu Bridge and Neighbourhood* (Kannosuke Kaminishi, 1927), RCC Broadcasting Company (Hiroshima).
41. *Central Hiroshima City Crowd Celebrating the Birth of the Crown Prince* (Shigeo Fukuichi, 1937), RCC Broadcasting Company (Hiroshima).
42. *Ebisu-ko Festival Crowd* (Shinichi Yoshioka, 1937), RCC Broadcasting Company (Hiroshima).
43. *Nakajima Honmachi and Kamiyacho* (Nobuichi Yoshioka, 1937–40), Hiroshima Peace Memorial Museum.
44. In this sequence, a woman and her young daughter stand on the bank of the Motoyasu River in front of the Prefectural Industrial Promotion Hall. At 8.15 a.m. Little Boy explodes over the city. After the blast the woman dies and her daughter is alone on the streets of the city. Suzu and Shūsaku find the girl near the surviving building of the railway station and decide to take her to Kure. The closing titles reveal that the little *hibakusha*, adopted by Suzu and Shūsaku, will survive radiation sickness and grow up with them as their daughter.

Part 2

Cold War Spaces

CHAPTER 5

San Fernando, Buenos Aires, Argentina, 11 May 1960, 8:05 p.m.

> *A fifty-four-year-old man from Solingen, North Rhine-Westphalia, is ambushed and wrestled to the ground by three Mossad agents while he is on his way home from work. He goes by the name of Ricardo Klement and this happens on the evening of 11 May 1960 in Buenos Aires.*

On the day of the atomic bombing of Hiroshima, former *SS-Obersturmbannführer* and architect of the Final Solution Adolf Eichmann was imprisoned under the name of Otto Eckmann at a POW camp in Weiden, Bavaria. Eichmann later fled Germany and arrived, via Italy, in Argentina on 14 July 1950 under the alias of Ricardo Klement. He was then apprehended by Mossad intelligence agents, taken to Jerusalem, put on trial, sentenced to death and finally executed on 1 June 1962. The operation which took place on 11 May 1960 and which led to the capture of Eichmann in Buenos Aires is the subject of Chris Weitz's historical drama *Operation Finale* (2018). The film details the role played by Lothar Hermann, a half-Jewish German who had immigrated to Argentina in 1938, and his daughter Sylvia, who began dating Eichmann's eldest son Klaus in 1956, in exposing the identity of the Nazi war criminal. Paradoxical at first, the narrative of the daughter of a Jewish refugee dating the son of Eichmann against the background of a tropical landscape captures the aftermath of the Holocaust in Latin America, a place where both survivors and perpetrators sought a new life.

After the war, a number of Nazis escaped, through Italy and Spain, to Argentina, Brazil, Bolivia, Chile, Colombia, Ecuador, Guatemala, Mexico, Paraguay, Peru and Uruguay via the system of escape routes known as ratlines.[1] Some lived in Latin America as free men until their death; others were captured and brought to justice. The fate of Adolf Eichmann thus epitomises a type of narrative of escape, trail and retribution, which unfolded in Latin America and repeated itself with many variations. The landscapes exemplified by the events narrated in *Operation Finale* are at the core of this chapter; in place of the cinematic image of the specific sites and buildings which I have explored in the previous chapters, in what follows I focus on the larger picture of the continent which emerges from film narratives rooted in the reality of Latin America during the Cold War and which surfaces in imaginative retellings of the afterlife of Nazism in unexpected locations across the Atlantic Ocean.

This is a landscape disseminated with unpredicted topographical connections and historical associations. The cityscapes of Brazil, for example, are directly connected to the forests of Eastern Poland, and more specifically to the location of the Sobibór death camp and to the events which took place in the Lublin district of the General Government and which I discussed in Chapter 3. This topographical connection was determined by the decisions which were taken by Franz Stangl, Gustav Wagner and Stanisław Szmajzner in the years which followed the Sobibór uprising. In 1951 *SS-Hauptsturmführer* and Sobibór commander Stangl escaped to Brazil, where he ended up working at the Volkswagen plant in São Bernardo do Campo. On 28 February 1967, he was found by Nazi hunter Simon Wiesenthal and arrested. Stangl was extradited to West Germany, where he was tried for mass murder, found guilty and sentenced to life imprisonment on 22 December 1970; Stangl died from heart failure a few months after his sentencing. His deputy, *SS-Oberscharführer* Gustav Wagner, also escaped to Brazil after the war and was exposed by Wiesenthal and arrested on 30 May 1978. Extradition requests from West Germany, Israel, Austria and Poland were rejected and on 3 October 1980 Wagner was found dead with a knife in his chest in São Paulo. His death was ruled a suicide.

Stangl and Wagner were both identified by Stanisław Szmajzner, one of the Jewish survivors of the Sobibór death camp who participated in the uprising. Soon after the war Szmajzner migrated to Goiânia, the capital and largest city of the state of Goiás in central Brazil, and lived there until his death in 1989. Pavel Kogan and Lily Van Den's documentary *Opstand in Sobibór* (*The Uprising in Sobibór*, 1990) includes a long interview with Szmajzner which was filmed shortly before his death. The Sobibór escapee gave an account of the German occupation of his hometown Puławy, in Eastern Poland, and the captivity in the Opole Lubelskie ghetto, which was located 30 miles west of Lublin. Szmajzner also talks about the deportation of his family to Sobibór, the camp where his parents and siblings were murdered, the escape from the camp and his work in the Resistance with Russian partisans. Szmajzner's testimony is given in Brazilian Portuguese against the background of the landscape which has become his home and which seems a world away from the ghettos of Eastern Europe and the forests of Sobibór evoked by the survivor. Resting on a hammock, riding a horse at the ranch, watering plants on a sunlit balcony, with the diegetic sound of *bossa nova* and Brazilian radio advertisements in the background, Szmajzner's testimonial performance is situated in a setting which is at once exotic and domestic.[2] By means of Szmajzner's testimonial performance, *The Uprising in Sobibór* thus illustrates how the tropical landscapes and cityscapes of Latin America became the setting for the epilogue of a long and painful history which had begun in Europe and which, after the war, continued to unfold in multiple contexts and directions across the world. In what follows I investigate the ways in which the presence of Nazi war criminals in Latin America, following their escape across ratline routes after the war, has been portrayed on film since 1946. My main objective is to explore how this theme has unfolded in a diverse range of case studies including classical Hollywood cinema and Latin American films, and spanning different genres including drama, espionage and science fiction. Additionally, these films are made to dialogue with archival footage and recent documentaries on Jewish migration from Europe to Latin America as it unfolded before and after the war.

A significant Latin American reverberation of the events which took place in Europe is addressed in Slawomir Grunberg's *The Legacy of Jedwabne* (2005), a documentary account of the pogrom which took place on 10 July 1941 in the town of Jedwabne, Eastern Poland. On that day at least 340 Jews were rounded up by their Polish neighbours on the main square of Jedwabne, corralled into a barn located near the Jewish cemetery, and burned to death.[3] In *The Legacy of Jedwabne*, two Jewish women named Regina and Sara and brothers Mieterk and Berek return to their *shtetl* Jedwabne, the place where they were born and which they left when they moved to Latin America in the 1930s.[4] Regina, Mieterk and Berek have since lived in Argentina while Sara has lived in Mexico. As they explore the streets of Jedwabne, these men and women articulate with their memories of interwar Jedwabne a deep sense of nostalgia for the lost world of Eastern European Jewry and, by means of a spatial engagement with history, they experience the pain associated with the knowledge of the destruction of that world. Several sequences from *The Legacy of Jedwabne* follow Regina, Mieterk, Berek and Sara as they identify faint traces of the Jewish heritage of Jedwabne and explore familial sites of memory in the company of their children and grandchildren. These members of the second and third generations speak Rioplatense Spanish, their first language, against the background of the old wooden houses and the cobbled streets of the former *shtetl* in a juxtaposition which appears as incongruous as Szmajzner's use of Brazilian Portuguese in the testimony included in *The Uprising in Sobibór*.

A significant number of Polish Jews resettled to Latin America with the support of relief organisations such as the Jewish Joint Distribution Committee (JJDC). Based in New York City, the JJDC was one of various relief organisations assisting those who, faced with the emergence and consolidation of fascism, decided to leave Europe. Among other charitable activities, this committee sent American lawyer David Glick on a long journey to Latin America in 1939 as part of its effort to identity suitable destinations for the resettlement of the European Jews who feared persecution. During his trip, David Glick used a 16 mm camera to film the places he visited and the resulting silent colour footage includes evocative images of indigenous men, women and children wearing traditional clothing and carrying packages on their heads or backs (Figure 5.1), views of the lively streets of Rio de Janeiro, unidentified colonial buildings and churches in Uruguay, shanty towns, and spectacular panoramic views of mountainous landscapes taken from an airplane.[5] In addition to Brazil and Uruguay, several scenes were filmed in Trinidad and in the Andean towns, their streets and marketplaces, and in the mountains, forests and waterfalls of Ecuador, Peru and Venezuela.[6] These images depict sceneries which appear a world away from the events which were taking place in Europe in the 1930s and from that war which was about to obliterate the lives of so many. Even their vivid colours, including the clear blue skies which characterise most of these scenes, can be seen as a striking visual opposition to the monotonous black and white world of the newsreels which reported on the unfolding of the incidents which led to the Second World War. And yet, this distant landscape had profound connections with what was happening on the other side of the Atlantic Ocean and was destined to become one of those unexpected contexts where, as Michael Rothberg has argued in his discussion of the concept of multidirectional memory, Holocaust memory can be situated.[7] Multidirectional memory enables the articulation of the aftermath of the Holocaust along with another history of victimisation, and specifically the political and racial violence perpetrated by the military juntas of Latina America from the 1960s to the 1980s. This connection emerges from both fiction films and documentaries and, as I explain later in this chapter, it illustrates a cyclical reading of history not dissimilar from the reverberations of past conflicts onto the present, brought out in the films of the Italian front of the First World War which I have investigated in Chapter 1.

Historical and cultural multidirectional links to Europe are embedded in the cities and landscapes filmed across Latin America by David Glick at the end of the 1930s as they were to become the unlikely background for the new lives of both those who wanted to forget and those who wished to be forgotten. The presence of Nazi war criminals in Latin America, in particular, has inspired a diverse range of narratives spanning across different media; these tales have both been based on real events and on fantasies such as Adolf Hitler's survival. From Frederick Forsyth's novel *The Odessa File* (1972), a fictional version of *SS-Obersturmführer* Eduard Roschmann's escape to Argentina

Figure 5.1 Footage filmed by American lawyer David Glick for the Jewish Joint Distribution Committee (1939).

which was adapted into a film of the same title directed by Ronald Neame in 1974, to George Steiner's philosophical novella *The Portage to San Cristobal of A. H.* (1981), where Hitler is found alive in the Amazon rainforest over thirty years after the end of the war, and to the Führer's cameo appearance in the animated sitcom *The Simpsons* ('Bart vs Australia', S06–E16, 1995), where Hitler is seen struggling with his car phone in the Buenos Aires of the 1990s, the Latin American afterlife of the Third Reich, the trail which began in Europe and ended across the Atlantic Ocean, has continuously been reinvented in literature, film and television.[8]

The intricate web of connections between Nazi Germany and Latin America can also be illustrated by archival footage such as news reports predating the escapes via the ratlines of the post-war years. This material reveals how in the 1930s Nazi Germany was perceived and presented as a threat with the potential to affect life across the Atlantic Ocean. The factual film *War Comes to America* (Anatole Litvak, 1939), for example, addresses these fears in a long sequence where the narrator explains that one million Germans live in Brazil, a country where children can attend German schools, be taught by German teachers and study using German textbooks, while Argentina is said to be seeing a very significant increase in the number of

German sport associations allegedly similar to the *Hitler-Jugend* (Hitler Youth) movement; the narrator also elucidates the noteworthy presence of German stores, industrial plants, banks and other businesses supporting what he dramatically describes as 'a fifth column ready to take over'.[9] Additionally, an illustrated map of Latin America included in the film shows how the presence of German pilots and planes with built-in bomb racks in Ecuador, run by the aircraft carrier SEDTA (Sociedad Ecuatoriana de Transportes Aereos), could threaten American access to the Panama Canal. In a similar vein, a 1938 edition of the newsreel *March of Time* includes a close-up shot of a Spanish edition of Hitler's book *Mein Kampf* which anticipates a reportage about the decision taken by Brazilian President Getulio Vargas to outlaw Nazism upon learning that, in the narrator's words, 'Nazi organizers and agents are building up storm troop organizations among German colonists'.[10] Footage showing urban and rural views of Latin America, including a large city bustling with traffic and vast fields of wheat, is followed by images of Japanese, Italian, and German ships unloading goods at local harbours; this sequence is accompanied by the narrator's warning that Latin American is already being 'invaded by nations whose dictator-controlled economies challenge all competition.'

With their juxtaposition of verbal warnings and threatening images, *War Comes to America* and *March of Time* address what was clearly perceived as a menace to the entire world, beyond the battlefields of Europe, North Africa or the Pacific, and as a threat which could have engulfed Latin America in the midst of the Nazi attempt to reshape geopolitics on a global scale. And yet, even though Brazil and Mexico sent troops to Europe and the Pacific during the conflict, war did not come to Latin America. Fascism, however, eventually did get to the continent. It came during the Cold War in the shape of the planes which bombed the presidential palace *La Moneda* in Santiago de Chile on Tuesday 11 September 1973; it came with the annihilation of democracy, with killings and torture, and with the voids left behind by those who were made to disappear in Argentina, Chile and other countries led by military juntas. And before fascism spread in the form of authoritarian nationalism and state terrorism, its individual personifications represented by Nazi war criminals like Eichmann, Stangl, Wagner, *SS-Hauptsturmführer* Josef Mengele and so many others had already found a home in Argentina and other countries; their hideouts were later used as locations in a series of diverse cinematic narratives addressing the afterlife of Nazi Germany in Latin America as it unfolded on filmic spaces where historical reality was often mystified and reinvented.

The fabrication of cinematic landscapes has been investigated by Graeme Harper and Jonathan Rayner in their study of the ways in which cinema has 'delineated and disseminated images and ideas about landscape' and their articulation of the process of production of cinematic spaces as 'the imposition of order on the elements of landscape, collapsing the distinction between the found and the constructed.'[11] This distinction evokes that intertwining of real and filmic spaces with various degrees of topographical and historical coherence which I have discussed in Chapter 3 in regard to the use of Lublin and Majdanek as film locations. Similarly, the cinematic landscapes of Latin America are a territory where connections among sites and narratives evolve in ways which repeatedly negotiate various departures from and returns to the real locations. Charlotte Brunsdon has argued that 'all cinematic geographies are generic' regardless of their connection to real locations.[12] Two of the earliest Hollywood films dealing with the presence of Nazi war criminals in Latin America reflect this claim as they use a creative approach to the topography of their setting; *Notorious* (Alfred Hitchcock, 1946) and *Gilda* (Charles Vidor, 1946) are crime dramas set in the cities of Rio de Janeiro and Buenos Aires respectively. They were both released one year after the end of the Second World War, at a time when Nazi escapes had already begun to inform the popular imagery of Latin America. Both films were largely filmed in studio in Hollywood, with a small number of scenes shot on location in Brazil in the case of Hitchcock's film. *Notorious* and *Gilda* express therefore different connections between their thematic flows and their settings and locations, but both films are similarly constructed upon highly generic cinematic geographies which are used as the background of narratives based on the fictionalisation of the lives of the ratline escapees in Latin America; these films also articulate a fictitious threat of Nazi vengeance and narrate a type of fantasy which, as I explain later in this chapter, anticipates the plot of later science-fiction films such as *The Madmen of Mandoras* (David Bradley, 1963) and *The Boys from Brazil* (Franklin J. Schaffner, 1978).

In *Gilda*, a tungsten cartel run by Nazis who escaped from Germany after the war is financed by a secret organisation hiding behind the illegal Argentinean casino where much of the plot unfolds. Jon Burrows has used an evocative line from a review of *Broken Blossoms* (D. W. Griffith, 1920) in his article about the generic nature of the original London Chinatown in Limehouse as a film location which was described by *The Bioscope* as a 'vague Chinese quarter elsewhere'.[13] The shadowy docklands where the first scene of *Gilda* is set and the opening lines narrated by Glenn Ford's character Johnny Farrell, similarly establish Buenos Aires as a vague Latin American city elsewhere: 'To me a dollar was a dollar in any language. It was my first night in the Argentine and I didn't know much about the local citizens, but I knew about American sailors, and I knew I better get out of there.' Unlike *Notorious*, Vidor's film does not make any use of location shooting and sporadic night scenes filmed in the dark alleys of a city recreated in the studio provide the

Buenos Aires of *Gilda* with that vagueness which is reminiscent of the impreciseness of the fabrication of Chinese Limehouse discussed by Burrows. In *Gilda*, Ford's character recalls his first encounter with the casino's owner, Ballin Mundson (George Macready), with these words: 'I was born last night when you met me in that alley.' The capital city of Argentina and its Nazi conspirators are thus a fabrication giving shape to a generic geography where Latin America is merely serving the purpose of being the other America, a distant exotic place where men and women with a shady past seek a new life.

Notorious tells the story of the daughter of a convicted Nazi war criminal, Alicia Huberman (Ingrid Bergman), who is recruited by an American government agent, T. R. Devlin (Cary Grant), to infiltrate a secret fascist organisation in Brazil. One of the Rio de Janeiro sequences is set in Praça Floriano Peixoto, with Sugarloaf Mountain in the background (Figure 5.2); Huberman and Devlin are sitting on a bench in the foreground and plot to get access to the wine cellar where a cache of uranium is being stored by a group of Nazis. In this sequence, Hitchcock uses that in-camera effect which combines foreground performances with pre-filmed backgrounds and which is known as rear projection. Bergman and Grant were not involved with any location shooting but this sequence provides topographical coordinates to the film and uses the landmarks of Rio de Janeiro to inscribe the action onto

Figure 5.2 Alicia and T. R. Devlin in Praça Floriano Peixoto in *Notorious* (Alfred Hitchcock, *1946*).

a cityscape which appears more specific than the elusive and vague Buenos Aires of *Gilda*. And yet, like *Gilda*, Hitchcock's film makes use of the presence of Nazis in Latin America largely to advance a plot about the romantic involvement between the two characters portrayed by its stars. In the final sequences of the film, as *The Showmen's Trade Review* put it, Grant 'braves the risk of entering the nest of Nazis and rescues Bergman'.[14] American journalist Dorothy Mae Kilgallen was not too impressed with the Nazi plot of the film and with the ending where the hero saves his woman from a group of implausible villains:

> But why this talk of Nazis and undercover agents? Let's face it. Long after the story line is forgotten, *Notorious* will be remembered as the picture in which Ingrid Bergman gnawed at Cary Grant as if he were a pound of fresh caviar.[15]

While there might be more to the story narrated by Hitchcock than Kilgallen implied in her review, it is true that the Nazi plot device is largely used to frame themes such as trust, patriotism and love versus duty. But ultimately, the story of the uranium smuggled by the Nazis, as well as the Latin American location, can indeed be seen as an excuse for the unfolding of such themes against the background of a Rio de Janeiro which, despite the occasional use of rear projection of location footage, remains a vague Latin American city elsewhere, an exotic location populated by archetypal villains with unlikely plans.

The improbable stories narrated in *Notorious* and *Gilda*, where the Nazis are not merely planning to avoid prosecution for their crimes but have already regrouped for the purpose of a new war, are still more plausible than the later cinematic incarnation of Nazi post-war activity represented in the aforementioned films *The Madmen of Mandoras* and *The Boys from Brazil*. Both films exploit the notion of a Nazi resurgence organised by escapees on the background of the exotic landscapes of Latin America. These narratives effectively inverted the direction of the threat which was articulated in the newsreels on the 1930s: in that context the danger came from Europe and menaced Latin America. In *The Madmen of Mandoras* and *The Boys from Brazil*, the threat comes from Latin America and imperils the whole world. In both instances Latin America is rendered on screen through thematic connections neglecting topographical coherence; the implausible narratives of these films were framed by a creative geography where Latin America was either staged in studio or recreated elsewhere.

On 26 July 1963, the magazine *Boxoffice* announced: '*Madmen of Mandoras*, melodrama dealing with attempted conquest of the world through secret weapon, is scheduled for August 14 release in the US.'[16] Set in a fictional country named Mandoras, this film includes a scene where a dance performance vaguely resembles flamenco; this is one of a handful of scenes revealing the extremely vague Latin American location of the story. The unlikely label of melodrama given to *The Madmen of Mandoras* by the film magazine *Boxoffice* does not really capture the plot of the film, a science-fiction narrative focusing on a group of Nazis plotting to conquer the world under the orders of Adolf Hitler (Bill Freed), whose head is being kept alive inside a glass jar.[17] As *The Madmen of Mandoras* resorts to this bizarre expedient in order to bring back the Führer, a long chase sequence seeing Hitler's head placed on the back seat of a car tells the viewer more about the exploitative nature of the film than about the escape of Nazi war criminals to Latin America. And yet, in its elusive and absurd manner, *The Madmen of Mandoras* captures a fantasy lingering in the post-war decades, a sense of unfinished business with that Nazi threat which had been vividly articulated in factual footage from the 1930s like *War Comes to America* and *March of Time*.

An equally improbable experiment is narrated in *The Boys from Brazil*, Schaffner's adaptation of Ira Levin's novel of the same title (1976), a film where Josef Mengele (Gregory Peck), who has established himself as a leading figure of a powerful secret Nazi organisation in Latin America, succeeds in cloning Adolf Hitler ninety-five times in the hope of creating a group of Nazi leaders for a forthcoming Fourth Reich. Filmed in Lisbon, the opening sequence of the film is set in Asunción, the capital city of Paraguay, during a military parade and a clandestine Nazi meeting; soldiers goose-stepping on a public square inscribe the authoritarian rule of Paraguay which was still in place in 1978 into the urban space of the capital city of a country, Portugal, which had done away with its own military regime only four years earlier.[18] James Mason, who played the role of one of Mengele's associates, told Roger Ebert during an interview: 'When I arrived on the set in Lisbon I asked if Paraguay had pine trees. "It does now", I was told.'[19] The capital city of Portugal is here made to play the role of the capital city of a former Spanish colony and, as Manson's statement suggests, the setting of *The Boys from Brazil* is thus a fabrication which saw a limited effort in the attempt to make Lisbon perform convincingly as Asunción. *The Madmen of Mandoras* and *The Boys from Brazil* are thus fantasies of a Fourth Reich attempting to emerge from its exile, from the cities and villages of Latin America where the Nazis went into hiding after the war. Whereas Bradley's film is entirely disconnected from real events which took place after the war, *The Boys from Brazil* makes a reference to the Mossad operation which led to the capture of Eichmann in the sequence where Mengele claims to have been a Nazi hunter who identified the Nazi's home address and passed it on to Mossad.[20] Beside this fictitious claim, Mengele's life in Argentina as portrayed by Gregory Peck has otherwise no references to historical events and certainly it does not capture his mundane life on the run from the Mossad and other agencies.

On 7 February 1979, Mengele suffered a stroke and drowned while swimming in the Atlantic Ocean off the Brazilian coast in Bertioga. At the time of his death he had lived in Latin America for thirty years during which time he worked as a carpenter and as a farmer. Several films have used the mystery surrounding his escape from Europe, the fruitless search led by Wiesenthal and Mossad, and Mengele's later years as the source for narratives departing from historical verisimilitude.[21] Mengele's escape to Latin America and his hideouts have inspired Lucia Puenzo's *Wakolda* (*The German Doctor*, 2013), a drama which fictionalises his life in Argentina by returning to the theme of Mengele's experiments which had already informed the plot of *The Boys from Brazil*. Set in 1960 near the town of San Carlos de Bariloche, in Argentina's Patagonia region, *Wakolda* focuses on a fictional encounter between Mengele (Àlex Brendemühl) and an Argentinean family, as well as on his special interest in the daughter of the family, Lilith (Florencia Bado), who was born prematurely and is considerably shorter than her classmates. Lilith's mother, Eva (Natalia Oreiro), allows Mengele to investigate her daughter's condition and supports his attempt to help her grow more rapidly; towards the end of the film, Eva also gives birth to premature twins and Mengele begins to study their physiology, just before escaping on a seaplane after his identity is discovered and made public.

Wakolda opens with the chance meeting between Mengele and Lilith's family. The first sequences of the film unravel as a road movie which sees the Nazi doctor following their car on the *Ruta del desierto* (Desert Route), a straight section of Provincial Route 20 in the desert of La Pampa, in the direction of Bariloche (Figure 5.3). A series of tracking shots introduce the transition from the sandy and windy desert to the forests and the craggy mountains of Patagonia. On the background of a wintry landscape where the events which took place in Europe during the war seem very remote, Mengele resembles a hunter who is chasing his prey all the way to his chosen terrain in Bariloche. In the following sequences, *Wakolda* establishes a thematic and geographical connection between Europe and Latin America as the mountainous lakes and the deep woods of Bariloche provide the setting for the re-enactment of the experiments which Mengele had already carried out more viciously and gruesomely in Auschwitz.[22] Additionally, a sequence filmed at Villa Tacul, a place situated 18 miles northeast of Bariloche and at the core of the Parque Municipal Llao Llao, establishes a very specific topographical connection between this Latin American landscape and the *Führerbunker*, the air raid shelter located near the Reich Chancellery in Berlin where Hitler died in 1945. Mengele and one of his associates, Klaus (Guillermo Pfening), visit the ruins of a mysterious concrete bunker of unclear origin. Klaus first mentions the hearsay that Adolf Hitler survived the war and fled to Latin America,

Figure 5.3 Desert route in *Wakolda* (*The German Doctor*, Lucia Puenzo, 2013).

where he was rumoured to be hiding in a similar bunker, and then shares his memory of a recent dream where he saw Hitler buried alive in a dark underground passageway. Mengele stands in silence as Klaus thus evokes the infamous fate of their Führer in the Berlin bunker where the dictator took his own life; *Wakolda* does not resuscitate Hitler in the improbable manner of films like *The Madmen of Mandoras* and *The Boys from Brazil* but the ghostly presence of the Führer permeates this sequence and haunts the remote landscapes of Patagonia.

The snow-capped mountains of the Nahuel Huapi National Park can be seen in the background of most sequences and seem to isolate Bariloche from the rest of the world. This landscape, in its apparent irreconcilability with the events which took place in Europe during the war, is reminiscent of the aforementioned footage filmed by David Glick in 1939 on behalf of the JJDC. And yet, in *Wakolda* this is not a safe haven for those who were persecuted but rather a place where the threat embodied by Mengele insinuated itself in the present. The past makes timid incursions into this landscape by means of the use of archival photographs of the Third Reich and footage of the war played on a television screen, while it is in the history evoked by Mengele's actions, in the re-enactment of the experimentation he carried out during the Holocaust, that past events make a more vigorous and disturbing appearance. Additionally, *Wakolda* also sees evocative incursions of what was to be the future of the country in a narrative saturated with a sense of foreboding and with omens of the arrival in Argentina, fourteen years later, of fascism as an authoritarian regime. Mengele's interest in Eva's unborn children and his brief appropriation of the twins after their birth is reminiscent of both the separation of families at their arrival at Auschwitz and of the ways in which Argentina's military junta would steal new-born babies from political opponents who were made to disappear during the Argentinean Dirty War

(1974–83); made thirty years after the return to democracy, *Wakolda* is set at an earlier time in the history of Argentina, and in the diegesis of the film Mengele's work anticipates what would soon happen in the country upon the emergence of a local brand of fascism with profound connections with its European progenitors and counterparts. In *Wakolda*, Mengele's actions thus talk of the re-emergence and the future of fascism in a way which reinterprets in a more evocative and intimate way the unlikely resurgence of the Reich represented in *The Boys from Brazil*. This sense of foreboding is rendered all the more evocatively by location shooting and the film's topographically coherent use of the landscapes of Patagonia in opposition to the creative geography of *The Boys from Brazil* and its use of Lisbon in the role of Asunción.

The testimonies of Holocaust survivors have often provided a factual counterpart to the fictional narratives of films such as *Wakolda* and *The Boys from Brazil*. More specifically, there are a significant number of documentaries addressing Mengele's criminal work in Auschwitz and providing information on his later years in Latin America. *Forgiving Dr. Mengele* (Bob Hercules and Cheri Pugh, 2006), for example, is a documentary about the life of Holocaust survivor Eva Mozes Kor, a woman who, aged eleven, was deported from the Romanian village of Porț to Auschwitz, where she and her twin sister Miriam Mozes were subjected to experimentation under Mengele and his staff. The experimentations evoked in Mozes Kor's testimony have also been recalled by the Holocaust survivors who moved to Latin America after the war and who were interviewed by the Survivors of the Shoah Visual History Foundation between 1996 and 1998. Directed by Luis Puenzo, the Argentinean documentary *Algunos que vivieron* (*Some Who Lived*, 2002) uses twelve of these interviews with a group of survivors who were living in Argentina at the time of filming and who were born in Poland (Jack Fuchs, Liza Zajak-Novera, Benjamin Mehl, Mira Kniazniew-Stupnik, Eugenia Unger, and Moises Borowicz), Hungary (Valeria Wollstein-Cohn and Pedro Boschan), Czechoslovakia (Robert Lamberg and Alejandro Horvath), Romania (Victor Oppel), and Rhodes (David Galante).[23]

Filmed in Argentina, and mostly in and around Buenos Aires, these interviews are all recorded in the private spaces of the apartments of the survivors, and are located on the sites of the genocide by their juxtaposition to archival footage of the concentration and death camps, to images of the ghettos and the battlefields of Europe, as well as to familial photographs from the 1930s and 1940s depicting the survivors and members of their family who died in the Holocaust.[24] Like Szmajzner's testimony in Brazilian Portuguese given in *The Uprising in Sobibór*, the interviews included in *Some Who Lived* hint at a linguistic displacement inasmuch as the variety of languages that these men and women spoke in their youth has been replaced by Rioplatense Spanish.

And as in the account given by Szmajzner, the testimonies of these survivors establish links between their own resettlement in Argentina and the escape of Nazi war criminals. Both Alejandro Horvath and David Galante recall meeting Mengele in Auschwitz and evoke the experiments the Nazi war criminal would perform in the camp and which were later reinvented in the fictional cinematic narratives of *The Boys from Brazil* and *Wakolda*. The paradox of survivors and perpetrators crossing paths and living in the same Argentinean cities, towns and neighbourhoods, is described by Liza Zajak-Novera as she explains that her holiday home in the city of Miramar was located near the house inhabited by *SS-Oberscharführer* Josef Schwammberger, a former commander of various forced-labour camps in the Kraków district of occupied Poland who was eventually extradited to Germany in 1990 and sentenced to life imprisonment two years later. *Some Who Lived* thus articulates the complexity of the process which saw the departure of perpetrators and victims alike from Europe to Latin America, and inscribes into reality what fiction films such as *Notorious*, *Gilda* or *The Boys from Brazil* had delivered to myth.

The connection between the emergence of fascism in Europe and its resurgence in the Argentina of the 1970s is discussed in *Some Who Lived* by Pedro Boschan.[25] This Hungarian survivor talks about the Argentine coup d'état which took place in 1976 and his words are juxtaposed with archival images showing arrests carried out by order of the junta and footage of political demonstrations which took place after the return to democracy in the name of the *desaparecidos*, the Argentines who were secretly arrested and murdered by the military junta.[26] The transversal themes, spaces, narratives and contexts of *Some Who Lived*, and to some extent of Mengele's actions as portrayed in *Wakolda*, can be illustrated by means of the use of Rothberg's aforementioned concept of multidirectional memory inasmuch as Puenzo's documentary draws attention to 'dynamic transfers that take place between diverse places and times during the act of remembrance'.[27] Accordingly, both *Wakolda* and, in particular, *Some Who Lived* draw attention to a dynamic transfer between Europe and Argentina, and between the events of 1939–45 and the Dirty War of 1974–83. As Rothberg explains, the idea of multidirectional memory leads to thinking about and framing 'the public sphere as a malleable discursive space in which groups do not simply articulate established positions but actually come into being through their dialogical interactions with others.'[28] Rothberg also argued that Holocaust memory can be situated in unforeseen contexts enabling the articulation of other histories of victimisation, and can emerge thanks to post-war events that apparently have little to do with it;[29] framed as a reflection of this process, the memories excavated in *Some Who Lived* evolve in multiple directions in a way which thus capture the processes of multidirectional memory envisaged by Rothberg. The unexpected locations of *Some Who Lived*, and the film's attempt to articulate a discourse on the Dirty War while talking about the Holocaust, embody multiple histories, continuous negotiations and multiple interactions, and thus illustrate Rothberg's idea that 'the borders of memory and identity are jagged; what looks at first like my own property often turns out to be a borrowing or adaptation from a history that initially might seem foreign or distant.'[30] This is achieved by means of Boshan's testimonial performance and the way it connects the Holocaust to the tragedy of the *desaparecidos*; his account of the coup d'état and of the Dirty War reveals that the threat of Nazism as it was articulated in the newsreels of the 1930s would eventually materialise in Latin America in a dramatic and unexpected manner.

The presence of Nazi war criminals in Latin America, and its depiction in films with various degrees of authenticity, borrows and adapts from a history that seems geographically distant. Similarly, the memory of the Holocaust evolves in the unpredicted contexts of the Latin American landscapes filmed by David Glick for the JJDC at the end of the 1930s and discussed earlier in this chapter. Those places were destined to become a new home for thousands of Jews who survived the Holocaust, including the witnesses interviewed by Puenzo in *Some Who Lived* and many others who would join the Jews who had already escaped to Latin America before the war, such as the Sobibór survivor interviewed in *The Uprising in Sobibór* or the men and women who left Jedwabne and would later return to their *shtetl* for the filming of *The Legacy of Jedwabne*. In parallel with the reality depicted in these documentary films, in this chapter I have tried to chisel a more mysterious, threatening and legendary cinematic landscape where the Nazis are plotting vengeance and resurgence from their Latin American hideouts. Films such as *Notorious*, *Gilda*, *The Madmen of Mandoras* and *The Boys from Brazil* recreate vague Latin American scenery elsewhere, in the film studios where the first three films were shot or on the Portuguese locations of the latter. Unlike those films, *Wakolda* uses its Patagonian scenery in a coherent way while taking liberties with historical authenticity and portraying a fictitious episode in Mengele's life. This diverse group of films shapes a multifaceted and multilayered landscape where myth and reality, history and fantasy wrestle one another, and where creative transfers between different places and times enact a negotiation between memory and invention as well as an intervention in the processes of recalling and reinventing historical events. In continuity with the cinematic landscapes which I have explored in earlier chapters, the case studies investigated here thus articulate a reflection on the ways in which filmic spaces are produced by means of a dynamic relation between history and memory which is articulated through both documentary and fiction films. More specifically, these films have mapped a continent where the fictitious afterlife of the Third Reich anticipates the emergence of an autochthonous form of fascism; they have enunciated a cinematic image of a paradoxical safe harbour for survivors and perpetrators alike, a place where the threat of capture or the fear of new persecution lingers in a landscape that appears incredibly distant from the battlefields and murderous sites of the war in Europe and yet is intrinsically related to them.

Had they not successfully escaped to Latin America, Franz Stangl and Gustav Wagner would possibly have been sentenced to life imprisonment, soon after the war or perhaps at the Sobibór trials for war crimes which took place in Hagen, West Germany, between 1965 and 1966.[31] On 20 December of that year, six *SS-Oberscharführer* and one *SS-Scharführer* who had served in Sobibór were given sentences ranging from four years to life imprisonment.[32] The war-crime trials of the 1960s were part of an effort to cleanse the image of West Germany in the years which followed the Eichmann trial in Jerusalem, an event which had revived the world's attention for what the Nazis did during the war. Persecution of war criminals was not the only way in which West Germany tried to deal with the past. A few months before the end of the Sobibór trials, on 26 April 1966, the city of Munich won the bid to host the 1972 Summer Olympic Games over bids presented by Detroit, Madrid, and Montréal. Even more so than the trials, hosting the Olympics was seen as a chance to promote a new image for West Germany as a safe, tolerant and open society. In the course of that sports event Jewish blood would be spilled again on German soil and, more specifically, on the sites of a Luftwaffe airfield established by the Nazis in the 1930s and that of a mass grave for victims of the Allied air raids which was turned into the Olympic Park. Seen from behind the Iron Curtain as the epicentre of the Western revanchist plans, Munich, as David Clay Large suggests, had a 'troubling Nazi past' and a 'prominent place on the frontline of the Cold War'; thousands of anti-Soviet refugees lived in a city which also hosted USA-funded Radio Liberty and Radio Free Europe and, in one of its suburbs, the headquarters of the *Bundesnachrichtendienst* (Federal Intelligence Service).[33] Its Olympic Park and airfield would become hot battlefields of the Cold War and would be captured in news reports made at the time of the events, memorialised in documentaries and staged in fiction films depicting the events of 5 September 1972.

Notes

1. See Gerald Steinacher, *Nazis on the Run: How Hitler's Henchmen Fled Justice*, Oxford: Oxford University Press, 2012, pp. 1–43.

2. Here, the survivor also talks about the presence of Nazi war criminals in Brazil and discusses the death of Wagner, hinting that though it was ruled as a suicide the man had in fact been assassinated.
3. See Richard S. Levy (ed.), 2005, *Anti-Semitism: A Historical Encyclopaedia of Prejudice and Persecution (Volume One)*, Santa Barbara: ABC-CLIO, pp. 366–7. Jedwabne was occupied by the Germans in 1939 and then again in 1941, after Hitler declared war on the Soviet Union. The Jews who survived the pogrom lived in a small ghetto which was liquidated in November 1942, when they were deported to a transit ghetto and from there to Auschwitz II-Birkenau. Only seven of the 1,000 Jews who lived in Jedwabne before the war survived the Holocaust (Miron, 2010, p. 268).
4. For a closer analysis of Grunberg's documentary *The Legacy of Jedwabne*, its use of locations and contribution to the debate on the responsibilities of the Poles in the pogrom, see my book *Journey to Poland: Documentary Landscapes of the Holocaust*, pp. 29–33.
5. This footage is now held in the collections of the United States Holocaust Memorial Museum in Washington, (USHMM); 'David Glick's JDC mission to South America in the late 1930s', USHMM, Accession Number: 2004.320.2, RG Number: RG-60.4310, Film ID: 2703.
6. 'David Glick's JDC mission to South America in the late 1930s', USHMM, Accession Number: 2004.320.2, RG Number: RG-60.4309, Film ID: 2702.
7. Michael Rothberg, *Multidirectional Memory: Remembering the Holocaust in the Age of Decolonization*, Redwood City: Stanford University Press, 2009, pp. 6–7.
8. Frederick Forsyth, *The Odessa File*, London: Hutchinson, 1972; George Steiner, *The Portage to San Cristobal of A. H.*, London: Faber and Faber, 1981.
9. *War Comes to America* is part of the *Why We Fight* series, produced by the War Department under the supervision of Lt. Col. Frank Capra and included in 'Army film showing Nazi aggression, refugees, FDR & Hull Film', Orientation Film No. 7, Reel 5 (1939–1940), USHMM, Accession Number: 1994.119.1, RG Number: RG-60.1114, Film ID: 932.
10. 'US Foreign Service and diplomats; Good Neighbor Policy; recall of ambassador from Germany', *March of Time*, Vol. 5, No. 4, 1938, USHMM, Accession Number: 2006.73.1, RG Number: RG-60.4512, Film ID: 2820.
11. Graeme Harper and Jonathan Rayner, 2010, 'Introduction', in *Cinema and Landscape*, Harper and Rayner (eds), Bristol and Chicago: Intellect, pp. 13–28 (16).
12. Charlotte Brunsdon, *London in Cinema: the Cinematic City Since 1945*, London: BFI Publishing, 2008, p. 96.
13. Jon Burrows, '"A vague Chinese quarter elsewhere": Limehouse in the cinema 1914–36', *Journal of British Cinema and Television*, Vol. 6, No. 2, 2009, pp. 282–301 (293).
14. 'Notorious', *The Showmen's Trade Review*, 27 July 1946, p. 31.
15. Dorothy Mae Kilgallen, 'Dorothy Kilgallen selects *Notorious*', *Modern Screen*, Volumes 33–4, July–December 1946, p. 138.

16. 'Crown sets three releases for August-September', *Boxoffice*, 29 July 1963, p. 8.
17. Six years after its theatrical release, *The Madmen of Mandoras* was adapted for television into a longer film under the title of *They Saved Hitler's Brain*. The film has had an impact on popular culture and, for example, the episode of the animated sitcom *The Simpsons'* titled 'They Saved Lisa's Brain' (S10–E22, 1999) plays with the title of the television version of *The Madmen of Mandoras*.
18. Paraguay was ruled by dictator Alfredo Stroessner from 1954 to 1989 while Portugal saw the authoritarian rule known as *Estado Novo* (New State), which had begun in 1933, overthrown by the *Revolução dos Cravos* (Carnation Revolution) of the Spring of 1974.
19. Roger Ebert, 'James Mason: *The Boys from Brazil*', *Chicago Sun-Times*, 12 October 1978, p. 14.
20. The events of spring 1960, when a team of Israeli intelligence officers captured Adolf Eichmann near his home on Garibaldi Street in the industrial district of San Fernando, have been portrayed in a number of fiction films including *Operation Eichmann* (R. G. Springsteen, 1961), which was filmed in studio in Hollywood soon after the event, *The Man Who Captured Eichmann* (William Graham, 1996) and the aforementioned *Operation Finale*, two films which were both filmed on location in the Argentinean capital and its environs. *Eichmann* (Paul Young, 2007) is a biographical film specifically focusing on his interrogation in Israel. Similarly, *Hannah Arendt* (Margarethe von Trotta, 2013) and *The Eichmann Show* (Paul Andrew Williams, 2015) address the political and historical implications of the trial in Jerusalem which saw Eichmann being sentenced to death by hanging on 15 December 1961. With their focus on the Mossad operation and despite various narrative liberties – for example, in *Operation Finale* the period between the identification of Eichmann and his capture is considerably shorter than in reality and, in a departure from the facts, the doctor on the operation is a woman – these films present a shift from the fictitious characters and events of films like *Gilda*, *Notorious*, *The Madmen of Mandoras* and *The Boys from Brazil* in the direction of a more accurate historical representation of a specific event related to the subject of Nazi escapees in Latin America.
21. Other films focusing on and reinventing the life of Mengele include *Rua Alguem 5555: My Father* (Egidio Eronico, 2003), *Nazis at the Center of the Earth* (Joseph Lawson, 2012), and *Nichts als die Wahrheit* (*After the Truth*, Roland Suso Richter, 1999), *Rua Alguem 5555: My Father* portrays a fictional encounter between Mengele and his son set in a Brazilian shanty town, while in the direct-to-video film *Nazis at the Center of the Earth* Mengele and a group of Nazi soldiers are hiding at the centre of the Earth and plotting a strategy to create and lead a Fourth Reich. *After the Truth* depicts the fictional trial of an eighty-seven-year-old Mengele upon his return to Germany at the end of the 1990s.
22. The same scenery is used in the opening sequence of *Pacto de silencio* (*Pact of Silence*, Carlos Echeverría, 2007), an Argentinean documentary about the Nazi war criminals, including former *SS-Hauptsturmführer* Erich Priebke, who were protected by the German community of Bariloche.

23. *Some Who Lived* was produced by filmmakers Steven Spielberg and James Moll as part of *Broken Silence* (2002), a series of five documentaries based on the testimonies of Holocaust survivors from various European countries, including Janos Szasz's *Eyes of the Holocaust*, Pavel Chukhraj's *Children from the Abyss*, Andrzej Wajda's *I Remember*, and Vojtech Jasny's *Hell on Earth*.
24. It is worth noting the difference between this strategy and what Lanzmann has done in *Sobibór, October 14, 1943, 4 p.m.*, as well as in *Shoah*. As discussed in Chapter 3, the French filmmaker places Lerner's remote testimony recorded in his apartment in Jerusalem in *Sobibór* by juxtaposing the interview with present-day footage of the site of the camp.
25. Before *Some Who Lived*, Luis Puenzo also directed one of the earliest films addressing the Argentinean Dirty War. *La historia oficial* (*The Official Story*, 1985) deals with the kidnapping of the children of those who were murdered by the regime and their adoptions by wealthy Argentinean families often in collusion with the military junta.
26. Additionally, Boschan also remembers the suicide bombing attack on the Israeli embassy in Buenos Aires, which took place on 17 March 1992 and resulted in the death of 29 civilians and the wounding of 242 men and women. The Hezbollah militia was suspected of being behind the attack. Boschan's testimony thus establishes another connection between the Second World War and later events, and specifically between the Jews who died during the Holocaust and the victims of Islamic terrorism.
27. Rothberg, p. 11.
28. Rothberg, p. 5.
29. Rothberg, pp. 6–7.
30. Rothberg, p. 5.
31. While Wagner was never put on trial, Stangl would be captured and put on trial in Germany in the following year.
32. Six *SS-Scharführer* were acquitted on the same day.
33. David Clay Large, *Munich 1972: Tragedy, Terror, and Triumph at the Olympic Games*, Lanham: Rowman & Littlefield, 2012, p. 5.

CHAPTER 6

Olympiapark, Munich, Germany, 5 September 1972, 4:30 a.m.

> *A forty-one-year-old wrestling referee is awakened by an unusual noise and then sees the front door of the apartment beginning to open and masked men with weapons on the other side; he throws his weight against the door in an attempt to stop the intruders. His name is Yossef Gutfreund and this happens on the night of 5 September 1972 in Munich.*

In the mid-1930s the Nazi regime established a Luftwaffe airfield near the town of Fürstenfeldbruck in Bavaria and also began the construction of a new airport in the city of Munich. Munich-Riem Airport opened in May 1939 and replaced an old airfield in Oberwiesenfeld, a suburban area which was due to be transformed into a large trading complex including a slaughterhouse and marketplace. The outbreak of the Second World War halted the plans made by the Nazis for the redevelopment of this district and, after the conflict, Oberwiesenfeld was used as a dumping ground for the rubble removed from the inner city and as a mass grave for the bodies of the many unidentified victims of the seventy-four Allied air raids on Munich. Twenty years later, Fürstenfeldbruck was serving as a West German air base while Oberwiesenfeld was chosen as the location of the Olympiapark München (Olympic Park Munich) in view of the 1972 Summer Olympics.[1] The Games of the XX Olympiad would be inaugurated on 26 August 1972 and on that day, as the Israeli team entered the Olympiastadion (Olympic Stadium), American Broadcasting Company (ABC) sports news presenter Jim McKay aptly accompanied footage of those athletes, coaches and referees with these words:

> Of course you can't be in Munich, Germany and not remember. We are just about 15 miles from Dachau, but it is perhaps a measure of the fact that people and times and nations do change. Israel is here and Germans are cheering Jewish athletes.[2]

As McKay explained, the entrance of the Israeli team in the Olympic Stadium had a great historical and political significance; the event took place thirty-six years after German Jewish athletes were prevented from taking part in the 1936 Summer Olympics in Berlin and just twenty-seven years after the liberation of the Dachau concentration camp. The images of the arrival of the Israeli athletes, captured by cameramen from countless countries, had an enormous symbolic meaning and could be read as the pinnacle of West Germany's intention to use the games to promote a new image of the country and to mark a clear break from that past which kept re-emerging during the war crimes trials of the 1960s.

Ten days after the opening ceremony of the games, and soon after Yossef Gutfreund heard alarming noises outside the door of one of the apartments occupied by the Israeli team, Jewish blood would be spilled again on German soil. On 5 September, the Olympic Village in Oberwiesenfeld and the airfield in Fürstenfeldbruck became the background of the assassination of eleven Israeli athletes, coaches and referees at the hands of the Palestinian terrorist group *Aylūl Al-Aswad* (Black September), a faction of the Palestine Liberation Organization.[3] Yosef Romano and Moshe Weinberg were killed in Apartment 1 at 31 Connollystraße; Yosef Gottfreund, Eliezaar Halfen, Yakov Springer, Andre Spitzer, Zeev Friedman, Kehat Schur, Mark Slavin, Amitzur Shapira and David Berger were murdered in Fürstenfeldbruck, the airfield from where the Palestinians had requested to be flown to Cairo with their surviving hostages. Five members of Black September were killed by the police and one West German police officer also lost his life during a failed rescue operation. Three of the terrorists, who had initially demanded the release of 234 Palestinians jailed in Israel and that of the founders of the Red Army Faction in West Germany, survived; they would be released from prison on 29 October 1972 following the hijacking of Lufthansa Flight 615 by a Palestinian group seeking to obtain their liberation.[4]

The dramatic outcome of Black September's attack in Munich and the failed police intervention, accompanied by images of the charred wreckage of the two Bell UH-1 military helicopters inside which the Israelis were killed by the terrorists with machine guns and grenades, was famously announced at the end of a long live broadcast presented by McKay for the ABC:

> We've just gotten the final word. When I was a kid my father used to say our greatest hopes and our worst fears are seldom realized. Our worst fears have been realized tonight. They've now said that there were eleven hostages. Two were killed in their rooms yesterday morning. Nine were killed at the airport tonight. They're all gone.[5]

The unfolding of the attack was covered by ABC along with countless other international radio and television networks; their crews were already setting up at the Olympic Park with the expectation of focusing on the games and their presence gave the terrorists a large global audience for their political cause and their demands. Accordingly, as Eva Maria Gajek has argued, the organisers of the Olympics 'increasingly aligned themselves with the needs of

TV-creators' and the 'architecture, opening ceremony, as well as the course of the sports competitions were considerably adapted to the work methods of television.'[6] The exceptional visibility of the Olympics thus gave Black September what they had wanted, a unique televised stage for the demands of the group and for an act of terrorism which would be broadcast globally, thus bringing the Palestinian struggle to the attention of the entire world.

Yair Galily, Moran Yarchi and Ilan Tamir have argued that the Israeli–Palestinian conflict had never received the level of attention which was generated by the Black September attack:

> The terrorist group had chosen to act at the Olympics because it knew that communication resources had been set up at the games to reach a global audience. For the first time, many people learned about the Israeli–Palestinian conflict or that there were groups willing to resort to violence for the Palestinian cause.[7]

The television coverage of the Munich massacre transmitted the event across borders on the day of the attack and through time as the news reports eventually became archival footage accounting for one of the defining events of the 1970s. The images filmed by various television crews and broadcast on 5 September 1972 were later used and repurposed in a number of documentaries in order to illustrate the unfolding of the incident. This material also provided the basis for dramatic reconstruction in a small number of fiction films. In both instances film narratives have thus been defined by the impact of the multiple live television coverage of the events and by what Galily, Yarchi and Tamir have aptly called 'the availability of communications to transmit that incident to a global audience.'[8] The village and the airfield are now associated with the murder of the Israeli athletes in a manner akin to the association between memory and the sites of the First World War and of the Spanish Civil War, the camps and ghettos of the Lublin district and the remains of the Hiroshima Prefectural Industrial Promotion Hall. Accordingly, in this chapter I look at the ways in which the Olympic Park in Oberwiesenfeld, and in particular the Olympisches Dorf (Olympic Village), and the airfield in Fürstenfeldbruck have been captured in a diverse range of films built on the narrative of the events which was established by the original news reports. The fiction and documentary films I have selected for this study articulate a vision of the locations of the Munich massacre where archival footage, dramatic reconstructions, present-day interviews and images of the site are intertwined; through a process which sees past and present wrestling one another, these films address the paradox of the unfolding of a terrorist attack against the background of what was meant to be a celebration of sport and of a new Germany.

The murder of eleven athletes, coaches and referees did not stop the games and the Men's Marathon was held five days after the attack on Sunday 10 September. British runner Ron Hill finished sixth in the race and his performance, as well as his training in Lancashire, was the subject of John Schlesinger's *The Longest*, a segment from the film *Visions of Eight* (1973). This documentary includes eight sections, each directed by a different filmmaker presenting a personal vision of the Olympic Games in Munich.[9] While the other seven segments entirely ignore the massacre, Schlesinger's film is the only one to address the event directly; and yet, *The Longest* acknowledges the incident through the apparent indifference of Ron Hill in response to what happened to those eleven members of the Israeli team. During the interview filmed soon after the massacre, Hill explains that he needs to focus on the race and that he cannot think about what happened in the apartment at 31 Connollystraße and in Fürstenfeldbruck. As Thomas Nachreiner has argued:

> Like runners with tunnel vision, the first seven contributing directors focus exclusively on the non-political aspects of the Olympics. Ironically, the concept of tunnel vision is personified by British runner Ron Hill, the ostensible subject of Schlesinger's episode whose utter refusal to see beyond his personal goal and whose outward indifference toward the incident disquieted the politically committed filmmaker.[10]

Hill's indifference, real or perceived, mirrored the feelings allegedly displayed by most athletes in the hours of the kidnapping. ITN reporter Gerald Seymour has explained the uneasy response of the athletes to the massacre in his recollection of the incident: 'It seemed like people having a noisy picnic in a churchyard. There was something unpleasant, selfish, slightly obscene about the atmosphere in the rest of the village.'[11] And yet, awareness of the killings pervaded the remaining races and, in *The Longest*, Schlesinger establishes a connection between the marathon and the massacre by including footage filmed during the attack, including the iconic image of the hooded terrorist on the balcony of the apartment in Connollystraße. Accordingly, by means of its editing technique *The Longest* articulates the incongruous association between the mundane setting of the games and the political and historical magnitude of the massacre which had just unfolded against the background of the Olympics. The film thus juxtaposes dramatic inserts from the front pages of the newspapers published in the days which followed the attack and footage of a wreath-laying outside the accommodation of the Israeli team at 31 Connollystraße. As with the ways in which the proximity of Dachau and the long shadow of the 1936 Olympics could not be ignored in the process of planning the return of the Olympic games to Germany, the massacre of the Israelis defined the public perception of all that was left of the event in spite of the decision made by the organisers to continue with the games after a day-long hiatus.

A similar incongruity is made explicit in later films by means of the use of present-day footage of the Olympic Park emerging as a vibrant sport venue which was inaugurated with a devastating act of terrorism. This duplicity emerges, for example, from *1972*, a 2008 documentary directed by Sarah Morris and focusing on the story of Georg Sieber, the police psychologist who was hired by the International Olympic Committee to be head psychologist of the Munich Police and to lead security during the Olympic Games. In his role, Sieber predicted twenty-six potential worst-case security scenarios which might possibly happen during the event. The terrorist attack carried out by Black September against the Israeli team unfolded almost in the exact same way described in one of Sieber's hypothetical situations. In *1972*, Sieber shares his thoughts on the massacre and the questionable ways in which the West German authorities dealt with the event, and he explains how he anticipated the intrusion of terrorists into the Israeli accommodation of the Olympic Village, the execution of the hostages and even the type of demands made by the Palestinians.

Most sequences from Morris' documentary consist of talking-head interviews with the retired police psychologist and a number of establishing shots at the beginning and in the middle of the film anchor Sieber's narrative to the sites of memory of the massacre. *1972* opens with a long shot of the top of the Olympiaturm, the Olympic Tower which was completed in 1968. This is followed by an extreme long shot revealing the full height of the tower and, behind it, the Olympic Stadium; the camera pans left to right and shows the Studentenviertel Oberwiesenfeld, also known as Olydorf, a student residency located on the site of the Olympic Village, the place where the terrorist attack unfolded. Additional shots of the Olydorf and of the rows of bleachers and the ceiling of the stadium are followed by two close-up shots of one of the original posters from 1972 showing four male athletes jumping a barrier in a steeplechase competition. Later in the film other panoramic views include the stadium, the Olympiahalle (Olympic Sports Hall), the Schwimmhalle (aquatics centre), the Olympic Lake and the Olympiaberg, the hill where a memorial for the civilian victims of the Second World War is located.

In the context of the memorialisation of the terrorist attack, these shots of the impressive sports venues are as incongruous as the absence of the massacre in most of the segments of *Visions of Eight*. Equally disquieting is the absence of a tangible memorial on the grounds of the Olympic Park. The attack is unavoidably inscribed onto the sites filmed by Morris and yet, as the memorial to the victims would only be inaugurated ten years after the making of the film, nothing really seems to bear witness to the events other than the film itself. The thriving Olympic Park appears as an embodiment of what Pierre Nora has called 'hopelessly forgetful modern society' and yet, akin to similar archival indicators, the shots of the park included in *1972* act as sites of memory.[12] Echoing the type of relationship between memory and space evoked by Nora's words, Katharine Hodgkin and Susannah Radstone have argued that landscape is 'little touched by human concerns for memory: give or take a few centuries, and the battlefields will be ordinary meadows; the memorials insisting on the reality of the deaths that took place will become illegible and crumble away.'[13] Even the unchanged built environment of the Olympic Park seems to be little touched by such human concerns for memory; for a day this location was a battlefield akin to those seen across Europe at the time of earlier hot wars, and then it became an ordinary place whose dark past is made to survive in a film such as *1972* as it deciphers the meaning inscribed onto its mundane locations.

Barely four years after the incident discussed in *1972*, the Olympic Village in Munich was filmed for *21 Hours at Munich* (William A. Graham, 1976), a television fiction film set and shot on the sites of the massacre. As the opening credits explain:

> The motion picture you are about to see is a dramatic recreation of events which occurred at the games of the XX Olympiad in Munich 1972. This entire film was made in West Germany on the actual location where the events took place.

21 Hours at Munich begins with two aerial shots of the city of Munich, including views of the building of the Bavarian State Ministry of Justice in Karlplatz, and the Neis Rathaus (New Town Hall), Peterskirche (St. Peter's Church) and Frauenkirche (Cathedral of Our Lady) in Marienplatz, in the Old Town; the Olympic Tower can be seen in the distance. These shots are followed by an aerial view of the Olympic Park, including the stadium and the tower. While the aerial shots provide the topographical coordinates of the narrative, the following archival footage from the inaugural ceremony of the Olympics, which includes the arrival of the Israeli team at the Olympic Stadium, establishes the historical context of the film.

The opening sequence of *21 Hours at Munich* is accompanied by the voice of Jim McKay covering the inaugural ceremony of the Olympic Games for the ABC; as I have observed earlier in this chapter, the same voice would later announce the murder of all Israeli hostages and, as David Scott Diffrient has argued, the result of this juxtaposition is that 'two seemingly unrelated things – spectator sports and terrorist reports – begin to slip into one another.'[14] This is particularly evident in the incongruous association of the content of the dramatic news delivered by McKay on live television and the stylised images of various sports on the back wall of the studio (Figure 6.1). This montage sequence provides the only use of archival footage in *21 Hours at Munich*; the fictional re-enactment of the incident is thus made to originate from factual footage which would have been familiar to the viewers who had been exposed to the attack during the broadcast of 5 September. Additionally, the fictional reconstruction which follows is at times closely based on the television footage filmed in 1972; this is particularly evident in the scenes of the negotiations between the commander and chief negotiator of the *fedayeen* (militia), Luttif Afif alias Issa, and the West German police and local authorities. Television broadcasts thus shaped the memorialisation of the massacre and informed later reconstructions of the event. In the context of heritage studies, David Lowenthal has argued that the past 'is not only recalled; it is incarnate in the things we build and the landscapes we create' and that 'physical residues of all events may yield potentially unlimited access to the past.'[15] Television footage of the Munich Massacre can also be read as a tangible residue of a past that is not only recalled but incarnated in the archival footage used in later films as much as in the way in which such footage has informed reconstructions of the incident; this past is also embedded in the physical residues of the incident, the buildings of the Olympic Village and the ground of the airfield.

The narrative and the filmic spaces of *21 Hours at Munich* are thus articulated on the basis of that singularity of the terrorist attack which, as Diffrient has argued, can be:

Figure 6.1 ABC television coverage of the Munich Massacre (1972).

... partly attributed to the presence of not one but several film and television cameras, positioned by news organizations and reporters outside 31 Connollystraße, where they not only recorded the terrible event for posterity but also transmitted it globally, in real time, to nearly one billion homes.[16]

Those film and television cameras also transmitted the incident through time as the footage was repurposed for a retrospective narrative of the massacre in documentary films such as *One Day in September* (Kevin Macdonald, 1999) and *Munich '72 and Beyond* (Stephen Crisman, 2016). Both documentaries combine archival footage, including the ABC coverage of the massacre, with present-day interviews with family members of the victims, eyewitnesses including the Olympic and government officials who engaged the terrorists in the negotiations. As I explain later in this chapter, *One Day in September* also uses the testimony of one of the Israeli survivors and that of the only living member of the Black September commando, with the aim of retrieving and unlocking memories of the events.

In order to establish a historical and topographical parallel, *Munich '72 and Beyond* uses a juxtaposition between the archival footage from the opening ceremony of the 1936 Olympics in Berlin and that of the 1972 Olympics in Munich. The black and white footage of the Berlin Olympics with its Nazi flags, symbolism and salutes, seems worlds away from the colourful and multiethnic images emerging from the footage of the opening ceremony in Munich. And yet, with this simple juxtaposition the film establishes a connection between the German Jews who were barred from participating in the Berlin Olympics, and who later died in the Holocaust, and the Israeli Jews who were killed in Connollystraße and Fürstenfeldbruck. This montage elucidates the ways in which the reverberations of the past affect the experience of the 1972 Olympics as well as the memorialisation of the event on later films. In order to illustrate the unfolding of the attack, *Munich '72 and Beyond* uses several aerial views of the Olympic Village as if they were maps where the name of the buildings and streets are imposed onto the actual locations. This technique is employed to explain in detail how the terrorists entered the village and made their way to the apartment in Connollystraße; it also reveals the proximity of the ABC control room to the accommodation of the Israeli team. Three-hundred feet separated the two buildings and the film thus implies that the ABC coverage was also facilitated by the topography of the Olympic Park and the vicinity of the two locations. *Munich '72 and Beyond* thus uses a topographical approach to address the unfolding of the events and to place the testimonies given by its witnesses onto the specific locations of the Olympic Park.

A similar spatial engagement with the sites of memory of the Munich Massacre is articulated in *One Day in September*. Sparsely narrated by Michael

Douglas, Macdonald's documentary is based on the juxtaposition of archival footage and present-day footage of the locations as well as on interviews with relatives of the victims, including Ankie Spitzer, the widow of fencing coach Andre Spitzer, West German authorities, and a member of the Black September commando Jamal Al-Gashey.[17] *One Day in September* combines archival photographs and footage of the races and other sports, the infamous images of the hooded terrorist on the balcony of the apartment in Connollystraße, extracts from the ABC and ITV news reports including the unfolding of the final phases of the incident at Fürstenfeldbruck. It also includes images of the negotiation led by Issa, who can be seen in television footage with his face covered with shoe polish and wearing a beach hat, a linen safari suit and holding a hand grenade. This material is juxtaposed with the accounts of the incident given by former Chief of Munich Police Manfred Schreiber and former Mayor of the Olympic Village Walther Tröger. The film also includes archival footage of the squad of thirty-eight West German police officers wearing Olympic sweat suits as they try unsuccessfully to crawl down from the ventilation shafts of the building in Connollystraße in order to free the hostages. These images were broadcast live on television and the terrorists were able to watch the failed police operation on the television screen in the Connollystraße apartment. As we shall see, the way in which television footage had an impact on the unfolding of the events by means of its own visibility is also used in Steven Spielberg's fiction film *Munich* (2005).

One Day in September also anchors its narrative to the sites of memory in the Olympic Village in Oberwiesenfeld and the airfield in Fürstenfeldbruck with the use of archival footage of these places. Like Morris' documentary *1972*, Macdonald's film opens with a long shot of the Olympiaberg with the Olympic Tower in the background; a canopy bed can be seen in the foreground and the camera zooms in to reveal a young woman who is waking up in that bed and being served breakfast by a butler (Figure 6.2). This is the opening shot from a 1972 advertisement for the Munich Tourism Bureau which continues with various shots of the Old Town, the Nymphenburg Palace and the Bavarian Alps. While the voice-over invites viewers to travel to Munich for the Olympics, two aerial shots of Oberwiesenfeld show the Olympic Park during the final phases of its construction. The repurposing of this advertisement in *One Day in September* establishes the location of the narrative and contributes to the articulation of the incongruous association between the Olympics and the massacre, and between the expectations of the organisers and the annihilation of their plans at the moment when the terrorists broke into the Olympic Village. Accompanied by the audio of various news reports on the unfolding of the attack, the opening credits put a blunt end to the advertisement and the promise of a safe and joyful Olympic

Figure 6.2 Advertisement for the Munich Tourism Bureau in *One Day in September* (Kevin Macdonald, 1999).

Games embedded in it. As it combines found footage with site-specific testimonies, *One Day in September* articulates that culturally enabling process defined by Andreas Huyssen in relation to the act of witnessing as 'a potential antidote to the freezing of memory into the one traumatic image'.[18] the meaningful use of archival footage and present-day testimonies thus enable memory by preventing it from freezing in the traumatic image of the terrorist on the balcony or that of the charred helicopters at the airfield.

The following sequences of *One Day in September* are constructed on the basis of similar juxtaposition of archival footage. Images of the arrival of the Israeli Olympic Team in Munich and during the opening ceremony at the Olympic Stadium are followed by footage from the 1936 Summer Olympics in Berlin showing swastikas, crowds making Nazi salutes and Adolf Hitler among the spectators. The Olympic Games of 1936 and 1972 are thus used as defining moments in the history of twentieth-century Germany; like *Munich '72 and Beyond*, *One Day in September* establishes a multidirectional connection between the persecution of the Jews in the 1930s and the assassination of Jewish athletes at the hands of Black September. These documentaries enable that understanding of memory based on the juxtaposition of the memories of the games in Berlin and Munich, and thus articulate a dialectic of remembering, revising historical events and establishing connections across time and by means of the use of archival footage.

The multiple layers of the historical meaning of the Olympics are also articulated in the scenes where the Rhythm and Blues song *Express Yourself*, performed by Charles Wright & the Watts 103rd Street Rhythm Band, accompanies a 1972 split-screen montage showing the athletes and the spectators of the Olympics with a strong emphasis on their racial and cultural diversity and their peaceful coexistence at the Olympic Village. This is followed by the testimony of Alex Springer, the son of wrestler and weightlifting coach Yakov Springer, who took part in the Warsaw Ghetto Uprising and was killed by the *fedayeen*, and by footage of the Israeli team attending the Olympic Memorial Service in Dachau and laying a wreath by the memorial sculpture designed in 1968 by Nandor Glid. This juxtaposition reveals how the Olympic Games were both defined by the memorialisation of the Second World War and characterised by an attempt to break free from the past. *One Day in September* here gives visibility to the memories of what happened in Germany and Occupied Europe in the 1940s, and establishes a connection with the present of the Olympics.

Like *Munich '72 and Beyond*, *One Day in September* engages with the locations of the attack and the accommodation of the Israeli team is filmed as the fundamental site of memory of the massacre. A tracking-shot from Gate 25A to 31 Connollystraße, and then up the staircase of the building to apartment 1, accompanies Al-Gashey's account of the unfolding of the attack starting with the moment when the *fedayeen* climbed over the fence of the Olympic Village with an oblivious group of American athletes who were returning to their accommodation after curfew. Another tracking shot takes the viewer to the balcony of the apartment where the hooded terrorist was photographed and filmed on 5 September 1972. Similarly, later in the film Gad Tsobari, the sole survivor among the six athletes housed in apartment 3, returns to Connollystraße and provides an account of his escape in the exact locations where it took place. Tsobari walks down the staircase of the apartment, and a tracking shot leads the viewer to the garage from which he managed to leave the building before jumping over the fence of the Olympic Village. Both the memories of the survivor and the narrative provided by Al-Gashey thus inscribe the past onto the built environment of the Olympic Village. To paraphrase the words of McKay which I have cited at the beginning of this chapter, one cannot be in the Munich Olympic Park and not remember and not think about the vicinity of Dachau; similarly, one cannot think of the testimonies of the events which took place in Munich and not think of multiple narratives of murder and survival in the context of the Holocaust emerging from documentary cinema. Connollystraße becomes the destination of a survivor's journey to a site of memory in a way which evokes the Sobibór documentaries discussed in Chapter 3 and their use of present-day footage of the sites.

A fictional reconstruction of the account given by Al-Gashey and Tsobari in *One Day in September* is re-enacted in Spielberg's *Munich*, a fiction film largely focusing on the Israeli government's secret retaliation against the Palestine Liberation Organization (known as 'Operation Wrath of God') in the years immediately following the Munich Massacre.[19] The first sequence of the film captures the events of 5 September 1972 in a way which brings together archival material and re-enactments while providing the context of Israel's retaliation against Black September. *Munich* opens with a shot of the 6-foot-high perimeter fence of the Olympic Village; the large sign of the Olympic Stadium can be seen in the background. While *21 Hours at Munich* was filmed on location, the role of the Olympic Stadium is here played by the now-demolished Puskás Ferenc Stadium located in the 14th district of Budapest, Hungary. Introduced by this shot, the first part of the film covers the events of that day, from the moment when the Palestinians enter the Olympic Village to the massacre at the airfield, in a 10-minute montage sequence.[20] Spielberg has here combined fiction and non-fiction in a sequence which juxtaposes dramatic reconstruction of the events with various international news reports broadcast on that day, including the ABC coverage and several extracts which have also been used in the documentaries discussed above.[21] As Nigel Morris suggests, the intertextual referencing provided by the use of television footage 'affords Spielberg's reconstruction an authenticating iconography' and articulates a sense of separation when 'optimism expressed on diegetic television/screens filters through the irony of knowing the outcome.'[22] Spielberg places television sets broadcasting the news reports of the attack within several scenes staged for the film and thus establishes an intertwined narrative of staging and found footage articulated both through editing and with the *mise-en-scène*. In *Munich*, this strategy enables multiple points of view including the responses to the television broadcasts given by the families of the hostages and those of the terrorists, by Israeli politicians and Palestinian refugees, as well as the point of view of the hostages and the *fedayeen* at 31 Connollystraße.

The opening sequence of the film starts at 4.10 a.m. on 5 September 1972 with one of eight tracksuit-clad heavily armed members of Black September trying to climb over the fence near Gate 25A. He is interrupted by a group of American athletes returning to their accommodation from an illicit night out; the Palestinian terrorists and the American athletes help one another to climb over the fence. The militants of Black September make their way to and break into apartment 1 at 31 Connollystraße; wrestling referee Yossef Gutfreund hears their arrival and tries to obstruct their entrance before he is overcome by the terrorists. The intertwining between fiction and non-fiction is immediately established as the opening scene is followed by the ABC news report where, with these words, sports commentator Jim McKay told the world about the Black September attack against the Israeli Olympic team:

> I'm Jim McKay speaking to you live at this moment from ABC headquarters just outside the Olympic Village in Munich, West Germany. The peace of what have been called the 'serene Olympics' was shattered just before dawn this morning about 5:00.

This ABC footage is not located anywhere specific within the *mise-en-scène* and it is used to deliver the news of the attack to the viewer of *Munich* with the same announcement which first revealed it to the world in 1972.

The following sequence takes the viewer to a crowded street in Haifa and to a bar with a television set showing a news report from the Israeli Broadcasting Authority; images of the hooded terrorist on the balcony are watched by a group of people and accompanied by this commentary:

> There is great uncertainty about how many Israelis are being held hostage in the apartment. It now appears that Black September has tossed a piece of paper out the window. A list of demands. They want what they call the 'Israeli war machine' to release two-hundred Arabs, which it insists are political prisoners or the hostages will be killed. The terrorist communiqué ends with an appeal for revolutionaries of the world to unite.

The dramatic report is emphasised by the previously mentioned iconic image of the terrorist on the balcony of Apartment 1; as Diffrient suggests, the photographs and the footage of 'a solitary terrorist standing on a balcony of the besieged building and gazing at the Olympic officials, German authorities, police forces and news correspondents below him, a wool ski hat pulled over his face and masking his identity' metonymically represented the whole event.[23] Accordingly, Spielberg uses this image to convey in the most immediate and powerful way the entirety of the Munich Massacre with its most recognisable imagery, a frightening vision in contrast to the festive images which had been broadcast from Munich in the previous days.

The parallel editing of this sequence leads to a Palestinian refugee camp where a group of men and women are cheering while watching the ABC report; McKay can be heard saying these words: 'This is building number 31. At this moment eight or nine terrified living human beings are being held prisoner. The demands have been many. There's someone right now. This certainly has to be one of the guerrillas.' Another topographical connection between West Germany and the Middle East is established as, in the following scene, the same ABC report continues in the apartment at 31 Connollystraße with McKay's words: 'A man with a stocking mask on his face. Weird. What's going on inside that head and that mind?'. This archival footage is played on a television set placed on the floor in the foreground of the shot; in the background the hooded terrorist can be seen with his back to the camera and making his way to that balcony (Figure 6.3). The apartment in Connollystraße in *Munich* is thus a reconstruction of the place where the drama unfolded and, at once, a location from which factual footage of the event itself is delivered to the viewers. Additionally these scenes establish a geographical connection between the apartment in Munich and the Palestinian refugee camps; they also articulate a site-specific interaction between fiction and non-fiction by means of the juxtaposition of the image of the hooded terrorist in the archival footage and that of his fictional counterpart. In *Munich*, this reconstruction is filmed from a perspective which was then only accessible to the hostages and to the *fedayeen* and works as a staged reverse shot of the factual image which was seen on television all around the world.

Spielberg uses archival footage to establish another geographical connection with the Middle East as the setting of the following scene shifts again from Connollystraße to Beit Aghion, the residence of the Israeli Prime Minister in Jerusalem; here Golda Meir (Lynn Cohen) is watching the ABC coverage of the events with journalist Peter Jennings explaining that: 'Just a short while ago, there was another in this long series of negotiations. The spokesman for the group came out, spoke, went back. It seems to be a process of speak and consultation.' In this instance, the film's viewer learns about the unfolding of the events just as Prime Minister Meir did and this

Figure 6.3 The Connollystraße apartment in *Munich* (Steven Spielberg, 2005).

scene illustrates the role played by television in the film, a spatial narrative device or, in the words of Thomas Nachreiner, 'an actor within the framework of the terrorist event'.[24] In his study of the relationship between media and memory in *Munich*, Nachreiner has explained that:

> All individual spectators see the same pictures of the event, thus becoming a unified mass audience despite their geographical separation. The staging of a (global) mass audience also indicates the permeation of society by television: The television screen becomes the centre of public attention as well as the centre of the private homes.[25]

Palestinian refugees, the Israeli Prime Minister, hostages and *fedayeen* are all exposed to the same images while, as Nachreiner suggests, television makes a violent intrusion into the homes of the spectators shown in the film while *Munich* itself overwhelms its spectators; Nachreiner concludes that central to this process is 'the production infrastructure of television, showing the studio, the cameras, and the reporters involved in the performance of the media event.'[26] The archival footage is thus intertwined with a fictional reconstruction in a rhythmic account of events which unfolded in the course of that day and which are summarised in a 10-minute sequence.

The following scenes return to the Olympic Park and are set in the television studios of the stadium and the apartment in Connollystraße. The ABC coverage of the attack can still be heard and seen on the studio monitors and on the television in the apartment. In this footage Jennings tells McKay that: 'Jim, there are now a great many, maybe a dozen already, of those security men in athletic uniforms.' These words, as explained in *One Day in September*, alerted the terrorists to the aborted rescued plan attempted by the West German police; the television set thus becomes an actor both within the framework of the film and of the actual event. In one of these scenes, as the terrorists in the apartment prepare to leave with their hostages, reporter Don Durbridge can be heard summarising the events for the BFBS (British Forces Broadcasting Service):

> It now appears that the siege of the apartment building where the hostages are being held has been called off and the German police are retreating from the area. Officials seem to have decided to abandon their plans when the leader of the *fedayeen* came out of the building and demanded they call off the siege pointing out that the entire operation was being watched on a television set within the apartment. Apparently, new demands have been made to move the *fedayeen* and their hostages, though it isn't yet known when or where this might occur.

The impact of the role of television in the context of the event is here made explicit by Durbridge's words. The paradox of an incident unfolding on a television screen located in the apartment in Connollystraße is embedded in the memorialisation of the attack and ultimately changed the course of the event.

Munich then covers the negotiations between the Palestinian commando and the West German authorities, and the operation which took the terrorists and their captives to nearby Fürstenfeldbruck airbase in order to be flown to Cairo and the ensuing chaos which led to the death of nine members of the Israeli team. Spielberg includes staged scenes set in the television studios of the Olympic Stadium and at Fürstenfeldbruck intertwined with television news reports edited with the reconstruction of the incident or shown on television screens as part of the *mise-en-scène*; a number of actors in the role of sport reporters talk into the cameras and the archival footage includes Jennings and Cosell's coverage for ABC. The multitude of voices and points of view here establishes a narrative of trauma. Nick Hodgin and Amit Thakkar explain that 'trauma on film is as much about individuals as it is about collectives, and the interaction between them needs always to be acknowledged.'[27] In *Munich*, individual and collective trauma is rendered by means of parallel editing juxtaposing the reaction of the family of an Israeli athlete and that of one of the terrorists in a sequence where the ABC coverage provides unity of time. The Palestinian family is following Lou Cioffi's report for the ABC in their sitting room: 'Yes, I just got back a little while ago and it was obvious that something quite serious was going on out there.' McKay's later announcement increases the traumatic tension: 'The latest word we get from the airport is that, quote, "all hell has broken loose out there."'

The Israeli family of one of the hostages is also watching the ABC report with Cosell's commentary offering the viewer misplaced hope: 'It's just arrived, Peter. The bus has arrived to the helicopters. We have reports now that all the hostages, all nine hostages are safe. We repeat, we have confirmed, it's just past 1.00 a.m. The fighting ceased at midnight.' This is juxtaposed with another scene set in the sitting room of the Palestinian family reacting with despair to the news, also inaccurate, that all terrorists died by West German gunfire. Later, McKay's dramatic announcement to the world, with the words I have quoted earlier in this chapter, is included in this montage sequence and placed in no specific diegetic context. The final scene of this opening sequence introduces one of the main characters, Mossad agent Avner Kaufman (Eric Bana). He is watching a news report with his wife and listens to a female Israeli journalist reading out the names of the members of the Israeli team who were murdered by the Arab terrorists. This announcement is edited in parallel with a scene where members of Mossad assemble photographs of their targets. This montage marks a transition between the reconstruction of the incident, with its intertwining of factual material and staged reconstructions, and the main narrative focus of the film, the preparation and execution of the Israeli revenge operation. What follows, the unfolding of the operation 'Wrath of God', is informed by the events which took place in Munich on 5 September 1972 and by the nature of the incident as accounted for in the montage sequence which opens the film; Spielberg crosses the bridge between fact and fiction and provides a reflection on the role of the media, and in particular television news reports, in the perception and reception of the Munich massacre.

The terrorist outrage in Munich placed the Olympic Park and the Fürstenfeldbruck airfield on the map of a series of sites and events which have defined the Cold War years and whose narrative has been captured in pictures at the time of their happening and retold on film in the years which followed. With multidirectional connections to other times, and specifically to the Nazi era and the persecution of the Jews, and to other places, the Middle East with its Israeli–Palestinian conflict, the Olympic Park in Munich and Fürstenfeldbruck became battlefields on that September day and then returned to their original function. And yet, like the sites of memory I have investigated in previous chapters, the Olympic Park can also tell a different story, not one built on sporting competitions, but one of death and violence exemplified in both fiction and documentary cinema. Film, as Fearghal McGarry and Jennie Carlsten have argued, is able to 'legitimize the codified narratives told about history, or it can subvert these by providing a range of competing images, symbols and discourses.'[28] Both fiction and documentary films studied in this chapter have legitimised the codified narrative of the event with unanimous condemnation of the attack and have inscribed the complex narrative of competing images and symbols of the Israeli–Palestinian conflict onto the sites of memory of the massacre.

Against the background of Olympic Park, the Black September commando made demands which were never accepted by the negotiators. Beside the release of hundreds of Palestinian prisoners from Israeli jails, the *fedayeen* requested that West Germany would set free Andreas Baader and Ulrike Meinhof, the founders of the *Rote Armee Fraktion* (Red Army Faction) who were held at the Stammheim Prison in Stuttgart. Meinhof and Baader would kill themselves in jail in 1976 and 1977 respectively and the Red Army Faction remained active until 1998.[29] On the day of the fifth anniversary of the Munich massacre, the far-left militant organisation kidnapped and later murdered Hanns Martin Schleyer, the president of the Confederation of German Employers' Associations and of the Federation of German Industries. His body was found in the boot of a green Audi 100 on the rue

Charles Péguy in Mulhouse, France. A few months later, the Italian far-left militant group *Brigate Rosse* (Red Brigades) would emulate the action of the Red Army Faction and kidnap Aldo Moro, the president of the political party *Democrazia Cristiana* (Christian Democracy). Moro was one of the minds behind *compromesso storico* (historic compromise), the political accommodation between Christian Democrats and the Italian Communist Party in the 1970s, and his kidnap and murder had enormous reverberation throughout Italian politics and society. This incident began on 16 March 1978, with an ambush in Via Fani, Rome, which gave Italy a glimpse of hot war in the midst of the Cold War. During the following weeks, the private space of an unassuming apartment in Via Montalcini, Rome, would play a historical role as significant as that of the apartment in Connollystraße. Moro would be found dead in the boot of a car in Via Caetani, also in Rome, fifty-four days after his kidnapping. The events unfolding on these three streets of Rome in the spring of 1978 and the ways in which, like the massacre in Munich, they were captured in news reports, memorialised in documentaries and re-enacted in fiction films is the focal point of the next chapter.

Notes

1. For a comprehensive history of the Olympic Games and the planning and the construction of the Munich Olympic Park, see: Large, pp. 51–93.
2. See Kay Schiller and Chris Young, *The 1972 Munich Olympics and the Making of Modern Germany*, Berkeley: University of California Press, 2010, p 188.
3. Seven members of the Israeli team were staying in Apartment 1 while other four athletes were brought in later on that morning from other apartments located in the same building at 31 Connollystraße. One of the Israeli wrestlers, Gad Tsobari, managed to escape via the parking garage located under the building.
4. The documentaries discussed in this chapter, among other sources, have voiced the suspicion that the hijacking of Flight 615 might have been staged by the West German government in a covert operation negotiated with Black September in order to remove terrorists whose trial would have created a security threat for West Germany. Among other reasons, the presence of barely thirteen passengers on a plane with a seating capacity of hundred and fifty has been deemed suspicious; the quick decision to have the members of Black September released, as well as alleged contacts between the West German Federal Intelligence Service and the Palestine Liberation Organization have also been listed as reasons for suspicion.
5. Schiller and Young, p. 187.
6. Eva Maria Gajek, 'More than Munich 1972. Media, Emotions, and the Body in TV Broadcast of the 20th Summer Olympics', *Historical Social Research*, Vol. 43, No. 2, 2018, pp. 181–202 (199).

7. Yair Galily, Moran Yarchi and Ilan Tamir, 'From Munich to Boston, and from Theatre to Social Media: The Evolutionary Landscape of World Sporting Terror', *Studies in Conflict & Terrorism*, Vol. 38, No. 12, 2015, pp. 998–1007 (1000).
8. Galily, Yarchi and Tamir, p. 1000.
9. The other segments of the anthology documentary *Visions of Eight* were directed by Miloš Forman (*The Decathlon*), Kon Ichikawa (*The Fastest*), Claude Lelouch (*The Losers*), Yuri Ozerov (*The Beginning*), Arthur Penn (*The Highest*), Michael Pfleghar (*The Women*), and Mai Zetterling (*The Strongest*).
10. Thomas Nachreiner, 'An Olympic Omnibus: International Competition, Cooperation, and Politics in *Visions of Eight*', *Film & History*, Vol. 35, No. 2, 2005, pp. 19–28 (24).
11. Testimony included in Simon Reeve's *One Day in September: the Full Story of the 1972 Olympics Massacre and the Israeli Revenge Operation 'Wrath of God'* (New York: Arcade Publishing, 2011, p. 66).
12. Pierre Nora, 'Between Memory and History: Les Lieux de Mémoire', *Representations. Special Issue: Memory and Counter-Memory*, No. 26 (1989), pp. 7–2 (8).
13. Katharine Hodgkin and Susannah Radstone, 'Introduction: Contested Pasts', in *Memory, History, Nation: Contested Pasts*, New Brunswick, NJ: Transaction, 2005, pp. 1–22.
14. David Scott Diffrient, 'Spectator sports and terrorist reports: filming the Munich Olympics, (re)imagining the Munich Massacre', *Sport in Society*, Vol. 11, No. 2–3, 2008, pp. 311–29 (315).
15. David Lowenthal, 'Past Time, Present Place: Landscape and Memory', *Geographical Review*, Vol. 65, No. 1, 1975, pp. 1–36 (6); David Lowenthal, *The Past Is a Foreign Country*, Cambridge: Cambridge University Press, 1985, p. 19.
16. Diffrient, p. 316.
17. At the time of the making of *One Day in September*, Al-Gashey had already given a short interview to a Palestinian newspaper in 1992 and was in hiding at an unspecified location in North Africa.
18. Andreas Huyssen, 'Monument and Memory in a Postmodern Age', *The Yale Journal of Criticism*, Vol. 6, No. 2, 1993, pp. 249–61 (258).
19. Operation 'Wrath of God' and its historical and political assessment are beyond the scope of the present investigation. On the unfolding of Israel's revenge against Black September, see Aaron J. Klein, *Striking Back: The 1972 Munich Olympics Massacre and Israel's Deadly Response*, London: Random House, 2007; George Jonas, *Vengeance: The True Story of an Israeli Counter-Terrorist Team*, New York: Simon and Schuster, 2005; Reeve, *One Day in September: the Full Story of the 1972 Olympics Massacre and the Israeli Revenge Operation 'Wrath of God'*.
20. *Sword of Gideon* (Michael Anderson, 1986), a Canadian television film about the Israeli response to the Munich Massacre, opens with a much-shorter sequence covering the events of 5 September while omitting many details which are included in Spielberg's film, such as the encounter between the Palestinian terrorists and the American athletes just outside the gate of the Olympic Village. This

brief sequence serves the purpose of providing a context for the main focus of the film, the revenge operation 'Wrath of God'.
21. Similarly, the documentary *Munich: Mossad's Revenge* (Tom Whitter, 2006) focuses on the Mossad operation known as 'Wrath of God' and the assassination of individuals involved in the Munich massacre. Like Spielberg's *Munich*, *Munich: Mossad's Revenge* opens with a sequence covering the events of 5 September and uses archival footage from the news reports including the ABC broadcast and the image of the hooded terrorist on the balcony of the apartment at 31 Connollystraße. Like *Munich*, Tom Whitter's documentary thus anchors the incident to the sites of memory of the massacre and repurposes archival footage to cover the unfolding of the events which took place on that day.
22. Nigel Morris, *The Cinema of Steven Spielberg: Empire of Light*, New York: Columbia University Press, 2007, p. 366.
23. Diffrient, p. 316.
24. Thomas Nachreiner, '"Inspired by real events" – Media (and) Memory in Steven Spielberg's *Munich* (2005)', *Imaginations: Journal of Cross-Cultural Media Studies*, Vol. 5, No. 2, 2016, pp. 67–87 (79).
25. Nachreiner, 2016, p. 79.
26. Nachreiner, 2016, pp. 80, 79.
27. Nick Hodgin and Amit Thakkar, 'Introduction: Trauma Studies, Film and the Scar Motif', in *Scars and Wounds: Film and Legacies of Trauma*, Nick Hodgin and Amit Thakkar (eds), Basingstoke: Palgrave Macmillan, 2017, pp. 1–30 (11).
28. Fearghal McGarry and Jennie Carlsten, 'Introduction', in *Film, History and Memory*, Fearghal McGarry and Jennie Carlsten (eds), Basingstoke: Palgrave Macmillan, 2015, pp. 1–17 (9).
29. The cause of death of both Baader and Meinhof has long been disputed and claims have been made that the two founders of the Red Army Faction were in fact assassinated (see Stefan Aust, *Baader-Meinhof: the Inside Story of the R.A.F.*, Oxford: Oxford University Press, 2009, pp. 154–5). The Red Army Faction was founded in 1970 and in the following thirty years it engaged in a bombings, assassinations, kidnappings, and robberies, with a peak in late 1977; the organisation has been held responsible for at least thirty-four deaths. Its earliest members were trained in Jordan with the Popular Front for the Liberation of Palestine and the Palestine Liberation Organization guerrillas (see J. Smith and André Moncourt, *The Red Army Faction: A Documentary History. Projectiles for the people*, Montreal: PM Press, 2009, p. 56).

CHAPTER 7

Via Mario Fani, Rome, Lazio, Italy, 16 March 1978, 9:02 a.m.

> *A sixty-one-year-old man from Maglie, Apulia, is kidnapped by a unit of the militant far-left organisation known as the Red Brigades and his five bodyguards are murdered. His name is Aldo Moro and this happens on the morning of 16 March 1978 in Rome.*

Today there is a children's room in one of the ground floor apartments of the building in Via Camillo Montalcini 8, a residential street named after a Piedmontese civil servant and located in Portuense, the eleventh borough of Rome. Two young girls play, do their homework and sleep in this room.[1] There are toys, children's books, notebooks and there is no trace of the infamous *prigione del popolo*, the small cell where the Red Brigades imprisoned and put on trial Aldo Moro, the president of Christian Democracy and a former Italian Prime Minister, in the spring of 1978 during the weeks which led to his assassination on 9 May.[2] In 1980 the apartment in Via Montalcini was identified by the police as the place where Moro had been kept in captivity and, at the beginning of the summer of that year, Ferdinando Imposimato, a prosecutor who was in charge of the investigation of the kidnapping of Moro, visited the apartment for the first time. Moro's captors had already dismantled the cell, sold the property and moved to a new location. All that was left of the cell was a mark on the wooden floor of the bedroom made by the bookshelves and fake wall behind which Moro spent almost two months during the most dramatic stage of the Years of Lead, that period of social and political struggle characterised by far-right and far-left political terrorism which began in the late 1960s and lasted until the late 1980s.[3] A phenomenon related to the Cold War, terrorism in Italy mirrored the international tensions between the West and the Eastern Block and reflected the country's alignment with NATO and the Red Brigades' revolutionary agenda. This is also the period of time which shaped the work of Francesco Rosi and, in particular, *Many Wars Ago*, a film which I have discussed in Chapter 1 in relation to how its take on the First World War served to provide a commentary on the political conflicts of the late 1960s and early 1970s; the pacifist vision articulated in Rosi's film framed the Years of Lead as yet another war with reverberations of the earlier conflicts which were fought in Italy during the Short Twentieth Century. In what follows, I investigate the ways in which Italian cinema has portrayed this war with a focus on how the kidnapping and murder of Aldo Moro has been used to exemplify the events of the Years of Lead.

The incident which unfolded in Rome in the spring of 1978 has been addressed in a significant number of films whose narratives develop across a precise Rome topography which, apart from the apartment in Via Montalcini, includes two other main sites of memory: Via Mario Fani at the crossroad with Via Stresa, the place where Moro was taken and where his five bodyguards were assassinated, and Via Michelangelo Caetani, the side street off Via delle Botteghe Oscure in the historic centre of Rome where Moro's dead body was found in the boot of a red Renault 4 on 9 May. In this chapter I focus on the ways in which the events which took place in Via Fani, Via Montalcini and Via Caetani have been represented in fiction films and documentaries which have repurposed archival footage, photographs, and radio and television news reports. In the case studies I investigate, multiple layers of time are intertwined and fictional and archival material juxtaposed in order to articulate a complex image of the events which took place in those months. Via Fani emerges from film as the most iconic battleground of the Years of Lead while Via Montalcini is the place of mystery whose role in the Moro case was unknown to the public; Via Caetani, finally, is a site of mourning. Shrouded in controversy, the exact unfolding of the events, the identity of the terrorists and the response given by politicians has been debated ever since, with multiple theories based on the later trials or on public inquiries leading to countless conspiracy theories.[4] The purpose of this chapter is not to review this debate but rather to understand the ways in which the memory of these sites has been shaped by multiple filmic narratives and to put forward a spatial reading of the Moro case where the topography of Rome can be read as a battlefield of the hot war fought by the Italian state and the Red Brigades in the midst of the Cold War. As in the case of the massacre perpetrated by Black September during the Munich Olympics, documentaries and fictional reconstructions of the events have dialogued in a multi-layered narrative providing a reflection on the ways in which the incident has been memorialised on the background of its three main locations.

Via Fani (Ambush)

Named after a young Catholic activist who lost his life to a pulmonary disease acquired as he saved a man from drowning, Via Mario Fani is located less than a mile west of what used to be Aldo Moro's home at 79 Via del Forte Trionfale, a street named after the fort which was built there in the 1880s.[5] On 16 March 1978, the day when this street became a hot front of the Cold

War, Moro left his house a few minutes before 9:00 a.m. in a blue Fiat 130 driven by a *carabiniere*;[6] a second officer sat next to the driver and a white Alfetta with other three bodyguards, members of the State Police, followed Moro's car. Just after 9:00 a.m., as the two cars entered Via Fani, a lookout alerted the terrorists; at the crossroads with Via Stresa a Fiat 128 cut the road in front of the Fiat 130 and four armed *brigatisti* wearing fake pilot uniforms jumped out from the bushes by Bar Olivetti firing machine guns. Moro's five bodyguards were killed and he was taken away in a Fiat 132.[7] The news of the attack was first given by state radio stations and later in the morning on public television channels. At 9.25 a.m. Giornale Radio 2 first told the country about the events in Via Fani and this was followed by a similar announcement on Giornale Radio 1 at 9.31 a.m. News reports on RAI, the national public broadcasting company of Italy, followed soon after the radio reports. Newscaster Giancarlo Santalmassi presented a special edition of the TG2 news report on Rete 2 at 10:01 a.m. while, almost simultaneously, a TG1 news report on Rete 1 was introduced by journalist Bruno Vespa.[8] This special edition of the TG1 included footage from Via Fani filmed by cameraman Andrea Ruggeri and reporter Paolo Frajese soon after the attack. As I explain in the second section of this chapter, this extraordinary first-hand account of the aftermath of the massacre has regularly been repurposed in documentary films about the kidnapping of Aldo Moro and used as a visual reference in fictional re-enactments of the ambush.

Both fiction and documentary films have focused on the attack and on its immediate aftermath, the gruesome war scene in Via Fani which was filmed and photographed in the hours which followed the kidnapping. The ambush has also been evoked by a handful of eyewitnesses who have provided partial accounts of the unfolding of the events. For example, actor Francesco Pannofino lived on that street and saw the ambush while on his way to university; in the documentary *Il Condannato. Cronaca di un sequestro (The Convict: Chronicles of a Kidnapping*, Ezio Mauro, 2018), Pannofino provides a vivid description of what he saw and explains that, paradoxically, he was only struck by the magnitude of the event when he watched the news reports later on that day. Pannofino's testimony and that given by other witnesses have contributed to establishing the dynamics of the attack and yet, in the absence of visual evidence, there have been contrasting views regarding the exact unfolding of the ambush.[9] In 1990 the investigation led by a parliamentary commission on the Years of Lead, for example, revealed the presence in Via Stresa of Camillo Guglielmi, a colonel of SISMI, the military intelligence agency of Italy, who also worked for *Operazione Gladio*, the codename for a clandestine stay-behind operation of armed resistance to a potential Soviet invasion of Italy and of opposition to the Communist Party. This revelation is used and dramatised in *Piazza Delle Cinque Lune* (*Five Moons Plaza*, Renzo Martinelli, 2003), a political thriller which includes fake archival footage of the attack. At the beginning of the film, chief prosecutor Rosario Saracini (Donald Sutherland) receives a parcel containing a Super 8 mm film which was taken from one of the upper floors of the building in Via Fani 109 on the day of the kidnapping. Saracini identifies Guglielmi as the man wearing a raincoat standing in Via Stresa during the ambush in the 8 mm footage, a fact which ignites a conspiracy narrative based on the many unanswered questions about the number of terrorists and the identities of those who took part in the attack. By embracing the idea of the involvement of the Italian secret services in the kidnapping, *Five Moons Plaza* exploits the authority inherent to archival footage in order to place the incident firmly in the context of Cold War conspiracy.

While *Five Moons Plaza* resorts to fake factual footage, other fiction films have entirely omitted a direct re-enactment of the events of Via Fani in an attempt to focus on the human tragedy embedded in the captivity of Moro. *Se sarà luce sarà bellissimo* (*If There Were Light, That Would Be Beautiful*, Aurelio Grimaldi 2004), for example, opens with a short scene where members of the Red Brigades are getting ready for the ambush, and then an elliptical cut leads to the immediate aftermath of the attack. In Marco Bellocchio's *Buongiorno, notte* (*Good Morning, Night*, 2003), the terrorist action in Via Fani is omitted in favour of a domestic focus on the preparation for Moro's arrival in the apartment of Via Montalcini; in Bellocchio's film, Moro (Roberto Herlitzka) enters the stage directly in what Giancarlo Lombardi has called the 'soundproofed heart' of that apartment.[10] Both *If There Were Light, That Would Be Beautiful* and *Good Morning, Night* can rely on the participation of their audiences inasmuch as the ambush in Via Fani is an episode engrained in the shared memory of the Years of Lead and most Italian viewers of a certain generation would be able to fill the narrative gap with their knowledge of the events, with the images of the aftermath of the ambush in Via Fani seen repeatedly on the news reports.

In *Aldo Moro: Il professore* (*Aldo Moro: Professor*, Francesco Miccichè, 2018), Moro (Sergio Castellitto) can be seen on the back seat of the Fiat 130 reading a thesis written by one of his students and the camera follows his car and the white Alfetta through the streets of Rome. An elliptical cut leads to the moments after the attack, with a scene where Moro's students are standing outside Montecitorio and are told by a *carabiniere* about what has just happened in Via Fani. *Aldo Moro: Professor*, a film which blends fiction and factual material, also includes a digital animation of the ambush in Via Fani made in 2017 by a scientific support unit of the state police. Projectile trajectories are identified and reconstructed on the basis of impact marks including the perforating of the bullets on the two cars and through the bodies of Moro's bodyguard. As it ignites a conspiracy theory in a way which is reminiscent of *Five Moons Plaza*, this animated version of the ambush is used to argue in favour of the presence of a highly-skilled marksman among the terrorists and thus suggest the possibility of a plan which could have involved national or international secret services. While *Five Moons Plaza* relies on fake footage, *Aldo Moro: Il professore* uses the results of police investigations and thus brings an element of authenticity to the speculation about the unfolding of the attack. Other films have staged the attack on the basis of the testimonies given by members of the Red Brigades during the trials of 1983–5 and have portrayed the ambush in Via Fani as the climax of the war between state and paramilitary left-wing organisations such as the Red Brigades. In *Year of the Gun* (John Frankenheimer, 1991), for example, the Via Fani sequence represents, as Alan O'Leary has argued:

> ... the culmination of a portrait of Italy as a country in such chaos that it cannot be trusted to govern itself and the film of less interest for what it might or might not say about the Moro kidnapping than for what it belatedly reveals about US Cold War attitudes to Italy.[11]

Frankenheimer's film thus uses the ambush in Via Fani as the epitome of the Years of Lead and acknowledges its impact on the country and on international relationships in the context of the Cold War.

Aldo Moro: Il presidente (*Aldo Moro: President*, Gianluca Maria Tavarelli, 2008) was filmed on location in Via Fani and contains aerial views of the street. In Tavarelli's television drama the reconstruction of the ambush includes images seen in news reports such as those of the body of Raffaele Iozzino and the fake pilot hat lost by one of the terrorists lying on the asphalt. *Aldo Moro: President*, as O'Leary suggests, thus uses these familiar cinematic topoi in order to provide 'a kind of review of what we remember and think we know about the man and the events.'[12] This is not the first film where the ambush in Via Fani is staged in front of the camera. Directed by Giuseppe Ferrara in 1986 and starring Gian Maria Volonté as Aldo Moro, *Il caso Moro* (*The Moro Affair*) opens with a close-up of the street sign in Via Fani and is followed by a camera movement revealing the residential street. A sequence covering the events which took place between 8:00 a.m. and 9:00 a.m. uses parallel editing in order to show the terrorists' preparation for the ambush and domestic scenes at the apartment where Moro lived with his family. As O'Leary suggests:

> *Il caso Moro* is fundamentally a 'human' story: the tale of a man and his suffering family. Indeed, our first sight of Moro is not in any governmental or even public context, but in his persona of *pater familias*, speaking softly at home with his little grandson Luca.[13]

The following sequence meticulously stages the ambush on the basis of the revelations made by the terrorists during the trials; this is the version of the attack which is ingrained in the shared memory of that day and which has also been included, in a transition from fictional re-enactment to factual evidence, in documentaries about the Moro case.

Four years after the release of *The Moro Affair*, the Via Fani sequence from Ferrara's film would be used in Sergio Zavoli's television documentary *La notte della Repubblica: Il sequestro Moro* (*The Night of the Republic: the Moro kidnapping*, 1990) in order to illustrate the unfolding of the ambush.[14] The images from *The Moro Affair* are juxtaposed with the audio recording of the testimony given by Valerio Morucci, a former member of the Red Brigades who took part in the ambush, during his trial at the Corte d'Assise d'Appello in 1985.[15] This fictional reconstruction thus provides a visual counterpart to the account provided by Morucci's voice-over mixed with the sound effects from the sequence from *The Moro Affair*. Fiction and documentary are here merged in an audiovisual juxtaposition which aims to approximate the unfolding of the events of the morning of that 16 March. As Isabella Pezzini has argued, the episodes of *The Night of the Republic* focusing on the Moro kidnapping 'gave credence to the importance of individual recollection, oral testimony, and the figurative inscription of events on the body, which television occasionally manages to convey to the viewing public.'[16] The scenes from Via Fani, Pezzini continues, thus bear 'all the traces of an act of inordinate violence, of a site of death dominated by the absence of the body of the abducted Moro.'[17] In order to fill this void and thus establish a further connection between fiction and reality, Zavoli's documentary includes a montage sequence of photographs of Moro and of the five bodyguards who died on that day in a powerful juxtaposition between personal memory and the fictional reconstruction of Ferrara's film.

Via Fani (Aftermath)

The ambush in Via Fani has been staged, animated by *a scientific police unit* and recreated through fake archival footage in the films discussed above. In other instances, it has been entirely omitted in films relying on the audience to fill the gaps in the narrative. The attack which was only witnessed by a handful of people has become part of a shared memory of the Years of Lead, and the retelling of the event has given the Italian nation, to borrow the definition used by Weissman and discussed in Chapters 3 and 4, the fantasy of witnessing a traumatic event which was not experienced directly. This fantasy has also been fuelled by the first-hand evidence of the immediate aftermath of the ambush, which was photographed and filmed by a number of reporters (Figure 7.1). The earliest footage shown on public television was that

Figure 7.1 The aftermath of the ambush in Via Mario Fani (ANSA).

recorded by Ruggeri and Frajese at 9:50 a.m. and broadcast by TG1 later on that morning.[18] Those graphic images of the dead, barely covered by sheets, are now ingrained in memory and they have been used widely in virtually every documentary on the event and in even some fiction films.[19]

The TG1 news report included a map of Rome showing the crossroads between Via Fani and Via Stresa which provided the topographical coordinates of the Moro kidnapping. Ruggeri and Frajese walked with a hand-held camera from Via Stresa to Via Fani and filmed shaky footage of the Fiat 130 with the corpses of two of Moro's bodyguards covered with sheets; another body can be seen on the Alfetta and both cars are riddled with bullets. The dramatic tension can be heard in the journalist's voice as he is exposed to the slaughter of Moro's bodyguards, Frajese describes the scene in great detail and speculates on what might have happened during the attack; a small crowd has gathered in Via Fani and a group of *carabinieri* is inspecting the scene. While one of the bodyguards was taken to hospital and would die later on that day, three bodies are still inside the vehicles while the corpse of policeman Raffaele Iozzino is lying on the street and is covered by a sheet. Ruggeri's footage and Frajese's frantic commentary largely focus on what can be seen on the asphalt: a significant number of bullets, a gun, one of Moro's briefcases, the loader of an automatic weapon, and a stream of blood. They also filmed what appears to be an Alitalia pilot hat; while its presence in Via Fani appears incongruous at first, it would soon be known that four of the attackers were wearing fake pilot uniforms which had been bought on 10 March in a shop called Cardia in Via Firenze by *brigatista* Adriana Faranda.[20]

The Moro Affair includes a reconstruction of the minutes which followed the ambush. The *mise-en-scène* of the sequence where Moro's wife (Margarita Lozano) arrives in Via Fani is based on the images broadcast on TG1: the fake pilot hat bought by Faranda, the bullets and the body of a bodyguard can be seen on the asphalt of the street just as in Ruggeri and Frajese's report. *Aldo Moro:* President includes both a fictional reconstruction of the aftermath of the attack and a sequence which uses the footage filmed by Ruggeri and Frajese; parallel editing shows both members of the Red Brigades expecting Moro in Via Montalcini, and Moro's family in Via del Forte Trionfale watching Ruggeri and Frajese's reportage on Rete 1. An even more explicit attempt to blur the boundaries between fiction and documentary is made through the juxtaposition of fictional material and factual footage in *Aldo Moro: Professor,* a docudrama combining archival films from the 1970s, overlaid with extracts from the footage filmed by Ruggeri and Frajese, and present-day interviews with Moro's former students and colleagues, as well as with fictional scenes set at La Sapienza, the university were Moro taught law. *Aldo Moro: Professor* thus includes two factual layers provided by the archival footage and the present-day interviews, and a fictional narrative focusing on the relationship between Moro and his students. The sequence dealing with the aftermath of the ambush combines archival material with interviews with Moro's assistant Saverio Fortuna; former students Valter Mainetti and Giorgio Balzoni; and former members of parliament Claudio Signorile and Guido Bodrato. Mainetti and Balzoni both explain that they went to Via Fani upon hearing the news on the radio and saw the bodies of Moro's bodyguards before they could be covered with sheets and thus before Ruggeri and Frajese had filmed their reportage. Balzoni's account is nevertheless juxtaposed with the footage broadcast on TG1 and followed by a segment of the news report where Bruno Vespa reads a message from the Red Brigades in which the terrorist group claims responsibility for the attack.21

The intricacies of the use of fictional scenes in documentaries and that of archival footage in fiction have a significant impact on the ways in which this group of films memorialises the aftermath of the ambush in Via Fani. In all instances filmmakers have tried to approximate the events of that day and provide a narrative of the Moro kidnapping which is based on the available visual evidence, on the traces left behind by the Red Brigades and on the testimonies of bystanders and terrorists. These films have thus drawn upon, or used directly, the imagery which was defined on that day by the frantic scenes broadcast on the public television network and which established Via Fani as a public and highly recognisable battlefield of the Cold War.

VIA MONTALCINI

From the crossroads between Via Fani and Via Stresa, Moro was taken, first in the Fiat 128 and then confined in a wooden box transported by a grey lorry Fiat 850T and later by a Citroën Ami 8, to his cell in the 100-square-foot apartment in Via Camillo Montalcini 8. The apartment had been bought in 1977 by Anna Laura Braghetti, a member of the Red Brigades and, together with *brigatisti* Germano Maccari, Mario Moretti and Prospero Gallinari, one of Moro's captors. The above-mentioned documentary *The Convict: Chronicles of a Kidnapping* includes several photographs of the building and details the characteristics which made Via Montalcini an ideal location for Moro's cell: there was no concierge, no shops or benches in front of the building and, more importantly, there was an internal garage. One of the photographs used in the documentary shows the mark left on the parquet floor of the bedroom by the fake wall of the tiny cell built by Gallinari and Maccari. This is the place where Moro's captors took the Polaroid snapshot which was attached to their first message, known as *comunicato numero uno*, and made public on 19 March. As Sarah P. Hill suggests, this photograph would acquire a highly symbolic meaning: 'The image of a dishevelled Aldo Moro beneath the Red Brigade star is often recalled as the iconic image that comes to mind in relation to that troubled period in Italy's history.'[22] The visual power of this photograph was built on a contrast between a familiar face and an unknown and mysterious place. When the country saw the photograph of Moro on the front page of all national newspapers the location of the cell was only known to the terrorists; today we can inscribe the photograph onto the physical space of that children's bedroom in Via Montalcini, one of the main sites of memory of the kidnapping of Moro and the most important location in *Good Morning, Night*.

Bellocchio's film is largely set in the apartment in Via Montalcini from 16 March to the early morning of 9 May 1978. The use of this private space in *Good Morning, Night* articulates an introspective reading of the events seen through the eyes of Chiara (Maya Sansa), the cinematic alter-ego of Anna Maria Braghetti.[23] Moro and his captors eat, read, pray and sleep in a space grounded in domesticity and in the routine of the kidnapping. With this self-reflexive narrative, as O'Leary suggests, *Good Morning, Night* is not a 'film about the Moro events as such, but about the representational means through which we construct our understanding of such events.'[24] In order to unfold this reflection within the limited space of the apartment, Bellocchio uses the images broadcast on the television set in the living room in order to connect the private space of the apartment to the public experience of the events unravelling in the news reports. The importance of the apartment is revealed in the first sequence of the film; an estate agent shows the first-floor apartment to two of the members of the Red Brigades, Chiara and Ernesto (Pier Giorgio Bellocchio). Ernesto, the cinematic alter-ego of Maccari, identifies and measures the space which will become Aldo Moro's small cell. The following sequence is set on 31 December 1977 and shows Chiara and Ernesto watching a performance from the New Year's Eve television programme *Buon Anno* (*Happy New Year*, Antonello Falqui), originally broadcast live from Teatro Tenda Bussoladomani (Viareggio). This sequence thus anticipates the function of the television set in the narrative of the film.

On the morning of the kidnapping, Chiara hears the noise of helicopters over the city. She turns on the television set and flips between channels; a culture programme on Rete 2 called *Argomenti* (*Topics*) focuses on *Opera dei Pupi*, a marionette tradition of Sicily, while Rete 1 is covering a golf tournament. The news of Moro's kidnapping had already been given by Cesare Palandri on Giornale Radio 2 at 9:25 a.m., and six minutes later on Giornale Radio 1, but it only reaches Chiara at 10:01 a.m., when *Argomenti* is interrupted by a breaking news report where journalist Giancarlo Santalmassi makes the following announcement (Figure 7.2):

> Good morning, the president of Christian Democracy Aldo Moro was the subject of a very serious attack. According to a first agency flash, Aldo Moro has been kidnapped. This has been confirmed by Agenzia Italia and the Home Office. There is talk of a bloody aftermath. There are five victims, all of them bodyguards of the president of the Christian Democrats.[25]

Figure 7.2 The Via Montalcini apartment in *Buongiorno, notte* (*Good Morning, Night*, Marco Bellocchio, 2003).

While the news report on the TV set shows a map of the site of the attack including Via Fani, Via Stresa and Via della Camillucia in the Trionfale district, Moro arrives at the apartment in a box and he is then taken to the cell concealed by a bookshelf-wall. As Gius Gargiulo observes the interior design of the apartment reflects:

> ... the crude symbolic contrasts of Maoist radicalism, according to which the noble and arrogant forms of the bourgeois 'Spirit' are ascribed to the library partition while Moro is hidden in the narrow little cell behind the books not only for practical reasons but also in order to reassert the BR judgment on his politics: that is to say, Moro is viewed as an aberration of the culture displayed on the bookshelf.[26]

This political and physical barrier would only be broken in a dream sequence where Moro leaves the *prigione del popolo* and walks freely in the apartment and in the imaginative final sequence of the film where the politician successfully makes his way out of the apartment.

A few feet away from Moro's cell and opposite the bookshelf, the television set continues to connect the public and the private experience of the kidnapping. The reportage made by Ruggeri and Frajese can be heard in the background and at times seen on the television set placed in the living room. In *Good Morning, Night*, these images are broadcast on television in a manner similar to the ways in which the reportages of the events in Munich were shown on television in the fictional reconstruction of the apartment at 31 Connollystraße in Spielberg's *Munich*. The private space of the apartment is intertwined with the location of the ambush by means of the juxtaposition between the re-enactment of the events in Via Montalcini and the use of factual evidence filtered through a television set placed within the *mise-en-scène*. This narrative device continues in sequences such as that where the four terrorists watch the news reports on the demonstration organised by the unions in Piazza San Giovanni in Laterano in Rome; the television set shows union leader Luciano Lama giving a speech condemning the action of the Red Brigades, and Prime Minister Giulio Andreotti reading a message to the nation later on that day.[27] On 19 March, the first message from the Red Brigades was found in the pedestrian subway between Largo Argentina and Via Arenula in an envelope which also contained the Polaroid photograph of Moro taken in his cell in Via Montalcini. Bellocchio articulates a further juxtaposition between private and public by showing the terrorists watching the news report showing the Polaroid photograph which they took in the very same space from which they follow the events on television. On this occasion, Bellocchio intervenes on the archival footage and replaces the face of real Aldo Moro with that of his actor Roberto Herlizka.

The Moro Affair, *Aldo Moro: President* and *If There Were Light, That Would Be Beautiful* are also partly set in the apartment in Via Montalcini. In these films the cell is considerably larger than the real space where Moro was detained which measured barely 9 × 3 ft. In Grimaldi's film the walls and ceiling of the cell are covered with acoustic soundproof foam while *The Moro Affair* and *Aldo Moro: President* use plaster and wooden panels respectively. In these films, the flag of the Red Brigades, with the five-pointed star and the words 'Brigate Rosse', covers one of the walls. A radically different approach to the representation of *prigione del popolo* is used in *Aldo Moro: Professor*, a film which embraces one of the alternative reconstructions of Moro's captivity. Later investigations have claimed that Moro could have been imprisoned in a building by the sea between Focene and Marina di Palidoro, a possibility suggested by the presence of sand and seawater in the boot of the car where Moro's body was found.[28] *Aldo Moro: Professor* accepts this hypothesis and rejects the idea that Moro spent fifty-four days in Via Montalcini; the film shows the statesman in a considerably larger and brighter prison, with a more comfortable bed and a regular desk (the flag of the Red Brigades covers only a small section of the wall).

While Via Fani and, as I explain in the next section, Via Caetani are public sites of memory of the Moro kidnapping, the apartment in Via Montalcini provides a private and obscure location. News reports and photographs of the ambush and, later, of the discovery of the body have provided a shared memory by recall of the events of that spring; the fiction films discussed in this section, and *Good Morning, Night* in particular, have contributed to establishing a shared and yet contested memory by imagination of the place where Moro spent his captivity. The humble image of Moro in a confined space dominated by the presence of the flag of the Red Brigades is ingrained in a national consciousness as one of the few certainties of an event surrounded by uncertainty, doubts, conspiracy and suspiciousness; *Good Morning, Night* has contextualised the place where the photograph was taken, that domestic space of an apartment connected to the rest of the city by the images broadcast on its television set.

Via Caetani

Aldo Moro's captivity in Via Montalcini ended in the early morning of Tuesday 9 May when he was taken to the garage of the building and was executed, most likely by *brigatisti* Mario Moretti and Germano Maccari.[29] Moro's murder in cold blood is used in the opening sequence of Paolo Sorrentino's *Il Divo* (2008), a biographical film based on the figure of former Prime Minister Giulio Andreotti. *Il Divo* opens with a montage sequence showing the assassination of public figures connected to Andreotti and includes the execution of Moro in the garage of Via Montalcini.[30] Covered with a thick blanket, Moro is lying in the boot of a red Renault 4 when he is killed by a loud round of bullets shot from a machine gun. This dramatised version of the execution serves the purpose of anchoring the assassination to other events which took place in Italy during the Years of Lead and raising questions in regard to the role of the state and the secret services in the fight against terrorism.[31] According to the testimonies given at the trials, Moretti shot Moro with a Walther PPK gun first and then with a Škorpion vz. 61 machine pistol. The use of such weapons in the confined space of a garage has been seen as incongruous and there are inconsistencies in the account of the execution but, regardless of the exact unfolding of the events earlier on that day, the unquestionable fact is that the Renault 4 containing the body of Moro covered by a blanket would be found on that day at around 2:00 p.m. in Via Caetani, in the historic centre of Rome.[32]

At 12:30 p.m., *brigatista* Valerio Morucci called Moro's assistant Francesco Tritto and explained that the body could be found in the boot of a red Renault 4, vehicle registration plate N57686, parked in Via Caetani.[33] Tritto's phone was under police control and the recording of this call has been used widely in the sequences of several films discussed in this chapter in their reconstruction of the events of that day, often in combination with the well-known photograph of the body taken by photojournalist Roland Fava (Figure 7.3). On that day, Fava used the back entrance of Palazzo Caetani and took a photograph of Aldo Moro lying dead in the boot of the Renault 4 from the window of the porter's apartment. The brutality of the image of Moro's contorted corpse embodies the public memory of the epitome of the Years of Lead and belongs to a shared experience of the Moro kidnapping. Fava's picture has thus been associated in the memorialisation of the event with the Polaroid photographs taken by the Red Brigades in Via Montalcini; as Hill argues:

> In their separation from the body but concentrated attention towards the dark square of the Renault's boot, the onlookers seem almost as though they are gazing at another Polaroid, composed and arranged by the Red Brigades for maximum visual impact, ready to be re-photographed and reproduced. Isolated in death as he was in the last 54 days of his life, Moro's body lies elevated as though on an altar towards which the crowd gazes.[34]

In addition to Fava's iconic photograph documentaries and fiction films used archival footage from the news reports broadcast on that day by RAI and by GBR, a local television network whose cameramen arrived in Via Caetani earlier than the reporters of the public broadcaster. In the early afternoon

Figure 7.3 The dead body of Aldo Moro in Via Caetani (Rolando Fava, 9 May 1978).

of that day police cordoned off Via Caetani while a large crowd assembled nearby. The news report on TG1 includes several views of Via Caetani filmed by Paolo Frajese from the building at 40 Via delle Botteghe Oscure and shows a large crowd close to the barricade tape marking the street, a number of police officers and *carabinieri*, and the Renault 4 (Figure 7.4).[35]

As with the portrayal of the ambush in Via Fani, the discovery of the body in Via Caetani has been approached in various ways in fiction and documentary films and on the basis of a meaningful overlaying of archival footage and staged sequences. This hybrid use of factual and fictional material is exemplified in *Romanzo Criminale* (Michele Placido, 2005), a drama inspired by the actions of the criminal organisation Banda della Magliana (Magliana gang) partly set against the background of the Moro kidnapping. *Romanzo Criminale* includes an insert from the footage filmed in Via Caetani on 9 May for TG1 combined with the original recording of the phone call made by Morucci to Tritto in an anachronistic juxtaposition: the phone call was made earlier in the day but it would only be made public in the summer of that year.[36] The non-diegetic insert turns into a diegetic component of the *mise-en-scène* as two characters watch a television set broadcasting the special edition of the TG1 news report while Morucci's voice is replaced by Bruno Vespa's commentary. Anticipated by the recording of Morucci's phone call to Tritto, the abovementioned documentary *The Night of the Republic* uses the footage of police and politicians in Via Caetani filmed by GBR and a close-up

Figure 7.4 TG1 coverage of the discovery of Aldo Moro in Via Caetani (9 May 1978).

of Fava's photograph focusing on Moro's face and upper body. The result is a combination of factual footage and audio filtered through a series of formal devices common to fictional narratives. Both *Romanzo Criminale* and *The Night of the Republic* thus use archival material in order to articulate the narrative of the discovery of the body and they place Via Caetani on the map of Rome in the final stages of the Moro case. *The Moro Affair* also employs the footage taken on that day in Via Caetani and re-enacts Morucci's phone call to Tritto at Termini railway station. The images from the news reports are edited with fictional close-ups of the discovery of the body, the opening of the boot and the removal of the blanket revealing Volonté taking up the same position as Moro in Fava's famous photograph, in a sequence built on archival images and re-enactments. *Aldo Moro: Professor* pushes the juxtaposition of fact and fiction further; archival footage of Moro's body in the boot of the car filmed by GBR from the upper floor of a building on that street is combined with Morucci's phone call, present-day interviews with politicians Marco Follini, Gero Grassi, Guido Bodrato and Giuseppe Fioroni, and Moro's former students Fiammetta Rossi, Giorgio Balzoni and Giuliana Duchini.[37]

During that long live broadcast on Rete 1 later repurposed in these films, news reporter Beppe Barletti also read a message from Holocaust survivor and writer Primo Levi: 'I am terribly upset; upset for this ferocious outcome. And I am angry at the institutions that failed to rescue Moro.'[38] The statement given by the Auschwitz survivor can be read as an articulation of multidirectional memory with power to situate the memory of the Second World War in the context of the Years of Lead and thus provide a sense of historical continuity, of causes and effects, of migration of meanings and memories across the Short Twentieth Century. A similar multidirectional connection with the war emerges from the sequence of *Good Morning, Night* where the letter written by Moro to his wife Eleonora is merged with that of a resistance partisan condemned to death by the fascists and with scenes from Roberto Rossellini's *Paisà* (*Paisan*, 1946). Bellocchio establishes here a connection which is reminiscent of that process of multidirectional memory articulated by Rothberg and which I have discussed in Chapter 5 in relation to the landscapes of Latin America and the Holocaust.[39] As Chiara read the final letter written by Moro to his wife, we hear the voice-over of Roberto Herlitzka reciting these words:

> Be strong, my sweetest, in this absurd and incomprehensible challenge. I would like to understand, through my mortal eyes, how we will be seen afterwards. If there were light, it would be beautiful. My love, keep me with you always and hold me tight.[40]

Herlitzka's voice is overlapped by the voice of actor Fabio Camilli reading a fragment of a letter written by a resistance partisan during the war: 'My love, tomorrow morning at dawn the execution platoon of the fascist republican guard will bring my days to an end.'[41] These words are juxtaposed with a sequence from the 'Porto Tolle' episode of *Paisan* which shows the execution of members of the Resistance at the hands of the fascists; in *Good Morning, Night*, as O'Leary suggests, 'Chiara has come to identify her captive with the partisans and their fate' and Rossellini's *Paisan* is thus used 'to move or to mythologize the struggle against Nazi-Fascism at the end of the Second World War in Italy.'[42]

Later in *Good Morning, Night*, the scene where Moro is taken out of the cell in Via Montalcini on the way to his execution in the garage of the same building is juxtaposed with a fantasy sequence where Chiara helps Moro to escape. While the other terrorists are asleep, he gets out of his cell, puts on his coat and leaves the apartment. Moro can then be seen walking free at dawn in Via Pietro Frattini with Palazzo della Civiltà Italiana visible in the background. The historic Via Caetani is replaced by this suburban street and by an iconic building which, as Alberto Zambenedetti has argued, is 'the most iconographical representation of the relationship between the Fascist dictatorship and modern Italian architecture.'[43] Palazzo della Civiltà Italiana features in a scene from Roberto Rossellini's *Roma città aperta* (*Rome Open City*, 1945) where partisans liberate a group of comrades from the Nazis and, as O'Leary argues, 'Bellocchio no doubt intends the allusion, given the references to the Resistance, and use of clips from the same director's *Paisà* (*Paisan*, 1946), elsewhere in *Buongiorno, notte*.'[44]

Following this train of thought, Dana Renga has suggested that the 'allusions to the finale of *Roma città aperta* in Moro's spectral walk through Rome, cogently align him to the Partisan Resistance.'[45] As Renga explains, in *Good Morning, Night* 'violence is not fictionalized and Moro's death is relegated to off-screen, its aftermath only allowed to creep into the closed quarters of the apartment through the television' which screens archival footage of the memorial service held on 13 May in the Basilica di San Giovanni in Laterano (Archbasilica of Saint John Lateran).[46] Here, as Gius Gargiulo observes, 'Bellocchio exacerbates the dilation of pace in the official news broadcast of RAI by employing the technique of slow-motion' in order to emphasise the 'terse stillness of the politicians who had been unable to save Moro.'[47] The footage of the memorial service re-establishes the actual course of the events and Herlitzka's Moro is seen blindfolded and escorted by the terrorists from the apartment to the garage and in the direction of the camera. And yet, in the final scene of the film, Moro returns to Via Frattini and walks again towards the camera, seemingly at peace. His expression evokes other images; the Polaroid photographs taken in Via Montalcini, Fava's brutal photograph of Moro's body in the boot of the Renault 4, the crowd assembling in Via Caetani on 9 May. It also summons Via Fani and the brutal aftermath of the ambush, the absence of Moro's body, dead or alive, from that scene; in the final scene of *Good Morning, Night*, Moro finally re-emerges alive in Via Frattini and dead in Via Caetani, a ghostly presence haunting Italian politics then and now.

Both the Munich massacre and the kidnapping and assassination of Aldo Moro were given a televised stage with exceptional visibility. The news reports broadcast in September 1972 and in the spring of 1978 would later inform the visuals and the narratives of films which memorialised the two incidents and their aftermath. They also contributed to providing specific topographical coordinates to those events and placed Connollystraße, Fürstenfeldbruck, Via Fani, and Via Caetani on the map of Cold War Europe. While the Munich massacre unfolded across a single day and captured the attention of a world which was following the games, the Moro case was primarily followed by a national audience across a much longer period of time nearing two months. In both instances, the private space of an apartment became a hotspot of the Cold War which was staged in later films where re-enactments are intertwined with the coverage of the events recorded in the news reports. Archival footage and fiction have thus defined how, in the aftermath of these incidents, film has memorialised the atrocities which unfolded in Munich and Rome and articulated complex narratives sprouting from defining images such as that of the hooded terrorist on the balcony of the apartment in Connollystraße or the contorted body of Moro in the boot of a car in Via Caetani. Film has also bridged the gap between the present of these incidents and the past with multidirectional connections to the Olympic Games of 1936 or the Italian Resistance during the Second World War. What happened in Munich and Rome exemplifies the multilayered complexity of the Cold War in a world divided by politics, religion, borders and by an Iron Curtain between East and West, and where the persistence of the past permeated the present and enhanced such divisions. This historical partitioning was also epitomised by the wall which divided East Berlin from West Berlin between the summer of 1961 and the autumn of 1989. Like the Hiroshima Prefectural Industrial Promotion Hall and other buildings discussed so far, the Berlin Wall was a structure where multiple memories, meanings and negotiations converged and, as I explain in the next chapter, a location relentlessly captured in news reports, documentaries and fiction films.

Notes

1. See Giovanni Bianconi, 'Aldo Moro, nella cella del rapimento oggi dormono due bambine', *Il Corriere della Sera*, Milan, 18 March 2018, p. 36.
2. Formed in 1970, the Red Brigades was an Italian far-left armed organisation and guerrilla group responsible for nearly fifty murders, numerous kidnappings, acts of sabotage and robberies during the Years of Lead. The Red Brigades demanded, to no avail, the release of their former leader Renato Curcio and other members of their group detained in Italian prisons, in exchange for Moro's life. See Robert C. Meade, *Red Brigades: The Story of Italian Terrorism*, New York: Springer, 1989.
3. See Ferdinando Imposimato and Sandro Provvisionato, *Doveva morire: Chi ha ucciso Aldo Moro. Il giudice dell'inchiesta racconta*, Milano: Chiarelettere, 2011, pp. 9–31.
4. The location of Moro's cell has been questioned throughout the years and claims have been made that the *prigione del popolo* was not in the apartment in Via Montalcini. Moro's brother, judge Carlo Alfredo Moro, claimed the prison was located at a seaside location by the delta of the river Tiber (see Carlo Alfredo Moro, *Storia di un delitto annunciato*, Roma: Editori Riuniti, 1998).
5. See Roberto Fagiolo, *Topografia del caso Moro. Da via Fani a via Caetani*, Roma: Nutrimenti, 2018.
6. *Carabinieri* are members of Italy's national gendarmerie of the same name.
7. The names of the victims included Oreste Leonardi, Raffaele Iozzino, Francesco Zizzi, Giulio Rivera and Domenico Ricci. While this is the broadly accepted

reconstruction of the attack, its dynamics have long been debated and there is uncertainty about the exact number of terrorists and the identities of those who took part in the action. See Imposimato and Provvisionato, pp. 45–68.

8. *TG2 Edizione Straordinaria: Il Rapimento di Aldo Moro* ('TG2 Breaking News: The Kidnapping of Aldo Moro', 16 March 1978, RAI Rete 2, 57 minutes); *TG1 Edizione Straordinaria: Il Rapimento di Aldo Moro* ('TG1 Breaking News: The Kidnapping of Aldo Moro', 16 March 1978, RAI Rete 1, 87 minutes).
9. In regard to the ambiguities and the many mysteries surrounding the Moro affair, see Imposimato and Provvisionato.
10. Giancarlo Lombardi, 'La passione secondo Marco Bellocchio Gli ultimi giorni di Aldo Moro', *Annali d'Italianistica*, Vol. 25 (Literature, Religion, and the Sacred), 2007, pp. 397–408 (399).
11. Alan O'Leary, 'Locations of Moro: The Kidnap in the Cinema', in *Remembering Aldo Moro: The Cultural Legacy of the 1978 Kidnapping and Murder*, Ruth Glynn and Giancarlo Lombardi (eds), London and Boston: Many Publishing (Legenda), 2012, pp. 151–70 (162).
12. O'Leary, 2012, p. 164.
13. O'Leary, 2012, p. 157.
14. *The Night of the Republic* was a series of eighteen documentaries about the Years of Lead broadcast by Rai 2 between December 1989 and April 1990. The three episodes on the kidnapping of Aldo Moro were broadcast on 21, 28 February and 7 March 1990.
15. Similarly, Vittorio Nevano's documentary *Aldo Moro: 55 Giorni di Passione* (*Aldo Moro: 55 Days of Passion*, 1998) opens with the Via Fani sequence from Ferrara's film.
16. Isabella Pezzini, 'Imago Moro: Medi-a-(c)tion on Aldo Moro', in *Remembering Aldo Moro: The Cultural Legacy of the 1978 Kidnapping and Murder*, Ruth Glynn and Giancarlo Lombardi (eds), London and Boston: Many Publishing (Legenda), 2012, pp. 136–50 (143).
17. Pezzini, p. 144.
18. *TG1 Edizione Straordinaria: Il Rapimento di Aldo Moro* ('TG1 Breaking News: The Kidnapping of Aldo Moro', 16 March 1978, RAI Rete 1, 87 minutes).
19. Among other documentaries, for example, *Les derniers jours d'Aldo Moro* (*The Last Days of Aldo Moro*, Emmanuel Amara, 2006) extensively uses the footage filmed by Ruggeri and Frajese.
20. These circumstances are explained in detail in Zavoli's *The Night of the Republic: the Moro kidnapping*.
21. This sequence also includes footage from the Chamber of Deputies of the Italian Parliament, the place where Giulio Andreotti was introducing a new government which obtained the vast majority of votes and the support of the Communist Party; a 1978 interview with MP Ugo La Malfa, who advocated a return to the death penalty; fictional scenes at the university followed by interviews with Moro's students from an edition of TG1 broadcast on the day after the attack.

22. Sarah P. Hill, 'Double exposures: The photographic afterlives of Pasolini and Moro', *Modern Italy*, Vol. 21 No. 4, 2016, pp. 409–25 (413).
23. *Good Morning, Night* was inspired by the book *Il prigioniero*, written by Moro's captor Braghetti and journalist Paola Tavella (Milano: Mondadori, 1998). The names of the members of the Red Brigades were changed in the film.
24. O'Leary, 2012, p. 159.
25. 'Buongiorno, il presidente della Democrazia Cristiana Aldo Moro è stato oggetto di un gravissimo attentato. Secondo un primo flash d'agenzia, Aldo Moro sarebbe stato sequestrato. Notizia che sarebbestata confermata dall'Agenzia Italia e dal Ministro dell'interno. Si parla di un bilancio sanguinoso di questo attentato. Sarebbero cinque le vittime, tutte della scorta del presidente della Democrazia Cristiana.'
26. Gius Gargiulo, 'Moro, Morucci, Moretti: Oxymoron and the Prison of Political Language', in *Remembering Aldo Moro: The Cultural Legacy of the 1978 Kidnapping and Murder*, pp. 96–106 (99).
27. In a later sequence, Chiara is ironing shirts while the television shows the funerals of the bodyguards killed in Via Fani live from San Lorenzo fuori le Mura (Basilica of Saint Lawrence); the news report includes panning shots of politicians from all parliamentary parties including Sandro Pertini, Ugo La Malfa, Enrico Berlinguer, Giovanni Leone, Benigno Zaccagnini, Guilio Andreotti and Francesco Cossiga. In the following days, the terrorists are both following the news reports on the Moro kidnapping, including the appeal for his liberation read by Pope Paul VI, as well as unrelated news reports such as that about the approval of the Basaglia Mental Health Act. The terrorists also watch television programmes like the variety show *Ma Che Sera*, including a scene where Raffaella Carrà sings and dances to the song *Tango*, and the television adaptation of *Madame Bovary* directed by Daniele D'Anza in that year.
28. See Moro, *Storia di un delitto annunciato*, p. 28.
29. Like most other aspects of the Moro case, the unfolding of his execution has also been the subject of multiple theories and versions.
30. Other victims include journalist Mino Pecorelli, General Carlo Alberto Dalla Chiesa, bankers Michele Sindona and Roberto Calvi.
31. The widely-disputed *strategia della tensione* (strategy of tension) would have seen the Italian state working with, or at least exploiting, far-right and far-left groups in order to isolate Partito Comunista Italiano (Communist Party) and generate support for Christian Democracy (see Mirco Dondi, *L'eco del boato: Storia della strategia della tensione 1965–1974*, Roma: Laterza, 2015).
32. Moro, pp. 28–32.
33. This is the same phone call used in *The Night of the Republic* and discussed earlier in this chapter.
34. Hill, p. 418.
35. *TG1 Edizione Straordinaria: Il Ritrovamento di Aldo Moro* ('TG1 Breaking News: The Discovery of Aldo Moro's Body', 9 May 1978, RAI Rete 1, 220 minutes).

36. This is the same juxtaposition used in *Aldo Moro: President*, where Morucci's phone accompanies the archival footage from Via Caetani.
37. *Aldo Moro: Professor* also uses colour photographs from the report of the Parliamentary inquiry and fictional scenes of Moro's student remembering their professor while walking on a beach by the Roman coast, Castellitto's Moro getting ready to leave his cell and, in the final scene, standing in front of an empty Senate while reading a speech about youth and women which Moro had originally given at Christian Democracy party conference in 1964.
38. 'Ho uno sconforto tremendo, uno sconforto per questa fine feroce. E poi un senso di rabbia per l'innefficenza delle istituzioni nel cercare di rintracciare l'onorevole Moro.' From 'TG1 Breaking News: The Discovery of Aldo Moro's Body'.
39. Rothberg, pp. 5–11
40. 'Sii forte, mia dolcissima, in questa prova assurda e incomprensibile. Vorrei capire, con i miei piccoli occhi mortali, come ci si vedrà dopo. Se ci fosse luce, sarebbe bellissimo. Amore mio, sentimi sempre con te e tienmi stretto.'
41. 'Amore mio, domattina all'alba il plotone d'esecuzione della Guardia Repubblicana Fascista metterà fine ai miei giorni.' From Pietro Malvezzi and Giovanni Pirelli, *Lettere di condannati a morte della Resistenza italiana (8 Settembre 1943–25 Aprile 1945)*, Milano: Mondadori, 1968.
42. O'Leary, 2008, p. 42.
43. Alberto Zambenedetti, 'Filming in Stone: Palazzo Della Civiltà Italiana and Fascist Signification in Cinema', *Annali D'Italianistica*, Vol. 28, 2010, pp. 199–215 (199). See also: Giacomo Lichtner, '"Io so": the absence of resolution as resolution in contemporary Italian cinema about the Years of Lead', Modern Italy, Vol. 22, No. 2, 2017, pp. 167–181.
44. Alan O'Leary, 'Dead Man Walking: The Aldo Moro kidnap and Palimpsest History in *Buongiorno, notte*', *New Cinemas: Journal of Contemporary Film*, Vol. 6, No. 1, 2008, pp. 33–45 (39).
45. Dana Renga, 'Moro Martyred, Braghetti Betrayed: History Retold in *Buongiorno, notte*', in *Terrorism, Italian Style: Representations of Political Violence in Contemporary Italian Cinema*, Ruth Glynn, Giancarlo Lombardi and Alan O'Leary (eds). London: IGRS Books, 2012, pp. 175–91 (189).
46. Renga, p. 189.
47. Gargiulo, pp. 98–99.

CHAPTER 8

Bornholmer Straße, East Berlin, GDR, 9 November 1989, 11:30 p.m.

> *As the barrier is raised at one of the crossings, over 20,000 people walk on a bridge and make their way to the other side of the border. These men and women are citizens of the soon-to-disappear German Democratic Republic and this happens on the night of 9 November 1989 in Berlin.*

Eight years after the fall of the Wall, Andreas Huyssen described the city centre of Berlin as the 'threshold between the Eastern and Western parts of the city, the space that now, in yet another layer of signification, seemed to be called upon to represent the invisible Wall in the head that still separated East and West Germans [...].'[1] Wolfgang Becker's *Good Bye, Lenin!* (2003) reflects upon the division which continued to linger in Berlin after the fall of the Wall and places its narrative firmly into the contested space of the city. The film opens with footage from a fictional home movie set in the summer of 1978 and showing a young boy and a young girl playing outdoors near a dacha located somewhere in the Deutsche Demokratische Republik.[2] These images are followed by footage of the boy wearing a T-shirt with a print celebrating the Soviet space programme *Interkosmos* and standing in a public space in East Berlin, with the Berliner Fernsehturm (Berlin Television Tower) in the background. East Berlin is explored further in the credits sequence, a montage of postcards from the 1980s showing iconic buildings including the Palast der Republik (Palace of the Republic, 1973–6), the Weltzeituhr (World Clock, 1969), the Brunnen der Völkerfreundschaft (Fountain of International Friendship, 1970), and the Haus des Lehrers (House of the teacher, 1962–4) in Alexanderplatz. Other vintage postcards show the granite statue of Vladimir Lenin created in 1970 by Nikolai Tomski and located in Leninplatz (today Platz der Vereinten Nationen, United Nations Square), Strausberger Platz in the district of Friedrichshain-Kreuzberg, Café Moskau (1961–4) and Kino International (1963), respectively at 34 and 33 Karl-Marx-Allee. The image of these buildings places the narrative of *Good Bye, Lenin!* in the East Berlin of the years leading to the fall of the Berlin Wall and the end of the Cold War. This is a location which has prominently been associated with spy films but Western filmmakers were regularly barred from the GDR and, as I explain later in this chapter, West Berlin was often made to play the role of the other sector of the divided city.

Filmed well after the end of the Cold War, the espionage thriller *Atomic Blonde* (David Leitch, 2017) makes accurate topographical use of East Berlin locations in a story set during the days leading to the fall of the Wall on 9 November 1989. Based on Antony Johnston's graphic novel *The Coldest City* (2012), *Atomic Blonde* follows MI6 field agent Lorraine Broughton (Charlize Theron) in her quest for a list of double agents who are being smuggled into the West in the final stages of the Cold War. Largely set in both East and West Berlin, *Atomic Blonde* is punctuated by the news reports from autumn 1989 announcing the escalation of the demonstrations in East Berlin and eventually the opening of the border between the two parts of the city. Staged scenes set near the Wall in locations such as the neoclassical Brandenburger Tor (Brandenburg Gate) or the streets of the Kreuzberg district are juxtaposed with news reports including the iconic images of the crowds of East and West Berliners climbing the Wall and celebrating its demise. Akin to the ways in which the news reports of the Munich massacre and of the kidnapping of Aldo Moro are used in *Munich* and *Good Morning, Night*, footage of the fall of the Wall is played on television sets placed within the *mise-en-scène* in the hotel room occupied by agent Broughton. *Atomic Blonde* thus articulates that particular intertwining of archival material and re-enactments which has been discussed in the previous chapters.

In a long sequence set in East Berlin and filmed in the same locations displayed in the postcards in the montage credit sequence of *Good Bye, Lenin!*, Broughton walks from Alexanderplatz to Kino International at 33 Karl-Marx-Allee and, in order to shake off the KGB agents who are chasing her, she enters the cinema during a screening of Сталкер (*Stalker*, 1979, Andrei Tarkovsky). The canopy at the entrance of the cinema on the Karl-Marx-Allee and a number of posters just outside the building advertise the screening of Tarkovsky's film while a second canopy and a smaller group of posters in the hall of the cinema promote the premiere of the East German film *Coming Out* (Heiner Carow, 1989), which was scheduled for the evening of 9 November. While *Stalker* had been released in the GDR in 1981 and its widely-advertised screening in the autumn of 1989 is implausible, the date of the première of *Coming Out* at Kino International is accurate. Carow's film deals with a high school teacher (Matthias Freihof) in the process of accepting his homosexuality and it was the first and only LGBT-themed film made in the GDR. The opening sequence of *Coming Out* follows an ambulance driving in the East-Berlin districts of Prenzlauer Berg, Mitte and Friedrichshain, and reveals snapshots of a city which will soon experience the most radical transformation. During the premiere of *Coming Out* in the cinema on the Karl-Marx-Allee, East

German guards let a small group of people leave for West Berlin through the border crossing in Bornholmer Straße. By the time the screening of *Coming Out* was over, 20,000 people had gathered in Bornholmer Straße and crossed the Bösebrücke after the authorities decided to raise the barriers; controls would be lifted at the other border crossings later in the night and other large crowds of East Germans would spill into West Berlin.

Set against this background, *Atomic Blonde* contains opening credits accompanied by Ronald Reagan's voice stating that 'East and West do not mistrust each other because we are armed; we are armed because we mistrust each other.' The credits cut to television footage of Reagan's speech at the Brandenburg Gate on 12 June 1987 with the President of the United States declaring: 'Mr. Gorbachev, tear down this Wall!' This is followed by a title card reading: 'In November 1989, after 28 years, the Berlin Wall came down and the Cold War ended.' Graffiti graphics are sprayed over those words and a large stamp suddenly appearing over the words on the title card reads 'This is not that story.' This chapter is not about that story either; it is about the Wall and the world which existed until that precise moment in time. And it is about the ways in which news reports, documentaries and fiction films have projected the image of that Wall into public consciousness by means of recurring tropes such as tunnels, barbed wire entanglements, bricked-up windows, watchtowers and graffiti. During its existence, the Wall was a reflection of the present of a divided country and at the same time the mirroring of the history of Germany in the twentieth century. As Brian Ladd explains:

> The Wall became an unintentional monument to the remarkable era in which two rival states simultaneously claimed Berlin. The division marked by the Wall, in turn, grew out of the shattering era of German history that culminated in World War II. Thus the Wall was built – literally and figuratively – atop the ruins of war, terror, and division. And it, too, is now among the ruins and memories of Berlin. The Wall – from concrete, to monument, to rubble – gives form to the story of Berlin and of Germany in our time.[3]

Exemplified by what Ladd calls an unintentional monument, the making of East and West Berlin during the Cold War is based on discursive strategies which, as Philip Broadbent and Sabine Hake have argued, include 'the legacy of the Weimar Republic and the Third Reich, the clash between tradition and modernity, the interplay of representation and perception, the dynamics of remembering and forgetting, and the construction of sameness and difference.'[4] The cinematic image of Cold War Berlin is also based on interconnected elements where past and present, memorialisation and destruction, oppression and freedom wrestle one another. The Wall which was built in the summer of 1961 embodies the discursive contradictions of Berlin; each of the sites torn apart by the Wall tells a complex history and, through film, these places have been used to articulate a reflection on the division of the city. Film thus mirrors the significance of the Wall to the fabric of Berlin through multiple narratives of espionage and escape; in this chapter I propose a site-specific reading of this process by exploring three Berlin locations which were swallowed up in the building of the Wall. Bernauer Straße, Potsdamer Platz and Friedrichstraße are the focus of my inquiry into the making of Cold War Berlin in film.

Bernauer Straße

In the night between Saturday 12 and Sunday 13 August 1961 East German military personnel and workers began to install barbed wire and fences around the entire perimeter of the French, British and American sectors of Berlin. Three days later, BBC TV (later BBC One) broadcast a news report including an item titled 'The Berlin boundary is sealed' where journalist Peter Woods witnessed and reported on the sealing of the border between East and West Berlin.[5] Various shots included in this story were filmed at the crossroads between Bernauer Straße and Schwedter Straße, in the Mitte district, and showed concrete blocks topped with barbed wire, border guards and bemused bystanders. Factual footage filmed by television troops in those days has been used widely in later fiction films. For example, *Escape from East Berlin* (Robert Siodmak, 1962) opens with shots of fence and barbed wire entanglement which was to develop into the Berlin Wall at the junction between Niederkirchnerstraße and Wilhelmstraße in Mitte. Twenty years later, *Night Crossing* (Delbert Mann, 1982), a drama about two men planning to escape from the GDR in a hot air balloon, would open with archival footage and photographs, including that of border guard Konrad Schumann jumping over barbed wire at the corner between Ruppiner Straße and Bernauer Straße on 15 August 1961.[6] Other films have avoided the use of archival footage and have staged re-enactments of the days which saw the building of the Wall. The chaotic urban scenes which accompanied the closing of the border were recreated in a short scene from *Berlin Tunnel 21* (Richard Michaels, 1981) and, in more detail, in a long sequence from *Bridge of Spies* (Steven Spielberg, 2015).

Spielberg's film is based on the real Cold War story of the negotiation between the United States, East Germany and the Soviet Union for the release of American pilot Francis Gary Powers (Austin Stowell) and student Frederic Pryor (Will Rogers), from a Russian and an East German prison respectively, in exchange for the release of Soviet spy Rudolf Abel (Mark Rylance). Lawyer James B. Donovan (Tom Hanks) travels to Berlin at the time when the border is being built and the film contains various scenes set in what was about to become the Berlin Wall. One of these scenes includes a tracking shot following Pryor cycling along the barbed wire barrier under the watchful eye of the East German police. This scene includes a re-enactment of the well-known footage of people escaping through the window of an apartment in Bernauer Straße and shots of the bricked-up windows of the buildings between East and West Berlin.

Fiction films such as *Bridge of Spies* have either used footage from news reports or created dramatic re-enactments in order to capture the events of a defining day in the history of the city with profound ramifications for world history. They have used the chaos, the absurdity and the disbelief of the days which saw the fences and barbed wire entanglements slowly being transformed into a deadly fortress subverting the urban fabric of the city. In few places has this process unfolded in a manner as unsettling and unnerving as in Bernauer Straße, a street where the windows were first bricked-up, and then the entire buildings demolished; beneath the road and pavement, tunnels were dug in several attempts to escape from the GDR. The evisceration of Bernauer Straße emerges clearly from documentaries and fiction films set and shot on location. The Berlin Wall ran along the East Berlin apartment blocks in Bernauer Straße but the street itself was located in the West. Before their windows were bricked up by the GDR border patrols, men and women tried to escape, sometimes successfully, by jumping from the building onto the street. The bricked-up windows eventually became one of the most evocative tropes of the divided city and were shown to the world in various news reports. A *Panorama* report broadcast by BBC TV on 30 October 1961 includes several shots of the bricked-up windows of Bernauer Straße; this footage revealed to the viewers the extent of the escalation of the Cold War in Berlin as it was embedded in the buildings of the street.[7] Similarly, the risky escapes from the windows of the apartment blocks were filmed for news reports and repurposed in later films. The opening sequence of *Escape from East Berlin*, for instance, includes footage of a man jumping from one of the windows and this image sets the claustrophobic atmosphere of the film and captures in one shot the theme implied by the title of the film.[8] *Funeral in Berlin* (Guy Hamilton, 1966) also included shots of the surviving bricked-up windows on the southern side of Bernauer Straße in a credit sequence including a panning shot revealing the façades of buildings which would soon be torn down (Figure 8.1).

Panorama, *Escape from East Berlin* and *Funeral in Berlin* capture a highly evocative location and take the viewer to a place where the significance of the Berlin Wall emerged from its devastating impact on the built environment of the city. Hope M. Harrison provides a vivid description of the ways in which the Wall tore apart the urban fabric of Bernauer Straße:

Figure 8.1 Bricked-up windows of Bernauer Straße in *Funeral in Berlin* (Guy Hamilton, 1966).

The end of Bernauer Straße, just two blocks from the parish centre, was closed off by the Wall on the two sides, making the area feel particularly isolated. In the first days after the border was sealed, some of the residents jumped from their houses on the eastern side of the street to freedom on the western side. Residents on the western side would help build tunnels in the following years to assist others in escaping from the East. The houses on the eastern side of the street were evacuated, walled up, and eventually demolished. Bernauer Straße was not a happy place to live. With scant optimism about the future of the area, many people resorted to alcohol and drug use.[9]

This account contextualises the footage used in *Panorama*, *Escape from East Berlin* and *Funeral in Berlin* and the complexities of the ways in which the division of the city affected this area. One of the symbols of resistance, capitulation and resurgence in the divided city was the parish centre mentioned by Harrison in the above quotation, the Versöhnungskirche (Church of Reconciliation, 1894) in Bernauer Straße. In 1945 this building found itself in the Soviet sector and, after the Wall was constructed, in the death strip between the eastern and the western sections of the Wall. Border guards used the church's bell tower as an observation post and the building was eventually demolished in 1985. Ten years after the fall of the Wall, the Kapelle der Versöhnung (Chapel of Reconciliation) was built on the same site. In the documentary *Behind the Wall* (Michael Patrick Kelly, 2011), Pastor Manfred Fischer, who served at the Church of Reconciliation from the late 1970s, gives his account of the demolition of the church accompanied by archival footage of the moment when the tower was made to collapse on the death strip.[10] His testimony contributes to anchoring the images of the demolition of the church tower to an individual experience of the disaggregation of the urban fabric of Bernauer Straße, an experience which repeated itself with infinite variations along the 87-mile long border around West Berlin.

Beside the Church of Reconciliation, other significant locations of Bernauer Straße were to be found not at street level but rather below its pavements. Once the windows of its buildings were bricked up, East Berliners tried to escape through tunnels leading from the privileged location of Bernauer Straße into West Berlin. The two most successful escape plans saw a number of men and women crawling through tunnels dug under Bernauer Straße in 1962 and 1964. On 14 September 1962, twenty-six people crawled 140 yards from 7 Schönholzer Straße, a side street of Bernauer Straße, to West Berlin with the help of students Luigi Spina, Domenico Sesta and Wolf Schroedtere.[11] Loosely based on this escape, *Der Tunnel* (*The Tunnel*, Roland Suso Richter, 2001) is a television drama set in 1961 and following a group of men and women digging a tunnel under the Wall. The film also includes a sequence mirroring the assassination of eighteen-year-old Peter Fechter and shows one of the main characters being shot and left to die by the East German border guards as he tries to cross the barbed wire and fences near Bernauer Straße.[12] Incidents like the killing of Fechter brought East Berliners to seek alternative escape routes including the tunnels under Bernauer Straße. The escape which inspired *The Tunnel* had already been the subject of a documentary of the same title, *The Tunnel* (Reuven Frank, 1962). In this film, the voice-over narration introduces the viewer to the urban fabric of Bernauer Straße:

> Above them, Bernauer Straße. The building they were digging from was a factory, one of West Berlin's half-ruins damaged by World War II bombings, but still used; used in fact for the manufacture of plastic swizzle sticks for cocktails. This window was directly above the tunnel opening. It fronted on Bernauer Straße, one of West Berlin's best-known streets. Bernauer Straße is famous among tourists and television audiences because the eastern sidewalk is still West Berlin. East Berlin starts at the building line on the right. In this street, which is barely a mile long, the communist authorities evacuated two thousand people and bricked up fifty doorways and thirteen hundred windows. The western side is the main street of West Berlin's principal working-class district Wedding. On a Sunday morning, the factory workers who lived hereabouts are

> out in force and leisure, crowding the western sidewalk. But the eastern sidewalk is blighted by the Wall. The grass rose among the cobbles because no one from the neighbourhood walks here, even on Sunday.

These words accompany shots of Bernauer Straße and anticipate scenes showing the actual digging of the tunnel, which was filmed exclusively by the NBC network in exchange for their financial contribution to the project.

Two years later Bernauer Straße witnessed an even more successful underground escape from East Berlin. In October 1964, fifty-seven citizens of the GDR escaped through a tunnel under the Berlin Wall dug by students from West Berlin from an abandoned bakery in the West-Berlin side of 97 Bernauer Straße to a dilapidated building at 55 Strelitzer Straße. This escape has been the subject of several documentaries including *Beyond the Wall* (Mark Byrne and Rob Dennis, 2010) and *The Secret Life of the Berlin Wall* (Kevin Sim, 2009). The former includes interviews with escape organiser Ralph Kabisch, combined with black and white photographs showing the digging of the tunnel and the arrival of the escapees at the abandoned bakery in West Berlin. The latter includes archival footage and an interview with Wolfgang Kockrow, another organiser of the escape. The camera follows Kockrow to the site of the tunnel from Bernauer Straße to Strelitzer Straße. An archival photograph of the area is juxtaposed with a present-day panoramic view of the same place revealing that the old buildings of Bernauer Straße and Strelitzer Straße have long been demolished. This juxtaposition testifies to a new absence on the map of Berlin, the void left by the Wall and the monumentalisation of its sparse remains. Witnesses like Kockrow place site-specific memories on the map of the shifting topography of Berlin at the time when tunnels have long been filled and borders dismantled.

The Wall at Bernauer Straße stood for the whole Wall and, as Gerd Knischewski and Ulla Spittler have argued, it could be read as a 'symbol of the inherent systemic weakness of the GDR, which was only able to survive through repression, imprisonment and the abuse of the human rights of its citizens' and 'as a constant reminder of the "unnaturalness" of the division of Germany.'[13] The Bernauer Straße sequences of the films discussed in this section embody the fluctuating and wavering nature of the built environment of Berlin as the Wall dislodged its people and tore apart its buildings. Tunnels were dug under the street while the dilapidated apartment blocks were turned into the Wall itself and church towers became watchtowers; eventually apartment blocks and churches were demolished in order to give way to an increasingly impenetrable barrier. The buildings were engulfed by a death strip constantly patrolled by border guards and saturated with what became filmic tropes of the Berlin Wall, including barbed wire entanglements, electric fences, watchtowers, tank barriers, guard dogs and gun emplacements. The widest point of this infamous death strip occupied the area which had once been known as the most lively and exciting square in Berlin, Potsdamer Platz.

POTSDAMER PLATZ

An American newsreel released by Castle Films in the 1930s and titled *Beauty and Berlin* contains a sequence introduced by the following text on a title card: 'In New York it's Times Square, in Berlin Potsdamer Platz is the centre of everything.'[14] This footage shows the bustling crowds, the lively shops, the electric cars and trams in the square located next to the Tiergarten. As revealed in *Beauty and Berlin*, before the Second World War, Potsdamer Platz was one of the liveliest places in Berlin, with department stores, cafés, including the famous Café Josty, and the iconic modernist office and shopping building called Columbushaus (Columbus House). As Brian Ladd suggests, in the interwar period the square 'came to symbolize above all the bustle, speed and motion of the modern metropolis.'[15] Located near the Reich Chancellery, Potsdamer Platz would be devastated during the Allied air raids on the city. After the war, the American, British and Soviet Occupation Zones would converge in Potsdamer Platz and, from 1961, the square would be divided into two parts by the Berlin Wall. These events turned the once bustling and lively square into an urban void or, as Ladd suggests, a 'significant void' whose 'significance can only be recovered through memory and history.'[16] Film has ultimately captured the square divided by the Wall in a manner that illustrates Ladd's claim that Potsdamer Platz is 'one of those Berlin places notable for what is not there.'[17]

The absence of Potsdamer Platz from the map of Berlin in the years of the Wall has been captured in films shot in its proximity and using this space as the epitome of the divided city. As Simon Ward suggests, film has played a pivotal role in evoking the significance of the dismembered square and the meaning embedded in its name even after the obliteration of its buildings:

> The physical state of the square before 1989 was that of a remnant of the end of the Second World War and its outcome: the bombing and the division of Berlin into four sectors, and the building of the Berlin Wall. The ongoing ruinous condition of Potsdamer Platz was directly linked to the low exchange value of the site, cut off from circulation of goods and commodities. Ironically, precisely that ruinous condition made possible a number of scenes set in the walled-in wilderness in Wim Wenders' 1987 film *Wings of Desire* (*Der Himmel über Berlin*) which demonstrated, however, that the invocatory power of the name had far from disappeared.[18]

Wings of Desire affirms the power embedded in the name of Potsdamer Platz and articulates that process of recovering the significance of the place to the memory and history of Berlin evoked by Ladd in the quotations above. This process unfolds in a sequence where an angel named Cassiel (Otto Sander) follows Homer (Curt Bois), an elderly poet, to the empty space of what used to be Potsdamer Platz.[19] On the ground of this personal and public site of memory Homer searches in vain for Café Josty, for the Loeser & Wolff tobacconist and the Wertheim department store but all he can find is rubble, trash and weeds;[20] the old man knows he is in the right place and yet he cannot make sense of the discrepancy between his memories and reality. As Jonathan Bordo suggests, in this sequence the character of Homer bears witness to the tragic history of Berlin in the twentieth century:

> [Wim Wenders] mobilizes the forces that Potsdamer Platz holds as a site of over-determined, ferocious history by injecting a dynamic narrative element in the figure of the storyteller named Homer. This storyteller is not an invention out of the blue. Wenders' Homer is the agent of the film's function as a document of Berlin.[21]

Beyond the narrative of the film, actor Curt Bois himself functioned as a document of Berlin or as the embodiment of a site of memory; as Wenders explained the actor mirrored the role of its character:

> Working with old Curt Bois, we filmed in Potsdamer Platz on a Sunday morning near the Wall and under the tracks of the M-Bahn, which was still in function there at that time. There was no one there. It was an urban desert, a steppe, a no man's land. The sun was shining, but it was still cold. Curt loved to joke. It made us all laugh. And he told us about the old square through which he had driven in his youth in his car.[22]

The Potsdamer Platz sequence begins with a long shot of Cassiel and Homer walking between the Wall and the elevated tracks of Magnet-Bahn (Figure 8.2). Tracking shots follow them as they walk along the Wall and then turn left towards the M-Bahn; the Television Tower in Alexander Platz can now be seen across the Wall; the angel follows Homer as he walks under the tracks through the weeds and to an abandoned armchair on which he sits and rests. This sequence also contains colour archival footage of the bombed out buildings of Berlin from the 1940s and these images, which are in stark contrast with the black and white footage filmed by Wenders, are used as a point-of-view reverse shot of what Homer is seeing as his tired eyes desperately seek the familiar buildings of Potsdamer Platz. Cassiel can hear the thoughts of the poet, his attempt to recover the significance of the square through recollection and by reviving history:

Bornholmer Straße, East Berlin 169

Figure 8.2 Cassiel and Homer in Potsdamer Platz in *Der Himmel über Berlin* (*Wings of Desire*, Wim Wenders, 1987).

> I cannot find Potsdamer Platz. Here? This cannot be it! Potdamer Platz; Café Josty used to be there. In the afternoons, I went there to chat and to drink a coffee, and to watch the crowd. Before that I would smoke my cigar at Loeser & Wolff, a renowned tobacconist just across the street. So this cannot be Potsdamer Platz. No. And there is no one to whom you can ask. It was a lively place, trams, horse-drawn carriages and two cars, mine and that of the chocolate shop. The Wertheim department store was here too. And then, suddenly, the flags appeared. The whole square was covered with them and the people were not friendly anymore, and neither were the police. I am not giving up until I find Potsdamer Platz.[23]

In this sequence, Homer the poet evokes the legacy of the Weimar Republic and the Third Reich and does not merely bear witness; he places himself as part of the hubbub of Potsdamer Platz and thus acts as a historian in the traditional sense described by Pierre Nora as 'the spokesman of the past and the herald of the future' but also as a new type of historian who has become, as a result of memory being engulfed by history, 'no longer a memory individual but, in himself, a *lieu de memoir*' (1989: 18).[24]

The history and memory of Potsdamer Platz as it emerges from this sequence in *Wings of Desire* can also be discerned from news reports filmed in this location and broadcast at the time of the building of the Wall. On 31 July 1961, BBC TV broadcast an episode of *Panorama* where Richard Dimbleby visited a number of Berlin locations in the dramatic days leading to the construction of the Wall.[25] A sequence filmed in Potsdamer Platz sees Dimbleby interviewing a family of four from West Berlin and asking them about the history of the square; Dimbleby revives memory by showing the interviewees and the viewers a photograph of a bustling Potsdamer Platz taken in 1935 from the building of Café Josty. This image is juxtaposed with a long shot of the empty square taken in 1961; *Panorama* uses that type of juxtaposition which, as we have already seen, would later characterise documentaries such as *The Secret Life of the Berlin Wall*, with its use of present-day and archival images of Bernauer Straße. This sequence also mirrors the quest for Potsdamer Platz seen in *Wings of Desire* and anticipates the overlaying of the image of the dilapidated square and the intact memories evoked by Homer. A few months after the broadcast of that BBC report, on 30 October 1961, a story from *Panorama* mentioned earlier in this chapter returned to Berlin and saw Robin Day visiting key locations along the Wall: Checkpoint Charlie, the Soviet War Memorial in the Tiergarten, the Brandenburg Gate, Bernauer Straße and, again, Potsdamer Platz (Figure 8.3). Day mentions the episode of Panorama broadcast in the summer and gives an account of the way in which Potsdamer Platz has gone through a further transformation, divided by the Wall and in the process of becoming a section of the death strip between the two concrete parallel walls isolating West Berlin. As Howard Caygill observes, Potsdamer Platz 'was once the main place to be seen in Berlin' but during the Cold War it 'became the place where to be seen meant death.'[26] As Caygill continues, the square 'took up its role as a memorial landscape combining architectural and political symbolism, but this time featuring as the front line of the global Cold War.'[27] *Panorama* captured this event with two reports documenting the ways in which the building of the Wall tore apart Potsdamer Platz and anticipating how a later fiction film such as *Wings of Desire* would use the square as an embodiment of the divided city.

With narratives migrating from novels to the screen by means of adaptation, spy films have made a particularly meaningful use of Potsdamer Platz as a site of memory.[28] Cold-War Berlin, as Oliver Buckton suggests, came to symbolise the political division of Europe and became 'a popular setting for Spy fiction, especially after the building of the Berlin Wall in 1961, which provided a physical barrier reflecting the abstract "Iron Curtain" separating Eastern from Western Europe.'[29] Trapped between the two concrete walls, the void of Potsdamer Platz embodied the physical and abstract barrier evoked by Buckton and was used as a location in *Funeral in Berlin* and in the

Figure 8.3 Robin Day in a *Panorama* report (BBC TV, 30 October 1961).

Granada television series *Game, Set and Match* (Ken Grieve and Patrick Lau, 1988), two adaptations from Len Deighton's novel and trilogy of the same title.[30] *Funeral in Berlin* opens with a panoramic view of the Europa-Center building (1965) and the Kaiser-Wilhelm-Gedächtniskirche (Kaiser Wilhelm Memorial Church) on Breitscheidplatz in the Charlottenburg district of West Berlin. This is followed by lively street scenes along Kurfürstendamm, with men and women going to work or sitting outdoors at local cafés.[31] Non-diegetic instrumental music ends and is replaced by silence as the film cuts to a panoramic view of the empty space, the barbed wire, warning signs and the watchtowers of what used to be Potsdamer Platz. A panoramic shot shows the back entrance of the building of the *Neue Zeit*, official organ of the Christian Democratic Union of the GDR, on Zimmerstraße (Mitte) looking east along that street from the junction with Friedrichstraße near Checkpoint Charlie; a group of people stand on a platform on the western side of the Wall and observe the crumbling buildings of East Berlin next to the Wall. Opening credits begin to run on this shot as the instrumental music returns; a staged shot of East German guards looking towards West Berlin is followed by a panoramic tracking shot returning to the death strip of Potsdamer Platz. A mere four years after the sealing of the border, *Funeral in Berlin* thus captures the division of the city, a reflection of the global opposition between East and West, between Capitalism and Communism; the Wall itself is here a *topoi* where change through time is embedded in its function and in its contribution to the deterioration of the urban fabric of Berlin.

Game, Set and Match focuses on Bernard Samson (Ian Holm), formerly an MI6 field agent based in West Berlin who, following the loss of a member of his team, works behind a desk in the London MI6 headquarters. In the first episode of the series, *Berlin Game: Part One*, Samson is instructing four young recruits and showing them footage of the construction of the Wall while implying he was sent to East Berlin on the night when its creation was commenced by the GDR. The training session is interrupted by a senior colleague and Samson is eventually left to reflect upon his time in the city; while he is still watching the footage of Berlin projected on the Wall of the room, a long flashback takes him back in time. A series of close-up shots of Samson's face are edited with a tilting shot of the graffiti on the western side of the Wall revealing the empty space of Potsdamer Platz with a panoramic shot reminiscent of the opening sequence of *Funeral in Berlin*. These shots are also redolent of the opening scene of *Octopussy* (John Glen, 1983), the thirteenth film in the James Bond series, with its tilting shot of the Wall filmed from West Berlin and looking at the watchtower in the section of Potsdamer Platz engulfed by the death strip. A second shot from *Game, Set and Match* zooms out from a detail of a mural painting on the same side of the Wall and shows again the death strip with St-Michael-Kirche (St Michael's Church) in Mitte in the background. Samson's internal monologue accompanies these images and explains the importance of the Berlin Wall to his own personal story: 'My whole life has been shredded from the last time I crossed the Wall.' The Berlin Wall and its border crossings had a significant impact on spy films and shredded the lives of innumerable real or fictional spies. The threatening emptiness of what used to be the lively Potsdamer Platz seen in 1930s newsreels such as *Beauty and Berlin* has been a recurring presence in later spy films; the void which had replaced the square has been revealed through montage as in *Funeral in Berlin* or with tilting shots like in *Game, Set and Match* and *Octopussy*. Potsdamer Platz has emerged as a site of memory whose destruction has been recorded as it happened in a variety of visual records, ranging from the BBC reports to celebrated adaptations of spy stories. Another location on the map of the divided city has played in reality and in fiction an equally significant role in the making of Cold War Berlin: a checkpoint nicknamed Charlie located on Friedrichstraße.

FRIEDRICHSTRAßE

Sonnenallee, a street connecting the districts of Neukölln and Treptow-Köpenick, was one of eight border crossings placed in the section of the Wall between East and West Berlin. In *Sonnenallee* (Leander Haußmann, 1999), this location is used as the background of a comedy looking back with nostalgia at the youth culture of East Berlin in the 1970s.[32] *Sonnenallee* is set at a border crossing which has otherwise largely been ignored in film; yet it adopts an entirely creative topographical approach to location and transforms a suburban area into an inner district of East Berlin with older buildings and more densely populated than the real district of Sonnenallee. Most documentaries, news reports and fiction films have instead focused on the border crossing located at the junction of Friedrichstraße with Zimmerstraße and Mauerstraße and called by the Western Allies Checkpoint Charlie (or Checkpoint C). This border crossing, simply named after Friedrichstraße on the eastern side, was located between Kreuzberg and Mitte and could be crossed by GDR citizens, foreigners, diplomats, and military personnel.

The checkpoint and the section of the Wall at Friedrichstraße have embodied the imagery of the divided city and the nature of the politicisation of the built environment of Berlin. As Brian Ladd explains, the public spaces of Berlin have been 'politicized in the extreme, and undisputed monuments are the exception' and 'recall controversial deeds, mostly of the recent past, deeds that prevent any consensus about the sort of things monuments are supposed to embody, such as national identity or a common ideal.'[33] Checkpoint Charlie was monumentalised and turned into a tourist attraction even before the fall of the Berlin Wall, and its imagery was defined by multiple appearances in spy films. As Ladd has argued, 'crossing into East Berlin represented a journey far greater than the short distance across the street' and Checkpoint Charlie thus 'became associated with mystery and intrigue, a reputation enhanced by dozens of spy novels.'[34] Similarly, spy films have made consistent use of this location on Friedrichstraße both through re-enactments there and staged in studio or elsewhere and by means of location shooting from the western side of the border.

Checkpoint Charlie was loosely recreated on set for the James Bond spoof *Casino Royale* (Ken Hughes, 1967) in a scene where villain Le Chiffre (Orson Welles) succeeds in creating an escape route in the Berlin Wall by blowing up a telephone booth near the border crossing; dozens of East Berliners and border guards are shown spilling into a vague version of Friedrichstraße. An adaptation of John le Carré's novel of the same title (1963), *The Spy Who Came in from the Cold* (Martin Ritt, 1965) uses a replica of Checkpoint Charlie and its iconic sign reading 'You are leaving the American sector' which was built next to the Jameson Distillery Chimney tower of Dublin's Smithfield Market, located on the north of the River Liffey and back in the 1960s a place still lined with yards housing livestock (Figure 8.4).[35] In the opening sequence of the film, Leamas (Richard Burton) is waiting at the checkpoint for one of his East German double agents to cross over to West Berlin. The MI6 agent is standing in the American booth and then walking nervously on the pavement of a vague replica of Friedrichstraße built in Smithfield Market. His agent makes it past the booth on the Eastern side but is then shot and killed while trying to reach safety on his bicycle. More recently, Checkpoint Charlie has also been recreated for *Bridge of Spies* and used as a location in the scene where Frederic Pryor is driven to the border crossing and released by East German police; the scene in Spielberg's film is reminiscent of the opening of *The Spy who Comes in from the Cold*, with the nerve-wracking waiting time in the checkpoint booth followed, in the case of *Bridge of Spies*, by a positive outcome.

In the *Panorama* report from 30 October 1961, Robin Day walked from the crossing of Friedrichstraße with Kochstraße in the direction of the booth and the sign at Checkpoint Charlie.[36] The journalist's walk to the border crossing anticipated scenes from two films which saw two of the most famous fictional spies of the Cold War reaching the booth and, unlike Day, crossing into East Berlin. Secret agent Harry Palmer (Michael Caine) walked through the border in *Funeral in Berlin* and James Bond (Roger Moore) followed the same route into East Berlin in *Octopussy*. Unlike the staged sequences from *Casino Royale*, *The Spy Who Came in from the Cold* and *Bridge of Spies*, the scenes from *Funeral in*

Figure 8.4 The replica of Checkpoint Charlie in *The Spy Who Came in from the Cold* (Martin Ritt, 1965).

Berlin and *Octopussy* were filmed on location in West Berlin. In Guy Hamilton's film, Palmer is driven by Johnny Vulkan (Paul Hubschmid), a German friend running the Berlin station for British intelligence, to the crossing of Friedrichstraße with Kochstraße; Palmer then walks across the border to meet Soviet Colonel Stok (Oskar Homolka) and to arrange his defection to the West. Once across the border, a taxi takes the MI6 agent to Spreewaldplatz, a West-Berlin location made to play the role of East Berlin's Marx-Engels-Platz (today Schloßplatz). The place where Palmer is dropped off is the former Görlitzer Bahnhof (Görlitzer Station), a building demolished soon after the making of *Funeral in Berlin*; Emmauskirche (Emanus Church) on Lausitzer Platz can be seen in the background. In *Octopussy*, Agent 009 is murdered by henchmen Mischka (David Meyer) and Grischka (Anthony Meyer) as he tries to flee East Berlin. In the second half of the film, James Bond is driven by Karl (Hugo Bower) to Checkpoint Charlie through the streets of West Berlin; landmarks such as the Kaiser-Wilhelm-Gedächtniskirche (Kaiser Wilhelm Memorial Church) and the crowded Kurfürstendamm Avenue are visible during the ride. The car turns right from Kochstraße to Friedrichstraße, and Bond is driven across the border to investigate the circumstances of the killing of Agent 009; Bond later makes his way from East Berlin to a circus in at Karl-Marx-Stadt (now Chemnitz). Both *Funeral in Berlin* and *Octopussy* use Checkpoint Charlie as the place where the two parts of the divided city collide and as a potential breech in the impenetrable wall. *Funeral in Berlin* resorted to having West Berlin, and in particular the Kreuzberg district, playing the role of East Berlin. *Octopussy* avoided East Berlin all together and saw 007 materialising in Karl-Marx-Stadt presumably through an implausible itinerary. These various creative approaches to the cinematic topography of Berlin have made of Checkpoint Charlie a highly recognisable and yet equally elusive point of access to a place surrounded by a sense of threat, paradoxically visible from the windows and the elevated platforms near the Wall on the Western side and, at once, remote and impenetrable.

Matthew Miller has argued that, 'Berlin invited critical artistic attempts to come to terms with the repercussions of the city's chilly division' and that the 'number and scope of site-specific artistic responses to urban division correlated to the existential, phenomenological, representational, and political challenges at hand.'[37] In film, the response to the division of the city emerges with particular emphasis in its relation to three liminal locations articulating a series of connections between the two parts of the divided city. In a way akin to various shots of the void of Potsdamer Platz or of the bricked-up windows of Bernauer Straße, the image of Checkpoint Charlie evokes the division of the city. In the case studies I have discussed in this chapter, the gaze on and over the Wall was from West to East Berlin. The forbidden city of East Berlin is revealed in shots where the Berlin Television Tower in Alexanderplatz can be seen from the West as it defines the familiar and yet disconnected cityscape of East Berlin. An exception to the exclusions of Western filmmakers from East Berlin was broadcast on 22 September 1970 as part of the BBC One Tuesday Documentary series; *Beyond the Wall* (Peter Ceresole, 1970) includes scenes filmed in East Berlin in the vicinity of the Wall such as a shot of the entry to the U-Bahn station Stadtmitte in Friedrichstraße. This area appears as a desolate place described in the accompanying words of reporter Alan Watson as follows:

> Stadtmitte, the old city centre, is now the central point of a no man's land. [...] At the end of empty streets squats the Wall, the only piece of self-confident architecture in this part of Berlin. In the end, all roads lead here and all trains of thought.

Watson's words capture the significance of the Wall as a commanding and powerful structure zigzagging through the wastelands of the former capital of the Third Reich, filmed at a time when the idea of its demise was highly unlikely. Nineteen years later, 20,000 people would spill into West Berlin through the border crossing in Bornholmer Straße. A year later Germany would reunify. Another year and the Soviet Union would dissolve. As Hobsbawm suggests:

> The end of the Cold War proved to be not the end of an international conflict, but the end of an era: not only for the East, but for the entire world. There are historic moments which may be recognized, even by contemporaries, as marking the end of an age. The years around 1990 clearly were such a secular turning-point.[38]

This historical juncture was embodied by the demolition of the Wall which took place between the summer of 1990 and the autumn of 1991. A few fragments of the Wall, including a stretch at Bernauer Straße, lampposts and watchtowers would remain in place as memorials and tangible traces of the Cold War; the location of the Wall at Potsdamer Platz is now marked by rows of cobblestones and sections of the death strip have been redeveloped into a hiking and cycling area. Other segments of the Wall were given to public and private institutions across the world. Commemorative markers for the victims of the Wall spread across the city are akin to those honouring the men who were murdered in Munich in 1972 or in Rome in 1978. As in the case of the trenches of the First World War in the Asiago Plateau, the ruins of Belchite, the ground of Majdanek or the Hiroshima Prefectural Industrial Promotion Hall, what is left of the structure which the GDR authorities called Antifaschistischer Schutzwall (Anti-Fascist Protection Rampart) is now made to memorialise a past inscribed in space.

Notes

1. Andreas Huyssen, 'The Voids of Berlin', *Critical Inquiry*, Vol. 24, No. 1, 1997, pp. 57–81 (66).
2. The official name of the country normally called East Germany outside its borders was Deutsche Demokratische Republik (German Democratic Republic), usually abbreviated to DDR (GDR). In this chapter I henceforth use the acronym GDR.
3. Brian Ladd, *The Ghosts of Berlin: Confronting German History in the Urban Landscape*, Chicago: University of Chicago Press, 2018 (first published in 1998), p. 12.
4. Philip Broadbent and Sabine Hake, 'Introduction', in *Berlin Divided City, 1945–1989*, Broadbent and Hake (eds), New York: Berghahn Books, 2010, pp. 1–10 (1–2).
5. *The Berlin Boundary Is Sealed* (BBC News, 16 August 1961).
6. Similarly, factual footage of the fall of the Berlin Wall was included in films such as *The Innocent* (John Schlesinger, 1993), an adaptation from Ian McEwan's novel of the same title (1990) largely set in 1950s Berlin and including an epilogue where the events of 9 November 1989 are broadcast on a television set in the crowded lobby of a hotel. Footage of East Berliners crossing the border to West Berlin and the Wall being torn down, including scenes from the opening of the Brandenburg Gate on 22 December 1989, was also repurposed in *Good Bye, Lenin!* in the sequences where Alex (Daniel Brühl) creates fake news reports claiming that the GDR has opened its border to refugees from the West. These news reports are used by Alex to make his dying mother (Katrin Sass) believe in an alternative history and ignore the fall of the Wall and the collapse of Communism.
7. *Panorama* (BBC TV, 30 October 1961).
8. A staged version of the escape from the windows of Bernauer Straße would later be included in *Bridge of Spies*.
9. Hope M. Harrison, *After the Berlin Wall: Memory and the Making of the New Germany*, 1989 to the Present, Cambridge: Cambridge University Press, 2019, pp. 74–5.
10. Fischer also explain that the original crucifix and altar were included in the design for the new Chapel of Reconciliation, while various shots reveal the present-day location with the clay-built chapel designed by architects Rudolf Reitermann and Peter Sassenroth and a replica of Coventry Cathedral's Statue of Reconciliation.
11. The same story is told in the documentary *Der Tunnel* (Marcus Vetter, 1999) and in the fiction film *Il tunnel della libertà* (*The Tunnel of Freedom*, Enzo Monteleone, 2004).
12. Peter Fechter was shot and killed by East German border guards while trying to climb over a 2-metre section of the Wall topped with barbed wire near Checkpoint Charlie with the aim of crossing over to the Kreuzberg district of West Berlin.

13. Gerd Knischewski and Ulla Spittler, 'Remembering the Berlin Wall: The Wall Memorial Ensemble Bernauer Straße', *German Life and Letters*, Vol. 59, No. 2, 2006, pp. 280–93 (287).
14. *Beauty and Berlin* (1930–1939, British Pathé: Film ID: 2741.07). Castle Films was a Californian film distributor founded by Eugene W. Castle in 1924.
15. Ladd, p. 116.
16. Ladd, p. 115.
17. Ladd, p. 115.
18. Simon Ward, 'Globalization and the remembrance of violence: Visual culture, space, and time in Berlin', in *Globalization, Violence and the Visual Culture of Cities*, Christoph Lindner (ed.), London: Routledge, 2009, pp. 87–106 (90).
19. In *Wings of Desire*, unseen and unheard, two angels, Cassiel and Damiel (Bruno Ganz), observe West Berlin and its people. The Berlin Wall, and the graffiti covering its west-facing partition and its watchtowers, appears in several sequences as Damiel and Cassiel walk by and even through the Wall of the divided city.
20. The Wertheim department store was located in the adjacent Leipziger Platz.
21. Jonathan Bordo, 'The Homer of Potsdamer Platz: Walter Benjamin in Wim Wenders's *Sky over Berlin/Wings of Desire*. A Critical Topography', *Images*, Vol. 2, No. 1, 2008, pp. 86–109 (91).
22. 'An die Arbeit mit dem alten Curt Bois. Wie wir da eines Sonntags morgens auf dem Potsdamer Platz gedreht haben, an der Mauer, unter der Magnetbahn, die damals da noch entlang fuhr. Kein Mensch weit und breit. Das war ja eine Stadtwüste, eine Steppe, ein Niemandsland. Die Sonne schien, es war aber trotzdem kalt. Curt war ein Witzbold. Der brachte uns alle ständig zum Lachen. Und was er alles zu erzählen hatte zu dem alten Platz, den er tatsächlich als junger Mann mit seinem Auto oft überquert hatte.' See, Wim Wenders in 'Muffensausen beim *Himmel über Berlin*', Peter Zander, *Welt Online*, 3 May 2007.
23. 'Ich kann den Potsdamer Platz nicht finden. Ah, nein hier – das kann er doch nicht sein! Denn am Potdamer Platz, da war doch das Cafe Jostin. Nachmittags habe ich mich da unterhalten und einen Kaffee getrunken, das Publikum beobachtet, vorher meine Zigarre geraucht. Bei Loeser & Wolff, ein renomiertes Tabakgeschäft, gleich hier gegenüber. Also das kann er hier nicht sein, der Potsdamer Platz. Nein. Man trifft keinen, den man fragen kann. Ah, das war ein belebter Platz. Straßenbahnen, Omnibusse mit Pferden und zwei Autos, meines und das vom Schockoladenharman. Das Kaufhaus Wertheim war auch hier. Und dann hingen plötzlich Fahnen dort. – Der ganze Platz war vollgehängt mit – und die Leute waren gar nicht mehr freundlich und die Polizei auch nicht. Aber ich gebe so lange nicht auf, bis ich den Potsdamer Platz gefunden habe.'
24. Nora, 1989, p. 18.
25. *Panorama* (BBC TV, 31 July 1961).
26. Howard Caygill, 'The futures of Berlin's Potsdamer Platz', in *The Limits of Globalization*, Alan Scott (ed.), London: Routledge, 1997, pp. 24–44 (35).
27. Caygill, p. 35.

28. Spy films based on original screenplays also used Berlin as a location. Written by Brian Moore, *Torn Curtain* (Alfred Hitchcock, 1966), for example, was set in East Berlin and includes a few scenes filmed on location in Fehrbelliner Platz (West Berlin).
29. Oliver Buckton, *Espionage in British Fiction and Film since 1900: The Changing Enemy*, Lanham: Lexington Books, 2015, p. 22.
30. *Funeral in Berlin* was published in 1964 (London: Jonathan Cape) and the novels *Berlin Game*, *Mexico Set* and *London Match* were published by Hutchinson (London) in 1983, 1984 and 1985 respectively.
31. This image of West Berlin provides a striking contrast to the nocturnal portrayal of the same locations in one of the most celebrated West German Berlin films of the 1980s, *Christiane F. – Wir Kinder vom Bahnhof Zoo* (*Christiane F.*, Uli Edel, 1981).
32. Other comedies using the Berlin Wall and its border crossings as locations include *Meier* (Peter Timm, 1986), *Helden wie wir* (*Heroes Like Us*, Sebastian Peterson, 1999), *Herr Lehmann* (*Berlin Blues*, Leander Haußmann, 2003) and *Liebe Mauer* (*Dear Wall*, Peter Timm, 2009). *Der Mann auf der Mauer* (*The Man on the Wall*, Reinhard Hauff, 1982) is a satirical drama which makes extensive use of the western side of the Wall at Sebastianstraße as a location. The Wall at Sebastianstraße also appears as a location in the action-drama *The Soldier* (James Glickenhaus, 1982).
33. Ladd, p. 11.
34. Ladd, p. 15.
35. The same words could be read on the sign in Russian, French and German: 'Вы Выезжаете Из Американского Сектора/Vous sortez du secteur américain/ Sie Verlassen den Amerikanischen Sektor'.
36. Twenty-eight years later, on the evening of 10 November 1989, *Newsnight* (BBC Two) would open with a report showing Peter Snow standing at Friedrichstraße with Checkpoint Charlie and the crowd of East Berliners crossing the border just behind him.
37. Matthew Miller, 'Divided Berlin and Cold War Aesthetics: Mediating the Wall in Literature and Film', *A Journal of Germanic Studies*, Vol. 55, No. 3, 2019, pp. 266–95 (270).
38. Hobsbawm, p. 256.

EPILOGUE

Venice, Los Angeles, California, USA, 10 January 1914, 1:30 p.m.

> *A spectator wearing a fake toothbrush moustache, baggy pants, large shoes, a tight coat, a cane and a bowler hat gets in the way of the camera at the Junior Vanderbilt Cup and ostensibly interferes with the race. He will be later known as the Tramp and this happens in Venice, California, on 10 January 1914.*

Harry Lehrman's Keystone comedy *Kid Auto Races at Venice* was filmed on location in the afternoon of 10 January 1914, two days after the making of *Mabel's Strange Predicament* (Mabel Normand). Charlie Chaplin had worn the costume of the Tramp for the first time in Normand's comedy, but that film would only be released on 9 February and so the improvised comic antics of *Kid Auto Races at Venice*, which came out on 7 February, offered cinema audiences a first glimpse of Chaplin's creation. The screening of Lehrman's film also marked the beginning of a process which, as Hobsbawm puts it, turned 'one figure from the entertainment world of the British poor [the music hall] into the most universally admired artist of the first half of the twentieth century.'[1] Twenty-six years later, the former vaudeville actor would play the role of Adenoid Hynkel, a parody of Adolf Hitler, in *The Great Dictator* (Charlie Chaplin, 1940), a film where the staging of military parades in the fictional state of Tomania is reminiscent of the newsreels produced in Nazi Germany. A photograph from the iconic sequence of Hynkel dancing with a large globe appears on the cover of most editions of Hobsbawm's *The Age of Extremes*. The juxtaposition of Chaplin's performance as the Tramp in *Kid Auto Races at Venice* and his presence on the cover of Hobsbawm's book performing a parody of one of the century's most murderous dictators captures the development of the Age of Catastrophe from the First World War to the collapse of ideals and the carnage of the Second World War. This historical narrative, which I introduced at the beginning of this book and which has underpinned all of its chapters, also talks of the Cold War which emerged in the aftermath of the Second World War and which was the result of the tumultuous years of hot wars unfolding between the shooting of Archduke Franz Ferdinand of Austria in 1914 and the atomic bombing of Hiroshima and Nagasaki in 1945.

The interplay between past and present has pervaded the study of the *topoi* discussed in this book. One of Aldo Moro's letters to his wife written in his cell and quoted in *Good Morning, Night* reads 'I would like to understand, through my mortal eyes, how we will be seen afterwards. If there were light, it would be beautiful.'[2] In *Film, Hot War Traces and Cold War Spaces* I have tried to summon the past and to elucidate, paraphrasing Moro, the ways in which history and memory can retrospectively be illuminated through film. Cinema emerged in the second half of the Age of Empire (1875–1914) and it did not stop providing entertainment with the beginning of the Age of Catastrophe;[3] on the other hand, cinema had already begun capturing war and its aftermath before the outbreak of the First World War. At the turn of the twentieth century, episodes of the Second Boer War in South Africa were filmed by British pioneer filmmakers as were incidents of the Boxer Rebellion in China.[4] And yet, from 1914 onwards film had to respond to the swelling proportion of the calamities unfolding across the world and to the speed with which humanity kept stumbling from one catastrophe to the next; as it did so by means of interwoven narratives made of newsreels, amateur footage, documentaries and fictional re-enactments, film has given a visual aftermath to the Short Twentieth Century and to its fears, anxieties and broken illusions.

Had a time traveller been sent back to Sarajevo in 1914 to stop Gavrilo Princip and to prevent the First World War, in a manner akin to that of the time traveller in *La Jetée* (Chris Marker 1962), would the world have witnessed a more peaceful century? Would the Moon landing, the event which I have used to introduce this book, have become the defining moment of the century to which people who lived before that war looked forward? These questions are, of course, paradoxical. In a scene from *La Jetée* a hand points to a place outside a sequoia tree at the Jardin des Plantes, to a place outside of time; and so *La Jetée* ultimately tells us that one cannot escape time and its final scene reveals that the image which marked the life of the time traveller was the image of his own death. This revelation is made at a specific location, Paris Orly Airport; history always happens in space and the aftermath of its incidents lingers in the ruins, traces, debris and memories of place. In *Film, Hot War Traces and Cold War Spaces* I have built on what Soja described as 'growing awareness of the simultaneity and interwoven complexity of the social, the historical, and the spatial, their inseparability and interdependence' and I have dealt with the filmic rendering of a range of historical events inscribed in space.[5] Trenches, ruins of villages and civic buildings, abandoned death and concentration camps, city streets, forests and sports venues have been investigated across the eight chapters of this book with a focus on the aftermath of traumatic events and on the ways in which film can capture the incidents at the time of their happening or moments, days, weeks, months and years afterwards. The passing of time and cultural and political flows have shaped my reading of filmic spaces through a process consisting of digging through layers of history and depictions of place. Like the noble metals recovered by scavengers on the sites of the battlefields of the First World War in Italy, the *topoi* I have tried to convey in this book evoke a historical imagery that resoundingly lingers in the memorialisation of the bloodied twentieth century.

1 December 2021, London

Notes

1. Eric Hobsbawm, *The Age of Empire: Europe 1875–1914*, London: Weidenfeld and Nicolson, 1987, pp. 237.
2. 'Vorrei capire, con i miei piccoli occhi mortali, come ci si vedrà dopo. Se ci fosse luce, sarebbe bellissimo.'
3. See Hobsbawm, *The Age of Empire: Europe 1875–1914*.
4. These events were also re-enacted in fiction films such as *Attack on a China Mission* (James Williamson, 1900); on the Second Boer War and the Boxer Rebellion in early cinema see my book *Of Empire and the City: Remapping Early British Cinema*, Bern: Peter Lang, 2014, pp. 215–36.
5. Soja, p. 3.

Bibliography

'Back from the Wars: A Street Scene in Hiroshima', *The Illustrated London News*, Vol. 125, Issue 3408, 13 August 1904, p. 226.
'Books of the Day', *The Illustrated London News*, Vol. 190, Issue 5118, 22 May 1937, p. 962.
'Crown sets three releases for August-September', *Boxoffice*, 29 July 1963, p. 8.
'Notorious', *The Showmen's Trade Review*, 27 July 1946, p. 31.
Aldgate, Anthony. *Cinema and History: British Newsreels and the Spanish Civil War*, London: Scolar Press, 1979.
Arad, Yitzhak. *Belzec, Sobibor, Treblinka: The Operation Reinhard Death Camps*, Bloomington: Indiana University Press, 1999.
Archibald, David. *The War That Won't Die: The Spanish Civil War in Cinema*, Manchester: Manchester University Press, 2014.
Aust, Stefan. *Baader-Meinhof: the Inside Story of the R.A.F.*, Oxford: Oxford University Press, 2009.
Barattoni, Luca. *Italian Post-Neorealist Cinema*, Edinburgh: Edinburgh University Press, 2012.
Basilio, Miriam. 'A Pilgrimage to the Alcázar of Toledo: Ritual, Tourism and Propaganda in Franco's Spain', in *Architecture and Tourism: Perception, Performance and Place*, D. Medina Lasansky and Brian D. McLaren (eds), Oxford: Berg, 2004, pp. 93–107.
Bianconi, Giovanni. 'Aldo Moro, nella cella del rapimento oggi dormono due bambine', *Il Corriere della Sera*, Milan, 18 March 2018, p. 36.
Black, Peter R. 'Rehearsal for "Reinhard"? Odilo Globocnik and the Lublin Selbstschutz', *Central European History*, Vol. 25, No. 2, 1992, pp. 194–226.
Bordo, Jonathan. 'The Homer of Potsdamer Platz: Walter Benjamin in Wim Wenders's *Sky over Berlin/Wings of Desire*. A Critical Topography', *Images*, Vol. 2, No. 1, 2008, pp. 86–109.
Braghetti, Anna Maria and Paola Tavella. *Il prigioniero*, Milano: Mondadori, 1998.
Broadbent, Philip and Sabine Hake. 'Introduction', in *Berlin Divided City, 1945–1989*, Broadbent and Hake (eds), New York: Berghahn Books, 2010, pp. 1–10.
Brunetta, Gian Piero. 'L'immagine della Prima Guerra Mondiale attraverso il cinema', in *Operai e Contadini nella Grande Guerra*, Mario Isnenghi (ed.), Bologna: Cappelli Editore, 1982, pp. 273–82.
Brunsdon, Charlotte. *London in Cinema: the Cinematic City Since 1945*, London: BFI Publishing, 2008.
Buckton, Oliver. *Espionage in British Fiction and Film since 1900: The Changing Enemy*, Lanham: Lexington Books, 2015.
Burrows, Jon. '"A vague Chinese quarter elsewhere": Limehouse in the cinema 1914–36', *Journal of British Cinema and Television*, Vol. 6, No. 2, 2009, pp. 282–301.
Calderoni, Franco. *La Grande Guerra: dal Soggetto al Film*, Bologna: Cappelli, 1959.

Caruth, Cathy. *Unclaimed Experience: Trauma, Narrative and History*, Baltimore: Johns Hopkins University Press, 2010.

Casey, Edward S. 'Boundary, Place, and Event in the Spatiality of History', *Rethinking History*, Vol.11, No. 4, 2007, pp. 507–12.

Caygill, Howard. 'The futures of Berlin's Potsdamer Platz', in *The Limits of Globalization*, Alan Scott (ed.), London: Routledge, 1997, pp. 24–44.

Cinquegrani, Maurizio. 'The cinematic city and the destruction of Lublin's Jews', *Holocaust Studies: A Journal of Culture and History*, Vol. 22, No. 2–3, 2016, pp. 244–55.

Cinquegrani, Maurizio. *Journey to Poland: Documentary Landscapes of the Holocaust*, Edinburgh: Edinburgh University Press, 2018.

Cinquegrani, Maurizio. *Of Empire and the City: Remapping Early British Cinema*, Bern: Peter Lang, 2014.

Cinquegrani, Maurizio. 'Place, Time and Memory in Italian Cinema of the Great War', in *The Great War in Post-Memory Literature and Film*, Martin Löschnigg and Marzena Sokolowska-Paryz (eds), Berlin: De Gruyter, 2014, pp. 321–34.

Cole, Tim. 'Crematoria, barracks, gateways. Survivors' return visits to the memory landscapes of Auschwitz', *History and Memory*, Vol. 25, No. 2, 2013, pp. 102–31.

Cosulich, Callisto. *Uomini Contro: dal Soggetto al Film*, Bologna: Cappelli, 1970.

D'Annunzio, Gabriele. '*Vittoria nostra, non sarai mutilate*', Corriere della Sera, 24 Ottobre 1918, p. 1.

De España, Rafael. 'Images of the Spanish Civil War in Spanish feature films, 1939–85', *Historical Journal of Film, Radio and Television*, Vol. 6, No. 2, 1986, pp. 223–36.

Diffrient, David Scott. 'Spectator sports and terrorist reports: filming the Munich Olympics, (re)imagining the Munich Massacre', *Sport in Society*, Vol. 11, No. 2–3, 2008, pp. 311–329.

Dondi, Mirco. *L'eco del boato: Storia della strategia della tensione 1965–1974*, Roma: Laterza, 2015.

Ebert, Roger. 'James Mason: *The Boys from Brazil*', *Chicago Sun-Times*, 12 October 1978, p. 14.

Edwards, Matthew. 'Suppression and Censorship: Japanese Cinema during the Occupation', in *The Atomic Bomb in Japanese Cinema: Critical Essays*, Matthew Edwards (ed.), Jefferson: McFarland, 2018, pp. 69–76.

Ethington, Philip J. 'Placing the Past: "Groundwork" for a Spatial Theory of History', *Rethinking History*, Vol. 11, No. 4, 2007, pp. 465–93.

Fabi, Lucio. *Gente di Trincea: la Grande Guerra sul Carso e sull'Isonzo*, Milano: Mursia, 2009.

Fagiolo, Roberto. *Topografia del caso Moro. Da via Fani a via Caetani*, Roma: Nutrimenti, 2018.

Fernández, Joxean. 'La memoria cinematográfica franquista de la Guerra Civil en el País Vasco', *Amnis. Revue de Civilisation Contemporaine*, No. 2, October 2011 (last accessed 17 April 2021, http://journals.openedition.org/amnis/1496).

Ferrándiz, Francisco. 'The Return of Civil War Ghosts: the Ethnography of Exhumations in Contemporary Spain', *Anthropology Today*, Vol. 22, No. 3, 2006, pp. 7–12.

Gajek, Eva Maria. 'More than Munich 1972. Media, Emotions, and the Body in TV Broadcast of the 20th Summer Olympics', *Historical Social Research*, Vol. 43, No. 2, 2018, pp. 181–202.

Galily, Yair, Moran Yarchi and Ilan Tamir, 'From Munich to Boston, and from Theatre to Social Media: The Evolutionary Landscape of World Sporting Terror', *Studies in Conflict & Terrorism*, Vol. 38, No. 12, 2015, pp. 998–1007.

Gargiulo, Gius. 'Moro, Morucci, Moretti: Oxymoron and the Prison of Political Language', in *Remembering Aldo Moro: The Cultural Legacy of the 1978 Kidnapping and Murder*, Ruth Glynn and Giancarlo Lombardi (eds), London and Boston: Many Publishing (Legenda), 2012, pp. 96–106.

Garrone, Giuseppe and Eugenio. *Lettere e Diari di Guerra 1914–1918*, Milano: Garzanti, 1974.

González-Ruibal, Alfredo. 'Museums and Material Memories of the Spanish Civil War: An Archaeological Critique', *Public Humanities and the Spanish Civil War: Connected and Contested Histories*, Alison Ribeiro de Menezes, Antonio Cazorla-Sánchez and Adrian Shubert (eds), Berlin: Springer, 2018, pp. 93–114.

Gruber Godfrey, Laura. *Hemingway's Geographies: Intimacy, Materiality, and Memory*, London and New York: Palgrave Macmillan, 2016.

Gundle, Stephen. *Mussolini's Dream Factory: Film Stardom in Fascist Italy*, New York and Oxford: Berghahn Books, 2013.

Haltof, Marek. *Polish Film and the Holocaust: Politics and Memory*, New York and Oxford: Berghahn Books, 2012.

Harper, Graeme and Jonathan Rayner. 'Introduction', in *Cinema and Landscape*, Harper and Rayner (eds), Bristol and Chicago: Intellect, 2010, pp. 13–28.

Harrison, Hope M. *After the Berlin Wall: Memory and the Making of the New Germany, 1989 to the Present*, Cambridge: Cambridge University Press, 2019.

Hay, James. 'Piecing Together What Remains of the Cinematic City', in *The Cinematic City*, Clarke David (ed.), New York and London: Routledge, 1997, pp. 209–29.

Hedges, Inez. *World Cinema and Cultural Memory*, Basingstoke: Palgrave Macmillan, 2015.

Hein, Laura E. and Mark Selden. 'Commemoration and Silence: Fifty Years of Remembering the Bomb in America and Japan', in *Living with the Bomb: American and Japanese Cultural Conflicts in the Nuclear Age,* Laura E. Hein and Mark Selden (eds), London and New York: Routledge, 2015, pp. 3–35

Hemingway, Ernest. *A Farewell to Arms*, London: Vintage, 2005 [first published by Jonathan Cape in 1929].

Hersey, John. *Hiroshima*, London: Penguin Classics, 2001 [first published in *The New Yorker* in 1946].

Hicks, Jeremy. *First Films of the Holocaust: Soviet Cinema and the Genocide of Jews 1938–1946*, Pittsburgh: University of Pittsburgh Press, 2012.

Hill, Sarah P. 'Double exposures: The photographic afterlives of Pasolini and Moro', *Modern Italy*, Vol. 21, No. 4, 2016, pp. 409–25.

Hobsbawm, Eric. *The Age of Empire: Europe 1875–1914*, London: Weidenfeld and Nicolson, 1987.

Hobsbawm, Eric. *Age of Extremes: the Short Twentieth Century 1914–1991*, London: Abacus, 1995.

Hodgin, Nick and Amit Thakkar. 'Introduction: Trauma Studies, Film and the Scar Motif', in *Scars and Wounds: Film and Legacies of Trauma*, Nick Hodgin and Amit Thakkar (eds), Basingstoke: Palgrave Macmillan, 2017, pp. 1–30.

Hodgkin, Katharine and Susannah Radstone, 'Introduction: Contested Pasts', in *Memory, History, Nation: Contested Pasts*, New Brunswick, NJ: Transaction, 2005, pp. 1–22.

Hogan, Michael J. 'Hiroshima in History and Memory: an Introduction', in *Hiroshima in History and Memory*, Michael J. Hogan (ed.), Cambridge: Cambridge University Press, 1996, pp. 1–10.

Huyssen, Andreas. 'Monument and Memory in a Postmodern Age', *The Yale Journal of Criticism*, Vol. 6, No. 2, 1993, pp. 249–62.

Huyssen, Andreas. 'The Voids of Berlin', *Critical Inquiry*, Vol. 24, No. 1 (1997), pp. 57–81.

Imposimato, Ferdinando and Sandro Provvisionato. *Doveva morire: Chi ha ucciso Aldo Moro. Il giudice dell'inchiesta racconta*, Milano: Chiarelettere, 2011.

Jarvie, Ian C. 'Seeing Through Movies', *Philosophy of the Social Sciences*, Vol. 8, No. 4, 1978, pp. 374–97.

Jonas, George. *Vengeance: The True Story of an Israeli Counter-Terrorist Team*, New York: Simon and Schuster, 2005.

Kilgallen, Dorothy Mae. 'Dorothy Kilgallen selects *Notorious*', *Modern Screen*, Volumes 33–4, July–December 1946, p. 138.

Klein, Aaron J. *Striking Back: The 1972 Munich Olympics Massacre and Israel's Deadly Response*, London: Random House, 2007.

Knischewski, Gerd and Ulla Spittler. 'Remembering the Berlin Wall: The Wall Memorial Ensemble Bernauer Straße', *German Life and Letters*, Vol. 59, No. 2, 2006, pp. 280–93.

Koslov, Elissa M. '"Going east": colonial experiences and practices of violence among female and male Majdanek camp guards (1941–44)', *Journal of Genocide Research*, Vol. 10, No. 4, 2008, pp. 563–82.

Labanyi, Jo. 'The Politics of Memory in Contemporary Spain', *Journal of Spanish Cultural Studies*, Vol. 9, No. 2, 2008, pp. 119–25.

Ladd, Brian. *The Ghosts of Berlin: Confronting German History in the Urban Landscape*, Chicago: University of Chicago Press, 2018 (first published in 1998).

Landy, Marcia. *Cinematic Uses of the Past*, Minneapolis: University of Minnesota Press, 1996.

Landy, Marcia. 'Introduction', in *The Historical Film: History and Memory in Media*, Marcia Landy (ed.), London: A. & C. Black, 2001, pp. 1–24.

Lanzmann, Claude. 'Site and Speech: An Interview with Claude Lanzmann about *Shoah*', with Marc Chevrie and Hervé Le Roux, in *Claude Lanzmann's* Shoah*: Key Essays*, Stuart Liebman (ed.), Oxford and New York: Oxford University Press, 2007, pp. 37–49.

Large, David Clay *Munich 1972: Tragedy, Terror, and Triumph at the Olympic Games*, Lanham: Rowman & Littlefield, 2012.

Launius, Roger D. *Apollo's Legacy: Perspectives on the Moon Landings*, Washington, DC: Smithsonian Institution, 2019.

Lefebvre, Henri. *The Production of Space*, trans. by Donald Nicholson-Smith, Oxford: Blackwell, 1991 [first published as *La production de l'espace* by Anthropos in 1974].

Levy. Richard S. (ed.), 2005. *Anti-Semitism: A Historical Encyclopaedia of Prejudice and Persecution (Volume One)*, Santa Barbara: ABC-CLIO

Lichtner, Giacomo. '"Io so": the absence of resolution as resolution in contemporary Italian cinema about the 'years of lead'', Modern Italy, Vol. 22, No. 2, 2017, pp. 167–81.

Lifton, Robert Jay. *Death in Life: Survivors of Hiroshima*, Chapel Hill: University of North Carolina Press, 2012.

Lombardi, Giancarlo. 'La passione secondo Marco Bellocchio Gli ultimi giorni di Aldo Moro', *Annali d'Italianistica*, Vol. 25 (Literature, Religion, and the Sacred), 2007, pp. 397–408.

Lowenthal, David. 'Past Time, Present Place: Landscape and Memory', *Geographical Review*, Vol. 65, No. 1, 1975, pp. 1–36.

Lowenthal, David. *The Past Is a Foreign Country*, Cambridge: Cambridge University Press, 1985.

Lucken, Michael. 'The Peace Statue at Nagasaki', in *Japan's Postwar*, Michael Lucken, Anne Bayard-Sakai and Emmanuel Lozerand (eds), New York and London: Routledge, 2013 [translated by J. J. A: Stockwin], pp. 179–202.

Lusso, Emilio. 'La Brigata Sassari e il Partito Sardo D'Azione', *Il Ponte*, No. 9–10, 1951.

Lusso, Emilio. *Un anno sull'altopiano*, Torino: Einaudi, 2005 [first published by Edizioni Italiane di Cultura in 1938].

Malvezzi, Pietro and Giovanni Pirelli. *Lettere di condannati a morte della Resistenza italiana (8 Settembre 1943–25 Aprile 1945)*, Milano: Mondadori, 1968.

McGarry, Fearghal and Jennie Carlsten, 'Introduction', in *Film, History and Memory*, McGarry and Carlsten (eds), Basingstoke: Palgrave Macmillan, 2015, pp. 1–17.

Meade, Robert C. *Red Brigades: The Story of Italian Terrorism*, New York: Springer, 1989.
Miller, Matthew. 'Divided Berlin and Cold War Aesthetics: Mediating the Wall in Literature and Film', *A Journal of Germanic Studies*, Vol. 55, No. 3, 2019, pp. 266–95.
Miron, Guy. *The Yad Vashem Encyclopaedia of the Ghettos during the Holocaust*, Jerusalem: Yad Vashem, 2010.
Monteath, Peter. *The Spanish Civil War in Literature, Film, and Art: An International Bibliography of Secondary Literature*, Santa Barbara: ABC-CLIO, 1994.
Moro, Carlo Alfredo. *Storia di un delitto annunciato*, Roma: Editori Riuniti, 1998.
Morreale, Emiliano. *L'invenzione della nostalgia. Il vintage nel cinema italiano e dintorni*, Roma: Donzelli, 2009.
Morris, Nigel. *The Cinema of Steven Spielberg: Empire of Light*, New York: Columbia University Press, 2007.
Nachreiner, Thomas. 'An Olympic Omnibus: International Competition, Cooperation, and Politics in *Visions of Eight*', *Film & History*, Vol. 35, No. 2, 2005, pp. 19–28.
Nachreiner, Thomas. '"Inspired by real events" – Media (and) Memory in Steven Spielberg's *Munich* (2005)', *Imaginations: Journal of Cross-Cultural Media Studies*, Vol. 5, No. 2, 2016, pp. 67–87.
Nicolle, David. *The Italian Army of World War One*. Botley, Oxford: Osprey Publishing, 2012.
Nora, Pierre. 'Between Memory and History: Les Lieux de Mémoire', *Representations. Special Issue: Memory and Counter-Memory*, No. 26 (1989), pp. 7–24.
Nora, Pierre. 'Entre Mémoire et Histoire', in *Les lieux de mémoire: La République*, Nora (ed.), 2.ª ed., París: Gallimard (Bibliothèque illustrée des histoires), 2001, pp. 23–43.
O'Leary, Alan. 'Dead Man Walking: The Aldo Moro kidnap and Palimpsest History in *Buongiorno, notte*', *New Cinemas: Journal of Contemporary Film*, Vol. 6, No. 1, 2008, pp. 33–45.
O'Leary, Alan. 'Locations of Moro: The Kidnap in the Cinema', in *Remembering Aldo Moro: The Cultural Legacy of the 1978 Kidnapping and Murder*, Ruth Glynn and Giancarlo Lombardi (eds), London and Boston: Many Publishing (Legenda), 2012, pp. 151–70.
Orwell, George. *Homage to Catalonia*, London: Penguin, 2000 [first published by Secker and Warburg in 1938].
Orwell, George. 'Looking Back on the Spanish Civil War', in *The Collected Essays, Journalism and Letters of George Orwell: Volume II My Country Left or Right, 1940–1943* (ed. Sonia Orwell and Ian Angus), London: Secker and Warburg, 1968, pp. 249–67.
Orwell, George. *Nineteen Eighty-Four*, London: Penguin, 2000 [first published in 1949 by Martin Secker & Warburg].
Penz, François and Andong Lu, 'Introduction: What is Urban Cinematics?', in *Urban Cinematics: Understanding Urban Phenomena Through the Moving Image*, François Penz and Andong Lu (eds), Bristol: Intellect Books, 2011, pp. 7–19.
Pezzini, Isabella. 'Imago Moro: Medi-a-(c)tion on Aldo Moro', in *Remembering Aldo Moro: The Cultural Legacy of the 1978 Kidnapping and Murder*, Ruth Glynn and Giancarlo Lombardi (eds), London and Boston: Many Publishing (Legenda), 2012, pp. 136–50.
Raack, Richard C. 'Historiography as Cinematography: A Prolegomenon to Film Work for Historians', *Journal of Contemporary History*, Vol. 18, No. 3, 1983, pp. 411–38.
Reeve, Simon. *One Day in September: the Full Story of the 1972 Olympics Massacre and the Israeli Revenge Operation 'Wrath of God'*, New York: Arcade Publishing, 2011.
Renga, Dana. 'Moro Martyred, Braghetti Betrayed: History Retold in *Buongiorno, notte*', in *Terrorism, Italian Style: Representations of Political Violence in Contemporary Italian Cinema*, Ruth Glynn, Giancarlo Lombardi and Alan O'Leary (eds). London: IGRS Books, 2012, pp. 175–91.

Richie, Donald. '"Mono no aware": Hiroshima in Film', in *Hibakusha Cinema: Hiroshima, Nagasaki and the Nuclear Image in Japanese Film*, Mick Broderick (ed.), New York and London: Routledge, 1996, pp. 20–37.

Rigoni Stern, Mario. *Amore di Confine*, Torino: Einaudi, 1986.

Roberts, Fifi. 'Girl Reveals Full Story of Seized British Ship', *Daily Mail*, Issue Number 12957, London, 3 November 1937, p. 13.

Rosenstone, Robert A. 'History in Images/History in Words: Reflections on the Possibility of Really Putting History onto Film', *The American Historical Review*, Vol. 93, No. 5 (1988), pp. 1173–1185.

Rothberg, Michael. *Multidirectional Memory: Remembering the Holocaust in the Age of Decolonization*, Redwood City, California: Stanford University Press, 2009.

Schiller, Kay and Chris Young. *The 1972 Munich Olympics and the Making of Modern Germany*, Berkeley: University of California Press, 2010.

Shibata, Yūko. 'Belated arrival in political transition: 1950s film on Hiroshima and Nagasaki', in *When the Tsunami Came to Shore: Culture and Disaster in Japan*, Roy Starrs (ed.), Leiden: Brill, 2014, pp. 231–48.

Shiel, Mark. *Italian Neorealism: Rebuilding the Cinematic City*, London: Wallflower Press, 2006.

Smith, J. and André Moncourt, *The Red Army Faction: A Documentary History. Projectiles for the people*, Montreal: PM Press, 2009.

Soja, Edward W. *Thirdspace: Journeys to Los Angeles and Other Real-and-Imagined Places*, Malden, MA: Blackwell, 1996.

Sorlin, Pierre. 'Cinema and the Memory of the Great War', in *The First World War and Popular Cinema: 1914 to the Present*, Michael Paris (ed.), Edinburgh: Edinburgh University Press, 1999, pp. 5–26.

Standish, Isolde. *A New History of Japanese Cinema*, London: Bloomsbury, 2006.

Steinacher, Gerald. *Nazis on the Run: How Hitler's Henchmen Fled Justice*, Oxford: Oxford University Press, 2012.

Steinlauf, Michael C. *Bondage to the Dead: Poland and the Memory of the Holocaust*, New York and Syracuse: Syracuse University Press, 1997.

Tachibana, Reiko. *Narrative as Counter-Memory: A Half-Century of Postwar Writing in Germany and Japan*, Albany: State University of New York Press, 1998.

Taylor, N. A. J. and Robert Jacobs, 'Introduction: on Hiroshima becoming history', in *Reimagining Hiroshima and Nagasaki: Nuclear Humanities in the Post-Cold War*, N. A. J. Taylor and Robert Jacobs (eds), New York and London: Routledge, 2017, pp. 1–12.

Taylor-Jones, Kate E. *Rising Sun, Divided Land: Japanese and South Korean Filmmakers*, New York: Columbia University Press, 2013.

Trompf, Garry W. *The Idea of Historical Recurrence in Western Thought: from Antiquity to the Reformation*, Berkeley: University of California Press, 1992.

Tusell, Javier. *Spain: From Dictatorship to Democracy*, Hoboken: John Wiley, 2011.

Ward, Simon. 'Globalization and the remembrance of violence: Visual culture, space, and time in Berlin', in *Globalization, Violence and the Visual Culture of Cities*, Christoph Lindner (ed.), London: Routledge, 2009, pp. 87–106.

Weissman, Gary. *Fantasies of Witnessing: Post-war Efforts to Experience the Holocaust*, Ithaca, New York: Cornell University Press, 2004.

Winter, Jay. *Remembering War: the Great War between Memory and History in the 20th Century*, New Haven: Yale University Press, 2006.

Winter, Jay. *Sites of Memory, Sites of Mourning: the Great War in European Cultural History*, Cambridge: Cambridge University Press, 1998 [first published in 1995].

Wiśnioch, Maria. *Majdanek: a Guide to the Historical Buildings*, Lublin: Państwowe Muzeum na Majdanku, 2012.

Yoneyama, Lisa. *Hiroshima Traces: Time, Space, and the Dialectics of Memory*, Oakland: University of California Press, 1999.

Zambenedetti, Alberto. 'Filming in Stone: Palazzo Della Civiltà Italiana and Fascist Signification in Cinema', *Annali D'Italianistica*, Vol. 28, 2010, pp. 199–215.

Zander, Peter. 'Muffensausen beim *Himmel über Berlin*', *Welt Online*, Berlin, 3 May 2007.

Zwigenberg, Ran. *Hiroshima: The Origins of Global Memory Culture*, Cambridge University Press, 2014.

Films by Location

ITALY

Archival Films

La guerra d'Italia a 3,000 metri sull'Adamello (*The Italian War at 3,000 Meters on the Adamello*, Luca Comerio and Paolo Granata), 1916, Comerio Milano Cinematografia, Archivio Storico Istituto Luce (Rome), Film ID: CF00302

Battaglia sulle colline italiane (*Battle on the Italian Hills*), 1918, Archivio Storico Istituto Luce (Rome), Film ID: RW55201

L'esercito americano in Italia durante la Prima Guerra Mondiale (*The American Army in Italy during the First World War*), 1918, Archivio Storico Istituto Luce (Rome), Film ID: 111H1228/D030401

Tra le Nevi e i Ghiacci del Tonale (*Amid Snow and Ice on Mount Tonale*), 1918, Cinematographic Section of the Italian Army, Imperial War Museum (London), Film ID: IWM 459

Dal Grappa al mare; ricordi di guerra e scene dei campi di battaglia (*From Monte Grappa to the Sea; War Memories and Battlefield Scenes*, 1925), 1925, Archivio Storico Istituto Luce (Rome), Film ID: M014801

Il Piave mormorò (*The Piave River Burbled*), 1934, Istituto Nazionale Luce, Film ID: D030401

Piave. Rievocata la Gloriosa Epopea (*Piave River. Recalling the Glorious Epic*), 1958, Settimanale CIAC/SC497, CIAC, Compagnia Italiana Attualità Cinematografiche, Archivio Storico Istituto Luce (Rome), Film ID: KB049701

Fiction Films and Documentaries

Maciste Alpino (*The Warrior*, Luigi Romano Borgnetto and Luigi Maggi, 1916)
La Guerra e il Sogno di Momi (*The War and the Dream of Momi*, Giovanni Pastrone, 1917)
Il Canto della Fede (*Song of Faith*, Filippo Butera, 1917)
Mariute (Eduardo Bencivenga, 1918)
A Farewell to Arms (Frank Borzage, 1932)
Cavalleria (*Chivalry*, Goffredo Alessandrini, 1936)
Ladri di biciclette (*Bicycle Thieves*, Vittorio De Sica, 1948)
Senza Bandiera (*Without Flag*, Lionello De Felice, 1951)
Fratelli d'Italia (*Brothers of Italy*, Fausto Saraceni, 1952)
La Leggenda del Piave (*The Legend of River Piave*, Riccardo Freda, 1952)
Bella Non Piangere (*Bella, Don't Cry*, Davide Carbonari, 1954)

I Cinque dell'Adamello (*The Adamello Five*, Pino Mercanti, 1954)
A Farewell to Arms (King Vidor, 1957)
La Grande Guerra (*The Great War*, Mario Monicelli, 1959)
I Recuperanti (*The Scavengers*, Ermanno Olmi, 1970)
Uomini Contro (*Many Wars Ago*, Francesco Rosi, 1970)
La Sciantosa (Alfredo Gianetti, 1971)
Novecento (*1900*, Bernardo Bertolucci, 1976)
L'Albero tra le Trincee (*The Tree in the Trenches*, Alessandro Scillitani, 2013)

Spain

Archival Films

Civil War in Spain: Troops in Action (Pathé Gazette, 1936)
Spain from Both Sides: Front-line Despatches from Government and Rebel (Gaumont British News, 1936)
Spanish Civil War (British Pathé, 1936, Film ID: 512.02)
Troubled Spain (British Pathé, 1936, Film ID: 895.0)
Troubled Spain: Fierce Fighting near the Portuguese Border (Pathé Gazette, 1936)
Bombing Madrid (British Pathé, 1937, Film ID: 524.07)
In Defence of Madrid (British Pathé, 1937, Film ID: 574.08)
In the Firing Line in Madrid (British Pathé, 1937, Film ID: 1903.01)
Guernica Wiped out by Air-Raid (Gaumont British News, 1937)
Franco Push: End Near? (British Paramount, 1938)
Francos Streitkräfte betreten Madrid (*Franco's Forces Enter Madrid*, Deutsche Monatsschau, 1939, British Pathé Film ID: 520.15)
Spain: A Rally By 100,000 Anarchists, Meeting In Barcelona For The First Time In 40 Years (Reuters, 1977)

Fiction Films and Documentaries

The Spanish Earth (Joris Ivens, 1937)
Blockade (William Dieterle, 1938)
Ispaniya (*Spain*, Esfir Shub, USSR, 1939)
L'Assedio dell'Alcazar (*The Siege of the Alcazar*, Augusto Genina, 1940)
Raza (*Race*, José Luis Sáenz de Heredia, 1942)
For Whom the Bell Tolls (Sam Wood, 1943)
Guernica (Alain Resnais, 1950)
Fünf Patronenhülsen (*Five Cartridges*, Frank Beyer, 1960)
La fiel infantería (*The Faithful Infantry*, Pedro Lazaga, 1960)
El camino de la paz (*The Way to Peace*, Rafael G. Garzón, 1961)
La Caza (*The Hunt*, Carlos Saura, 1966)
L'arbre de Guernica (*The Tree of Guernica*, Fernando Arrabal, 1975)
Inside the Revolution (David Hart, 1983)
Prelude to Tragedy: 1931–1936 (David Hart, 1983)
Revolution, Counter-Revolution & Terror (John Blake, 1983)

Battleground for Idealists (John Blake, 1983)
The Adventures of Baron Munchausen (Terry Gilliam, 1988)
Huidos (Sancho Gracia, 1993)
Land and Freedom (Ken Loach, 1995)
Libertarias (*Libertarians*, Vicente Aranda, Spain, 1996)
El laberinto del fauno (*Pan's Labyrinth*, Guillermo del Toro, 2006)
Guernica (Koldo Serra, 2016)
El silencio de otros (*The Silence of Others*, Robert Bahar and Almudena Carracedo, 2018)
Spider-Man: Far From Home (Jon Watts, 2019)

POLAND

Archival Films

Majdanek (Irina Setkina, 1944)
Majdanek: Cmentarzysko Europy (*Majdanek: Burial Ground in Europe*, Aleksander Ford, 1944)
The Tragic City Of Lublin (British Pathé, 1944, Film ID: 1370.22)
Lublin. Uroczystości na Majdanku (*Lublin: Commemoration at Majdanek*, Polska Kronika Filmowa, Ludwik Perski and Jerzy Bossak, 1948)

Fiction Films and Documentaries

Der ewige Jude (*The Eternal Jew*, Fritz Hippler, 1940)
Rzeczywistość (*Reality*, Antoni Bohdziewicz, 1960)
Czarne Chmury (*Black Clouds*, Andrzej Konic, 1973)
Żołnierze Wolności (*Soldiers of Freedom*, Jurij Ozierov, 1977)
Holocaust (Gerald Green, 1978)
Kronika Wypadków Miłosnych (*A Chronicle of Amorous Accidents*, Andrzej Wajda, 1985)
Shoah (Claude Lanzmann, 1985)
Escape from Sobibór (Jack Gold, 1987)
Past and Present, History Falsified (Thomas and Dena Blatt, 1987)
Kornblumenblau (*Cornflower Blue*, Leszek Wosiewicz, 1989)
Sobibór, October 14, 1943, 4 p.m. (Claude Lanzmann, 2001)
Chopin, Pragnienie miłości (*Chopin – Desire for Love*, Jerzy Antczak, 2002)
The Aryan Couple (John Daly, 2004)
Kryptonim <Puch> (*Codename 'Down'*, Adek Drabiński, 2005)
Tajna Sprawa (*A Matter of Secrecy*, Adek Drabiński, 2005)
Uczniowie Widzącego z Lublina (*Students of the Seer of Lublin*, Leszek Wiśniewski, 2005)
Spring 1941 (Uri Barbash, 2007)
The Reader (Stephen Daldry, 2008)
Z królestwa śmierci (*From the Realm of Death*, Urszula Hasiec and Grzegorz Michalec, 2008)
Simon Konianski (Micha Wald, 2009)
Sobibór: the Plan, the Revolt, the Escape (Karen Lynne and Richard Bloom, 2010)
Escape From a Nazi Death Camp (Hereward Pelling, 2014)
Sobibór (Собибор, Konstantin Khabensky, 2018)

Hiroshima

Archival and Amateur Films

At Restaurant Sushitoku, Hiroshima (Shuichi Fujii, 1925), RCC Broadcasting Company/ Kabushiki Gaisha Chugoku Hoso (Hiroshima)
Motoyasu Bridge and Neighbourhood (Kannosuke Kaminishi, 1927), RCC Broadcasting Company/ Kabushiki Gaisha Chugoku Hoso (Hiroshima)
Shokon-sai Festival (Kannosuke Kaminishi, 1928), RCC Broadcasting Company/ Kabushiki Gaisha Chugoku Hoso (Hiroshima)
Central Hiroshima City Crowd Celebrating the Birth of the Crown Prince (Shigeo Fukuichi, 1937), RCC Broadcasting Company/ Kabushiki Gaisha Chugoku Hoso (Hiroshima)
Hiroshima City in the Spring of 1936 (Genjiro Kawasaki, 1936), RCC Broadcasting Company/ Kabushiki Gaisha Chugoku Hoso (Hiroshima)
Ebisu-ko Festival Crowd (Shinichi Yoshioka, 1937), RCC Broadcasting Company/ Kabushiki Gaisha Chugoku Hoso (Hiroshima)
Nakajima Honmachi and Kamiyacho (Nobuichi Yoshioka, 1937–1940), Hiroshima Peace Memorial Museum
Nagasaki and Hiroshima (British Pathé, 1945, Film ID: 2319.12)
World News in Review (British Pathé, 04/10/1945, Film ID: 1165.21)
Hiroshima, Six Years After (British Pathé, 1951, Film ID: 1469.36)
Hiroshima, Nine Years After A-Blast (Warner Pathé News/British Pathé, 1954, ID: 2490.19)
Date With History: Hiroshima (British Pathé, 1964, Film ID: 2733.01/2)
Hiroshima and Nagasaki Today (British Pathé, 1964, Film ID: 3195.16)
Japan: Hiroshima Marks 22nd Anniversary of Atom Bomb (Gaumont British Newsreel, 08/08/1967)

Fiction Films and Documentaries

Genbaku no Ko (*Children of Hiroshima*, Kaneto Shindo, 1952)
Nagasaki No Uta Wa Wasureji (*I will Not Forget the Song of Nagasaki*, 1952)
Hiroshima (Hideo Sekigawa, 1953)
Ikimono no kiroku (*I Live In Fear*, Akira Kurosawa, 1955)
Hiroshima mon amour (Alain Resnais, 1959)
Jingi Naki Tatakai (*Battles Without Honour and Humanity*, 1974–76)
Hadashi no Gen (*Barefoot Gen*, 1976, Tengo Yamada)
Hadashi no Gen: Namida no Bakuhatsu (*Barefoot Gen: Explosion of Tears*, 1977, Tengo Yamada)
Barefoot Gen Part 3: Battle of Hiroshima (*Hadashi no Gen Part 3: Hiroshima no Tatakai*, 1980, Tengo Yamada)
Hadashi no Gen (*Barefoot Gen*, Mori Masaki, 1983)
Hadashi no Gen 2 (*Barefoot Gen 2*, Toshio Hirata, 1986)
Kuroi ame (*Black Rain*, 1989)
Hiroshima: Out of the Ashes (Peter Werner, 1990)
Yume (*Dreams*, Akira Kurosawa, 1990)
Hachigatsu no rapusodī (*Rhapsody in August*, 1991)
Barefoot Gen (*Hadashi no Gen*, Masaki Nishiura and Shosuke Murakami, 2007)

White Light/Black Rain: The Destruction of Hiroshima and Nagasaki (Steven Okazaki, 2007)
Kono Sekai no Katasumi ni (*In This Corner of the World*, Sunao Katabuchi, 2016)

LATIN AMERICA

Archival Films

'US Foreign Service and diplomats; Good Neighbor Policy; recall of ambassador from Germany' (1938), *March of Time*, Vol. 5, No. 4, USHMM, Accession Number: 2006.73.1, RG Number: RG-60.4512, Film ID: 2820

'David Glick's JDC mission to South America in the late 1930s' (1939), USHMM, Accession Number: 2004.320.2, RG Number: RG-60.4310, Film ID: 2703

'David Glick's JDC mission to South America in the late 1930s' (1939), USHMM, Accession Number: 2004.320.2, RG Number: RG-60.4309, Film ID: 2702

'Army film showing Nazi aggression, refugees, FDR & Hull Film' (1939–40), Orientation Film No. 7, Reel 5, USHMM, Accession Number: 1994.119.1, RG Number: RG-60.1114, Film ID: 932

Fiction Films, Documentaries and Animated Films

Gilda (Charles Vidor, 1946)
Notorious (Alfred Hitchcock, 1946)
Operation Eichmann (R. G. Springsteen, 1961)
The Madmen of Mandoras (David Bradley, 1963)
The Boys from Brazil (Franklin J. Schaffner, 1978)
La historia oficial (*The Official Story*, Luis Puenzo, 1985)
Opstand in Sobibór (Pavel Kogan and Lily Van Den, *The Uprising in Sobibór*, 1990)
The Man Who Captured Eichmann (William Graham, 1996)
Nichts als die Wahrheit (*After the Truth*, Roland Suso Richter, 1999)
Algunos que vivieron (*Some Who Lived*, Luis Puenzo, 2002)
Rua Alguem 5555: My Father (Egidio Eronico, 2003)
The Legacy of Jedwabne (Slawomir Grunberg, 2005)
Forgiving Dr. Mengele (Bob Hercules and Cheri Pugh, 2006)
Eichmann (Paul Young, 2007)
Pacto de silencio (*Pact of Silence*, Carlos Echeverría, 2007)
Nazis at the Center of the Earth (Joseph Lawson, 2012)
Hannah Arendt (Margarethe von Trotta, 2013)
Wakolda (*The German Doctor*, Lucia Puenzo, 2013)
The Eichmann Show (Paul Andrew Williams, 2015)
Operation Finale (Chris Weitz, 2018)

Munich

Television Broadcast

Munich 1972: Games of the XX Olympiad (ABC, 1972)

Fiction Films and Documentaries

The Longest, (John Schlesinger, 1973, fragment of *Visions of Eight*)
21 Hours at Munich (William A. Graham, 1976)
Sword of Gideon (Michael Anderson, 1986)
One Day in September (Kevin Macdonald, 1999)
Munich (Steven Spielberg, 2005)
Munich: Mossad's Revenge (Tom Whitter, 2006)
1972 (Sarah Morris, 2008)
Munich '72 and Beyond (Stephen Crisman, 2016)

Rome

Television Broadcast

TG1 Edizione Straordinaria: Il Rapimento di Aldo Moro ('TG1 Breaking News: The Kidnapping of Aldo Moro', 16 March 1978, RAI Rete 1, 87 minutes)
TG2 Edizione Straordinaria: Il Rapimento di Aldo Moro ('TG2 Breaking News: The Kidnapping of Aldo Moro', 16 March 1978, RAI Rete 2, 57 minutes)
TG1 Edizione Straordinaria: Il Ritrovamento di Aldo Moro ('TG1 Breaking News: The Discovery of Aldo Moro's Body', 9 May 1978, RAI Rete 1, 220 minutes)

Fiction Films and Documentaries

Il caso Moro (*The Moro Affair*, Giuseppe Ferrara, 1986)
La notte della Repubblica: Il sequestro Moro (*The Night of the Republic: the Moro kidnapping*, 1990)
Year of the Gun (John Frankenheimer, 1991)
Aldo Moro: 55 Giorni di Passione (*Aldo Moro: 55 Days of Passion*, Vittorio Nevano, 1998)
Buongiorno, notte (*Good Morning, Night*, Marco Bellocchio, 2003)
Piazza Delle Cinque Lune (*Five Moons Plaza*, Renzo Martinelli, 2003)
Se sarà luce sarà bellissimo (*If There Were Light, That Would Be Beautiful*, Aurelio Grimaldi 2004)
Romanzo Criminale (Michele Placido, 2005)
Les derniers jours d'Aldo Moro (*The Last Days of Aldo Moro*, Emmanuel Amara, 2006)
Aldo Moro: Il presidente (*Aldo Moro: President*, Gianluca Maria Tavarelli, 2008)
Il Divo (Paolo Sorrentino, 2008)
Il Condannato. Cronaca di un sequestro (*The Convict: Chronicles of a Kidnapping*, Ezio Mauro, 2018)
Aldo Moro: Il professore (*Aldo Moro: Professor*, Francesco Miccichè, 2018)

BERLIN

Archival Films and Television Broadcast

Beauty and Berlin (1930–39, British Pathé: Film ID: 2741.07)
Panorama (BBC TV, 31 July 1961)
The Berlin Boundary Is Sealed (BBC News, 16 August 1961)
Panorama (BBC TV, 30 October 1961)
Beyond the Wall (*Tuesday Documentary*, BBC One, Peter Ceresole, 22 September 1970)
Newsnight (BBC Two, 10 November 1989)

Fiction Films and Documentaries

Escape from East Berlin (Robert Siodmak, 1962)
The Tunnel (Reuven Frank, 1962)
The Spy Who Came in from the Cold (Martin Ritt, 1965)
Funeral in Berlin (Guy Hamilton, 1966)
Torn Curtain (Alfred Hitchcock, 1966)
Casino Royale (Ken Hughes, 1967)
Der Mann auf der Mauer (*The Man on the Wall*, Reinhard Hauff, 1982)
The Soldier (James Glickenhaus, 1982)
Octopussy (John Glen, 1983)
Berlin Tunnel 21 (Richard Michaels, 1981)
Christiane F. – Wir Kinder vom Bahnhof Zoo (*Christiane F.*, Uli Edel, 1981)
Meier (Peter Timm, 1986)
Der Himmel über Berlin (*Wings of Desire*, Wim Wenders, 1987)
Game, Set and Match (Ken Grieve and Patrick Lau, 1988)
Coming Out (Heiner Carow, 1989)
The Innocent (John Schlesinger, 1993)
Der Tunnel (Marcus Vetter, 1999)
Helden wie wir (*Heroes Like Us*, Sebastian Peterson, 1999)
Sonnenallee (Leander Haußmann, 1999)
Der Tunnel (*The Tunnel*, Roland Suso Richter, 2001)
Good Bye, Lenin! (Wolfgang Becker, 2003)
Herr Lehmann (*Berlin Blues*, Leander Haußmann, 2003)
Il tunnel della libertà (*The Tunnel of Freedom*, Enzo Monteleone, 2004)
Liebe Mauer (*Dear Wall*, Peter Timm, 2009)
The Secret Life of the Berlin Wall (Kevin Sim, 2009)
Beyond the Wall (Mark Byrne and Rob Dennis, 2010)
Behind the Wall (Michael Patrick Kelly, 2011)
Bridge of Spies (Steven Spielberg, 2015)
tomic Blonde (David Leitch, 2017)

Index

ABC, 8, 52, 113, 117–18, 122–5, 128–32, 136
Age of Catastrophe, 2–4, 6, 72, 91, 181–2
Apollo 11 (spaceflight), 1, 4
Arad, Yitzhak, 72–4
Archduke Franz Ferdinand, 6, 15–16, 28, 181
Archibald, David, 42–3, 47, 51–3
Armstrong, Neil, 1
Asiago (Italy), 17, 23, 27–30, 32, 176

Baader Meinhof Fraktion, 133, 136
Badajoz (Spain), 7, 37, 46, 48–50, 59
   Alcazaba, 48–9, 59
Barattoni, Luca, 17, 31
Bariloche (Argentina), 107–8, 114
Basilio, Miriam, 49, 53
Basque Country (Spain), 37–9, 41, 43
BBC, 11, 162–3, 170–2, 176–9
Belchite (Spain), 35–8, 40, 46–7, 49–51, 77, 176
Berlin, 8, 31, 53, 107–8, 117, 124, 126, 154, 159–79
   Alexanderplatz, 159–60, 176
   Berlin Wall, 6, 8–9, 154, 159, 161–3, 166–7, 170, 172–3, 177–9
   Bernauer Straße, 9, 162–6, 170, 175–8
   Brandenburg Gate, 160–1, 170, 177
   Checkpoint Charlie, 170–5, 177, 179
   Friedrichstraße, 9, 162, 171–6, 179
   Kreuzberg, 159–60, 173, 175, 177
   Potsdamer Platz, 9, 162, 167–72, 175–6, 178
   Sonnenallee, 173
Bianconi, Giovanni, 154
Black September Organisation, 118–19, 121, 124–6, 128–9, 133–5, 138

Bordo, Jonathan, 168, 178
Braghetti, Anna Maria, 145, 156–7
Broadbent, Philip, 161, 177
Brunetta, Gian Piero, 21–2, 32
Brunsdon, Charlotte, 103, 113
Buckton, Oliver, 170, 179
Buenos Aires, 7, 97, 99, 101, 103–5, 107, 109, 111, 113, 115
Burrows, Jon, 103–4, 113

Calderoni, Franco, 23, 32
Carlsten, Jennie, 133, 136
Caruth, Cathy, 85, 93
Casey, Edward S., 9–11
Caygill, Howard, 170, 178
Chaplin, Charles, 181
Cold War, 2–6, 8–11, 16, 18, 20, 22, 24–6, 28, 30, 32, 34, 36, 38, 40, 42, 44, 46, 48, 50, 52, 54, 56, 58, 60, 62, 64, 66, 68, 70, 72, 74, 76, 78, 80, 82, 84, 86, 88, 90–2, 94–5, 98, 100, 102, 104, 106, 108, 110, 112, 114, 118, 120, 122, 124, 126, 128, 130, 132–4, 136–8, 140–2, 144, 146, 148, 150, 152–4, 156, 159–64, 166, 168, 170, 172, 174, 176, 178–9, 181–2
Cole, Tim, 66, 73
Communism, 3, 31, 36–7, 41, 47, 52, 56, 59, 134, 139, 155–6, 165, 172, 177

D'Annunzio, Gabriele, 19, 31
De España, Rafael, 43, 52
Diffrient, David Scott, 122–3, 129, 135–6

Ebert, Roger, 106, 114
Eichmann, Adolf, 7, 97, 102, 106, 112, 114
Ethington, Philip J., 9–11

Fabi, Lucio, 21, 32
Fascism, 6, 18–19, 25–6, 28, 30–1, 40–1,
    43–4, 49, 52, 54, 100, 102, 104, 108–10,
    112, 152, 157, 177
Fernández, Joxean, 37, 43, 52
Ferrándiz, Francisco, 45–6, 53
First World War, 1–2, 6, 9–10, 15–19, 22–7,
    29–32, 37, 46, 50, 100, 119, 137, 176,
    181–3
Franco, Francisco, 7, 32, 35–9, 41, 43–4, 46,
    48–50, 53, 56, 59

Gajek, Eva Maria, 118, 134
Galily, Yair, 119, 135
Gargiulo, Gius, 147, 153, 156–7
Garrone, Eugenio, 25–6, 33
Garrone, Giuseppe, 25–6, 33
González-Ruibal, Alfredo 44, 47, 53
Gruber Godfrey, Laura, 15, 30
Guadalajara (Spain), 7, 37, 45–6, 50
Guernica (Spain), 7, 37–41, 50–2, 85
Gundle, Stephen, 18, 31

Hake, Sabine, 161, 177
Haltof, Marek, 56, 72
Harper, Graeme, 102, 113
Harrison, Hope, 163–4, 177
Hay, James, 4, 11, 61, 73
Hein, Laura E., 83, 87, 92, 94
Hemingway, Ernest, 15–17, 27, 30, 47, 53
Hersey, John, 76, 91
hibakusha, 77–8, 81–4, 86–7, 90, 93–4
Hicks, Jeremy, 61–2, 73
Hill, Sarah, 145, 149, 156
Hiroshima, 6–7, 11, 38, 72, 75–94, 97, 181
    Aioi Bridge, 76, 78, 81, 85–90, 94
    Hondōri, 88–9
    Motoyasu River, 76, 78, 80, 89, 93–4
    Nakajima Honmachi, 78, 86, 88–9, 94
    Ōta River, 85–6, 88, 93
    Prefectural Industrial Promotion Hall
        (Atom Bomb Dome), 7, 76–82, 86–90,
        92–4, 119, 154, 176
Hitler, Adolf, 100–2, 106–8, 112–14, 126,
    181
Hobsbawm, Eric, 2–3, 10–11, 32, 176, 179,
    181, 183
Hodgin, Nick, 132, 136

Hodgkin, Katharine, 122, 135
Hogan, Michael J., 75, 91
Holocaust, 6–9, 11, 44, 50–1, 55–7, 62–4,
    66–7, 70–4, 91, 97, 100, 108–11, 113,
    115, 124, 127, 151–2
    Auschwitz, 51, 62–6, 73, 107–10, 113, 152
    Bełżec, 55, 57, 66, 73
    Chełmno, 69
    Dachau, 117, 120, 127
    Sobibór, 7, 50, 55, 65–74, 73–4, 91, 98–9,
        109, 111–12, 115, 128
Huesca (Spain), 35, 42
Huyssen, Andreas, 29, 33, 126, 135, 159, 177

Imposimato, Ferdinando, 137, 154–5

Jacobs, Robert, 77, 91
Jarvie, Ian C., 3, 10
Jedwabne (Poland), 99, 111, 113
Jerusalem, 68–9, 72, 97, 112, 114–15, 130

Kilgallen, Dorothy Mae, 105, 113
Knischewski, Gerd, 166, 178
Koslov, Elissa M., 64, 73

Labanyi, Jo, 45–6, 53
Ladd, Brian, 161, 167–8, 173, 177–9
Landy, Marcia, 3, 10
Lanzmann, Claude, 67–9, 71, 74, 115
Large, David Clay, 112, 115
Launius, Roger D., 1, 10
Lefebvre, Henri, 59, 72
Lérida (Spain), 7, 35, 37, 42, 50
Levi, Primo, 152, 156
Lifton, Robert Jay, 82–3, 92
Lombardi, Giancarlo, 140, 155, 157
Lowenthal, David, 29, 33, 123, 135
Lu, Andong, 4–5, 11, 61, 73
Lublin, 7, 50, 55–63, 65–6, 69–73, 91, 98,
    103, 119
    Brama Grodzka, 60–1, 72
    Majdanek, 7, 50–1, 56–7, 61–5, 68–71, 73,
        77, 103, 176
Lucken, Michael, 80, 92
Lusso, Emilio, 23, 25, 27, 29, 32–3

Madrid, 17, 37, 39, 42, 45–8, 50–1, 53, 112
Malvezzi, Pietro, 157

McGarry, Fearghal, 133, 136
Miller, Matthew, 175, 179
Monteath, Peter, 43, 52
Moon landing, 1, 3, 182
Moro, Aldo, 6, 8, 26, 134, 137–57, 160, 182
Moro, Carlo Alfredo, 154
Morreale, Emiliano, 30, 34
Morris, Nigel, 128, 136
Mossad, 7, 97, 106–7, 114, 132, 136
multidirectional memory, 100, 110–11, 113, 126, 133, 152, 154
Munich, 6, 8, 112, 115, 117–36, 138, 147, 153–4, 160, 176
   Connollystraße, 8, 118, 120, 124–5, 127–32, 134, 136, 147, 153–4
   Fürstenfeldbruck, 8, 117–20, 124–5, 132–3, 153
   Olympiapark, 117, 119, 121, 123, 125, 127, 129, 131, 133, 135
Mussolini, Benito, 18–19, 31

Nachreiner, Thomas, 120, 131, 135–136
Nagasaki, 75, 79, 91, 94, 181
Nazism, 6–9, 41–3, 53, 55–8, 59–62, 64–6, 70–1, 73–4, 97–107, 110–14, 117, 124, 126, 133, 152–3, 181
newsreels, 3, 7–8, 15–22, 30, 35–8, 41, 43, 45, 50–1, 53–4, 56–7, 59, 61–2, 70–1, 77–81, 84–7, 90, 92–3, 100, 102, 105, 111, 167, 172, 181–2
Nora, Pierre, 5, 11, 62, 73, 122, 135, 169, 178

O'Leary, Alan, 141, 145, 152–3, 155–7
Olympic Games (1972), 6, 8, 112, 115, 120–2, 126–7, 134, 154
Orwell, George, 2, 6, 10, 35, 41–4, 52

Patagonia, 107–9, 111
Penz, François, 4–5, 11, 61, 73
Pezzini, Isabella, 142, 155, 189
photography, 18, 30, 38–41, 66, 73–4, 78, 88, 93, 108–9, 125, 127, 129, 132, 138, 139, 142, 145, 148–9, 153, 156, 157, 162, 166
Princip, Gavrilo, 6, 10, 15–16
propaganda, 17, 19, 22, 31, 38, 41, 43, 49–50, 52–3, 56, 59, 62, 72
Provvisionato, Sandro, 154–5

Raack, Richard C., 3–4, 10–11
Radstone, Susannah, 122, 135
RAI (broadcasting company), 11, 139, 149, 153, 155–6
Rayner, Jonathan, 102, 113
Red Brigades, 8, 134, 137–8, 140–2, 144–9, 154, 156
Renga, Dana, 153, 157
Richie, Donald, 88, 94
Rigoni Stern, Mario, 28, 33
Rio de Janeiro, 100, 103–5
Roberts, Florence 'Fifi', 39, 40, 51
Rome, 6, 8, 134, 137–8, 140, 143, 147, 149, 151, 153–4, 176
   Via Caetani, 8, 134, 138, 148–54, 157
   Via Fani, 8, 134, 137–45, 147–8, 153, 156
   Via Montalcini, 8, 134, 137–8, 140, 144–9, 152–4
Rosenstone, Robert A., 4, 11
Rothberg, Michael, 100, 110–11, 113, 115, 152, 157

Sarajevo, 6, 10, 15–17
Second World War, 2–3, 8, 16, 19, 25, 27–8, 31, 37–8, 43, 50, 52, 56, 71, 86, 91, 100, 103, 115, 117, 121, 127, 152, 154, 167, 181
Selden, Mark, 83, 87, 92, 94
Shibata, Yūko, 92–3
Shiel, Mark, 27, 33
Short Twentieth Century, 2–3, 5–6, 9–10, 16, 25, 37, 137, 152, 182
sites of memory, 5, 7, 17–19, 27, 30, 32, 36, 39, 40, 42, 45–6, 48–9, 50, 57, 66, 68–9, 71, 77, 85–7, 89–90, 99, 121–2, 124–5, 127–8, 133, 136, 138, 145, 148, 168, 170, 172
Soja, Edward, 5–6, 9, 11, 182–183
Sonderkommando, 67–8, 71
Sorlin, Pierre, 21, 32
Spanish Civil War, 6–7, 30, 35–9, 41, 43–7, 49–54, 56, 59, 119
   Aragón Offensive, 7, 35, 37, 42
Spittler, Ulla, 166,178
Steinlauf, Michael C., 56, 72

Tachibana, Reiko, 83, 93
Tamir, Ilan, 119, 135

Taylor, N. A. J., 77, 91–2
Taylor-Jones, Kate E., 78, 92
television, 57, 119, 134, 147, 162–3, 170–1, 177–8
terrorism, 8, 26, 29, 102, 115, 118–42, 144–5, 147, 149, 152–7
testimony, 10, 36, 40, 48–50, 66–71, 74, 88, 94, 98–9, 109–10, 115, 124, 126–7, 135, 139, 141–2, 144, 149, 165
Thakkar, Amit, 132, 136
Toledo, 7, 37, 46–7, 49–50, 53, 59
   Alcázar, 37, 47, 49–50, 53–4, 59

Trompf, Garry, 28, 33

Ward, Simon, 167, 178
Weissman, Gary, 69, 74, 85, 93, 142
Winter, Jay, 20, 24–5, 32–3

Yarchi, Moran, 119, 135
Yoneyama, Lisa, 78–80, 92

Zambenedetti, Alberto, 152, 157
Zwigenberg, Ran, 84, 93

EU representative:
Easy Access System Europe
Mustamäe tee 50, 10621 Tallinn, Estonia
Gpsr.requests@easproject.com

www.ingramcontent.com/pod-product-compliance
Lightning Source LLC
Chambersburg PA
CBHW071842230426
43671CB00012B/2044